Also by William Stevenson:

A Man Called Intrepid
Birds' Nests in Their Beards (Revolution in Indonesia)
The Bormann Brotherhood
The Bushbabies
Emperor Red
The Ghosts of Africa
Ninety Minutes at Entebbe
Strike Zion
The Yellow Wind (Revolution in China)
Zanek! A Chronicle of the Israeli Air Force

INTREPID'S LAST CASE

INTREPID'S LAST CASE

WILLIAM STEVENSON

THE LYONS PRESS
Guilford, Connecticut
An imprint of The Globe Pequot Press

The Lyons Press is an imprint of The Globe Pequot Press.

Originally published in 1983 by Villard Books, New York.

Printed in Canada
Design by Susan Mitchell

10 9 8 7 6 5 4 3 2 1

ISBN 1-58574-521-9

The Library of Congress Cataloging-in-Publication Data is available on file.

"Deception is an arrangement of light and dark . . . *chiaroscuro*. . . . The people must be made to see white where there is black when this is necessary to the progress of the Revolution. . . ."

—From the guidelines for "disinformation" and deceit as an arm of secret warfare, offered to Lenin by his German Communist escort, Willi Münzenberg, on that famous sealed train carrying Lenin like an incubus into Mother Russia in 1917. The German General Staff provided train and escort from Lenin's Swiss exile to Petrograd, counting on him to spread disaffection among the Russian soldiery at a critical phase in World War I.

"Little Bill Stephenson, in serious discussions with me concerning wartime operations, always conveyed a sense of unassuming but absolute authority which was based on moral integrity and an immense experience of the world and its affairs, of man's ambitions and follies, of international politics. . . . He had been through it all as a soldier, an airman, an escaper, setting up his own private intelligence service as the threat of war with Nazi Germany developed. . . . He was covering the whole world with his intelligence, and he knew what to look for. . . . One aspect of his operating technique was absolutely fascinating to me: He seemed rarely to leave his New York office, except for some operational purpose where he felt his presence was essential—or else to see some head of state or something that major. But everybody seemed to come and see him, drawn to his office as it were by some unseen thread.

"It was like ancient Greeks going to their oracle at Delphi to pose their multitudinous questions and to get a definitive answer. . . . We always seemed to get from Bill a definitive answer."

—General Sir Colin Gubbins,
chief of Special Operations Executive;
from a tape-recorded interview with the author.

by MAJOR-GENERAL
RICHARD HEATH ROHMER

The place: the library of Sir William Stephenson's Bermuda home. The time: just after eleven in the morning, 24 April 1983, four decades after the wartime heroics of the man called Intrepid. Intrepid's hooded eyes were bright, filled with intelligence. Would I listen to some tape-recorded notes he'd made that morning for a speech he was going to deliver in September to a gathering of members of the American Office of Strategic Services and others of the intelligence community. Where was the speech to be given? In New York aboard the dry-docked aircraft carrier the USS *Intrepid*. "Remember, they're just notes," he cautioned.

Notes or not, the voice that flowed from the tape recorder was strong and filled with urgency. Intrepid's message was typical of the man: concise and to the point. This was the heart of his warning:

> The enemy is not only at our door but inside our house and in prac-
> tically every room. The West is fortunate to have in the United States
> the most effective and knowledgeable leaders, standing firmly shoulder
> to shoulder with their British and Canadian allies. They are aware of
> the present danger, that Yuri Andropov is now sole dictator of all the
> Soviet Union.
> This is the moment that secret intelligence becomes not only the first
> line of defense but perhaps the only defense.
> The issue is quite clear. Death or slavery versus life and freedom.
> Remember important events—Hitler, Pearl Harbor, Hungary, Czecho-
> slovakia, Poland, Afghanistan and others. And remember, Russian
> infiltration and disinformation tactics after Stalin were all the work of
> Andropov!

Intrepid's exhortation to make the issue of "death or slavery versus life and freedom" clear to all the people was a plea to citizens free to speak and hear all manner of opinions in societies where liberty and justice are taken for granted; to citizens unaware of the powerful, pervasive forces of Soviet disinformation and the penetration of the Russian intelligence services into every level of the ruling bureaucracies, even into the very heart of the intelligence and counterintelligence organizations of the Western nations.

The months and years ahead would be marked by harsh new military and nuclear challenges from the Soviets, and by increased KGB efforts to infiltrate Western security systems, to create more "moles" and to steal or buy more and more secret technological information. The KGB agents who populate every Soviet embassy would encourage more marches and protests against the deployment of the weapons upon which the forces of the North Atlantic Treaty Organization and its leading member, the United States of America, must rely for their defense against Kremlin-originated aggression.

Intrepid's Last Case demonstrates the Kremlin's single-minded purpose, even from the early days of World War II, when the Soviet Union was an ally to the West. Even then Soviet belligerence prompted the defection in early September 1945 of a highly placed member of the secret cipher branch operating out of the Soviet embassy in Ottawa. The appalling ineptitude of the Canadian government and of its eccentric prime minister, Mackenzie King, in handling this defector brought an alarmed William Stephenson to Ottawa—to take on the *double* task of protecting the defector from both the vengeance of his Soviet masters and the incompetence of the Canadians. The man whom Intrepid sought to shield, while at the same time obtaining as much intelligence information from him as possible, was Igor Gouzenko.

Igor Gouzenko was Intrepid's last case. Author Bill Stevenson sees the Gouzenko affair, known as the Corby Case, and the crucial part Intrepid played in it, as the pivot for a cluster of events from September 1945 to Gouzenko's death in 1982, and beyond. Applying his own deep knowledge and consummate skills as a researcher to the facts provided by Intrepid, he has written an extraordinary chronical of the widespread strategies employed by the Soviets to undermine every aspect of Western government bureaucracies, from their security services to the reputations of powerful and trusted agents.

Such efforts to neutralize enemies of the Soviet Union by sowing seeds of mistrust and discord among members of the intelligence or counterintelligence services were exemplified by the KGB character assassination of Intrepid's wartime right-hand man, Dick Ellis. Shortly before his death in 1975, Ellis had done what I am doing now: he had written the foreword for a book by Bill Stevenson. Colonal Charles Howard ("Dick") Ellis, CMG, CBE, OBE, U.S. Legion of Merit, had been flattered to be invited to write an opening "historical note" for a book on the life and accomplishments of a man he and countless others admired, the man called Intrepid. Ellis finished his foreword to A *Man Called Intrepid* by explaining why the existence of Intrepid's New York–based intelligence organization, BSC (British Security Coordination headquarters), had been made public in 1962—the 1962 escape to the Soviet Union of Kim Philby, the brilliant Communist agent who had infiltrated the highest level of the British secret service. Ellis wrote:

We knew that Philby took with him the knowledge of BSC's existence, but we also knew that he was not aware of the full and far-reaching purpose of Intrepid's organization. Thus just enough of the truth was revealed for publication to blunt the effect of any disclosures that Philby or his supporters might reveal. But ten years later, in 1972, we knew also that the Russians had learned rather more and might use this information to bludgeon our friends and to hurt United States and Canadian relations with Britain. Full disclosure at last was the answer to this threat and to the demands of history. Hence this book.

What about *this* book, *Intrepid's Last Case*? Ironically, it grew out of Intrepid's resolve to counter posthumous charges that Ellis was a "German-Soviet mole" who, among other things, had suppressed parts of Gouzenko's evidence to protect himself and others. If Ellis's reputation were not cleared, future secret-intelligence analysts would think twice about making controversial, individual decisions. The KGB would have succeeded again.

Questions had to be answered. Did Ellis commit gross acts of treachery? Did Ellis help the Russians suppress or distort Gouzenko's disclosures of Russian agents in high places within the Western bureaucracies? Had Ellis confessed, as alleged, to spying for both German Nazis and Russians?

As the author says, Stephenson was "determined to shake the truth out of the Corby Case. He had the contacts. I had the mobility. Through the spring and summer of 1981 . . . we began our own investigation."

There was no choice. The results of that investigation had to be presented in such a way that all those interested in the protection of Western democracy against Communist subjugation could judge for themselves. To use Ellis's own words, "Hence this book."

As the story unfolded, it became apparent that Sir William's warning speech contained an important truth, unblemished by the passage of time from that distant day when it was spoken by one of the world's greats to another:

> Finally, I must repeat what my friend Winston Churchill included in his last-minute words of wisdom to me on the evening of the day that he became prime minister of Britain and sent me here as his personal representative. I quote: "The United States of America is the mightiest force in the world and can remain so. When the nation is united in a righteous cause, it will prevail over all evil interests, over *all* evil interests." (Sir William Stephenson)

REFLECTIONS
ON SOURCES AND
OFFICIAL
LIES

When the Soviet Union and ourselves were allies in World War II, Stalin's agents were also waging covert warfare against the West. They were helped by secret agreements by which Western secret intelligence assisted in moving Soviet agents into Nazi-held territories, and shared with the Soviets the weaponry and methods of guerrilla warfare. We seemed to be conspiring in our own undoing.

Then Igor Gouzenko, a Russian intelligence officer, defected with proof of aggressive Soviet operations against its allies. This brought all official secret collaboration between the West and the Soviets to an abrupt halt. It was September 1945, the war was over, and the significance of the secret arrangements was suddenly understood by the small handful who knew about them. Gouzenko exposed, for example, spies who had given atomic secrets to the Russians. How did this differ from the official handing over to Moscow of the West's other secrets?

That question has never been asked publicly because the existence of the secret wartime agreements has never been openly discussed. Gouzenko's lonely struggle against the KGB ended in his sudden death in the 1980s. The Soviets had infiltrated Western security, and during the forty years after Gouzenko decided to make his move, they worked to improve their situation. Gouzenko warned us. But he was silenced by the Russian moles he was talking about.

Gouzenko's life was first in danger when the West was treacherously advised to hand him back to the Soviet Union. He was then saved by Sir William Stephenson, known as Intrepid, who ran British Security Coordination with headquarters in New York.

"If Russia seizes the West's secret services, it controls Western policies," was Gouzenko's simple theme. "If it taps into Western intelligence services, it makes them serve the Kremlin. That's the prime Soviet objective."

Now, late in the day, we know he was right. Moscow has been continuously informed of our innermost secrets, from the first atom bomb to the present crop of aerospace weapons, from foreign policies to new satellite defense systems, because the warning was ignored.

The Gouzenko case was reopened in the 1980s after new betrayals were uncovered. When the Soviets failed repeatedly in their attempts to liquidate him, they buried him in a fog of lies generated by their increasingly efficient machinery for disinformation. Deceit, it became clear, was more than ever the instrument of Soviet policy. Weapons for the distortion of truth enjoyed a status equal to that of nuclear arms: they could be wielded aggressively under cover of a peaceful posture.

Gouzenko was a footnote to *A Man Called Intrepid*, and in that book, I called Gouzenko's case "Intrepid's Last." I never intended to write a sequel. Everything regarding Gouzenko was still classified. Secrecy had been used to cover up a conflict that had grown far beyond the dimensions of his early nightmares. Gouzenko's struggle to keep his integrity was that of any individual who believes we cannot remain free and at the same time let ourselves be governed by the weapons of secrecy and falsehood.

In the Soviet scheme of things, Gouzenko was small potatoes. Still, the KGB, the sword and shield of the state, had to crush him. The state could not suffer even one individual who uttered the blasphemy: "You're lying to me."

Soviet justice is mob justice. It condemns a man to death even if he lives outside legal Soviet jurisdiction. Gouzenko had few resources to help him escape. Yet what he did possess was formidable. He was in love with his wife, Svetlana, all his life. She returned that love in full. Their love story illuminates the case. They drew from each other courage enough to inspire an army.

No totalitarian regime can tolerate romantic love. As George Orwell noted in *1984*, only Big Brother is entitled to such devotion. Love between two people is subversive. The lesson of Gouzenko, as we survive 1984, is that romantic love can prevail. From Svetlana he drew the reassurance that he was not guilty of deserting Russia because he had challenged the leadership's claim of infallibility. At the end, surrounded by the love of Svetlana and the children they had raised in freedom, he knew he had been right, in spite of all the pain.

• ◆ •

Gouzenko's story is a journey through today's secret world. As the reader will see, secret reports can be altered secretly by the bureaucrats of secrecy to serve a government's secret needs. Those who guard such secrets have the freedom to tamper with history, and to open fire on amateurs reckless enough to cross their terrain in search of the realities.

Truth, according to Marxist doctrine, is whatever serves "the revolution." Our own strength depends on a decent regard for truth, and recognizing that "official versions" don't always serve it.

Trying to separate truth from falsehood, I finally followed the advice of a fellow combat pilot who crashed in the middle of a wartime mine field. Asked how he failed to blow himself up while walking out, he replied: "Any course I took was bound to trigger some hidden land mine. I made an educated guess on where the safe ground lay and marched straight out with my fingers firmly stuck in my ears."

That may not be the recipe for a scholarly work. By the close of this story, the reader may agree that journalistic objectivity or academic detachment would only lend a spurious gloss to the Gouzenko file. The visible terrain has been navigated with care, in the belief that the booby traps have been avoided; but in the final analysis, it remains a personal journey. Open sources are acknowledged in the text. Many events are described from personal knowledge. It seemed intrusive to project myself into a narrative dealing with matters of such gravity, and involving historical figures. Still, the reader is entitled to know when the author reports from direct experience. Thus, I was with nuclear physicist Niels Bohr when Soviet scientists in Kiev disclosed new space projects. It was I who was in the cell of Trotsky's killer, and showed him proof of his real identity. It was Communist China's premier who accurately warned of a plot to sabotage the *Kashmir Princess*, after inviting me to fly with him on that aircraft to the first Afro-Asian conference. These anecdotes illustrate points in the Gouzenko story, and I have tried to indicate when I myself am the source, without holding up the narrative. One anecdote concerns a Western ambassador who committed suicide in Cairo, fearing he might have to reveal suspected Soviet moles. I talked with him shortly before the tragedy. Now, a KGB-inspired book claiming to list British intelligence agents alleges I was expelled from Cairo while working for MI6. This is totally untrue. I was expelled from Cairo as a foreign correspondent for exposing a former Nazi Jew-baiter employed under an Arab name to direct propaganda against Israel. My talk with the ambassador was never made public.

Another source was Dick Ellis, a professional British intelligence officer all his working life. When reports circulated that he was the second ELLI named by Gouzenko as a Soviet mole, and that Ellis had been a Nazi spy too, the case underwent yet another review. This confirmed that Western secrets had been systematically handed over to the Soviets. But not by Ellis. The leaks have continued to the present day, and Ellis is dead.

I am indebted to the University of Regina whose archivists assumed the task of putting BSC papers in order. These will include summaries in the confidential British Security Coordination history, stamped TOP SECRET. I have drawn from these reports and the previously embargoed BSC file on Gouzenko's case.

The Soviets set out to smash the West's own wartime alliance for intelligence coordination, after the one-way flow of our intelligence secrets to Moscow was officially stopped. The flow began after Hitler invaded Russia in 1941. Prior to that, the Soviets had put their secret intelligence at Nazi disposal. The question of who set up the later Soviet-Western arrangements has never been answered.

It is my own conclusion that once the Soviets lost their access to these secrets, they set out with the help of "useful idiots" to break up the systems painfully assembled by Stephenson and General Donovan of OSS. I base this on the unpublished representations these two intelligence chiefs made to the U.S., Canadian and British governments in a last-ditch attempt to salvage wartime organizations. Bradley F. Smith, in his 1983 history *The Shadow Warriors—OSS and the Origins of the CIA*, records the newly declassified papers that reveal the secret wartime arrangements with the Soviet Union and how the facts were suppressed. I have quoted from my own conversations with personalities such as the former Canadian prime ministers, Lester B. Pearson, and Louis St. Laurent. The diaries of another former Canadian prime minister, William Lyon Mackenzie King, provide the substance of reconstructed conversations: unfortunately, some of the diaries are missing, specifically those covering the period after King consulted with Russian intelligence chiefs in London.

The fact that he did so without concealment, at the height of the Gouzenko crisis and while it was still highly secret, shows that even a prime minister saw nothing wrong, during World War II's immediate aftermath, in discussing Soviet spy-rings with Soviet spymasters. The fact that some relevant diaries have been inexplicably mislaid since then indicates some later embarrassment in the climate of the Cold War. The start of the Cold War was marked, in fact, by Gouzenko's disclosures.

Ian Fleming was the first to suggest I write about Stephenson's organization. That was when the creator of 007 was in Asia to research his last James Bond novel. Long before 007, Fleming was in British naval intelligence, where I first met him in connection with special wartime operations. I was then a navy fighter-pilot. Later, as a foreign correspondent, I kept in touch with Stephenson and Fleming, who ran a foreign news service.

Fleming always knew the Gouzenko case had a significance beyond its immediate impact. It had exploded the world of espionage as noisily as the atom bomb with which it seemed primarily concerned. But Fleming lived in the company of those who were bound by common traditions. A traitor in their midst was unthinkable. I don't believe he quite anticipated that Gouzenko's talk of a Russian mole would lead to the discovery of an entire society betrayed.

"Nothing is ever what it seems," Fleming wrote. And eventually an unsettlingly different picture of the Gouzenko case emerged. It was like a trick drawing in a nursery book. First, you see simple black-and-white shapes. Then the shadows become profiles and everything is inside out.

Such shadows had been burned into the rock at Hiroshima. I wandered through that wasteland after the bombing, before the public understood about radiation death. Suddenly the shadows of a mother and child appeared before me. Yet neither a mother nor her infant were anywhere to be seen. Nor was there light in the sky to cast such shadows.

It was absurd. There were these stark silhouettes on the ground, down to the bun of the mother's hair and the child bound to her back with its tiny head lolling in sleep. Then I saw that the real woman and the child had been vaporized. Only the shadows remained as proof they had ever existed.

If we risk becoming shadows on the stonework of terrestrial creation, as others have warned, it is in part because we did not see Gouzenko clearly the first time. He was obscured by chiaroscuro, that arrangement of dark and light advocated by Soviet ideologues: the deception said to be necessary to the progress of revolution. Misunderstanding is its purpose. Today, a misunderstanding between the superpowers can lead to MAD, "mutually assured destruction." Do the Soviets know what they're doing? Do we?

Officially sanctioned programs of deceit and defamation were assisted by the squabbles between Western intelligence groups after Gouzenko escaped. We cultivated prominent Nazis who lied about their anti-Communist dedication. Now, the Gouzenko case shows that many of those Nazi turncoats were planted by the Soviets to mislead and divide us. We set aside all moral scruples, and we got what we deserved.

Gouzenko believed we could survive on the common integrity and the freedom of ideas at the center of our society. If we surrender any part of these in fighting back, Gouzenko might as well have stayed in Moscow. There, men far more skilled and ruthless in setting aside moral principles would have advanced Gouzenko. His intelligence, stamina and courage would have taken him far—provided Svetlana had helped him kill his conscience. That, of course, was what neither of them could ever do.

William Stevenson   Blue Marlin
1983   Jamaica, West Indies

A GLOSSARY FOR
ATOMIC AND SPY WARS

New forms of warfare cast a pall over the human race when Hiroshima was atomized and a Russian intelligence officer exposed Soviet atomic espionage. The growth of nuclear weapons is only too familiar, whereas the public learns little about advances in spy warfare. We glimpse the underground conflict when, say, a defector is killed by a poison-tipped KGB umbrella. The nuclear-tipped missile, however, is the better-advertised threat. We know that a contemporary nuclear war would differ radically from the Japanese experience, and we know how it would differ. Atomic scientists share knowledge in order to progress, chronicling their work as part of their scientific discipline. By contrast, spy wars employ specialists in the art of concealment. *Their* discipline requires the destruction or distortion of records.

Each type of conflict has its own jargon. This brief glossary is a reminder that secret warfare hides its specialties in acronyms, except in the matter of terror. Our civilization has come under sustained terrorist attack, using all the secret-warfare weapons from deception to torture; it has forced the victims, people of the Jewish faith, to name one of Israel's unending wars the War Against Terror. There is no acronym for terror. No attempt is made here to list the many front organizations practicing this method of assault against the West.

For the sake of simplicity, the secret-intelligence agencies are generally mentioned under the groupings in use at the time of writing. The Russian Intelligence Services, designated RIS, cover the KGB Committee for State Security and the GRU of the Soviet Ministry of Defense.

This story begins when the KGB was known as the NKVD. To clear up the vexing question of the KGB's many predecessors, remember the original need was to control the Soviet Union's people with a secret police: first, Cheka, then OGPU, then NKVD. There has always been conflict between "Chekists," which is what KGB personnel are again officially called, and the GRU, dating from long ago when the KGB's predecessors tried to monopolize foreign activities. To keep both in line, the Soviet Union's Communist Party Central Committee has an international department to coordinate operations.

During and shortly after the Second World War, the Soviet Union's SMERSH operated against Stalin's enemies. SMERSH derived from an acronym of *Smert shpionam*, "death to spies." This has become absorbed into a larger KGB department dealing with *mokrie dela*, "wet affairs," sometimes involving assassination abroad. Action at home or abroad is symbolized by the KGB's device as "the Sword and Shield of the Party." The sword imposes the will of the Party oligarchy, and the shield protects the Party leaders. The KGB is known within the Soviet Union as "the Office of Crude Bandits."

In the United States, the Central Intelligence Agency, CIA, grew out of the first U.S. foreign-intelligence service, the Office of Strategic Services, OSS. There was, however, a chaotic period after the end of World War II when more than twenty different agencies competed to take up the OSS mantle. One of these was the State Department's Office of Policy Coordination, OPC. The OPC's existence was not even suspected, did not appear in official records, and was excluded from official CIA history until 1982,* when its brief existence was examined in the reinvestigation of Intrepid's last case.

Intrepid's last case covered several countries but was handled *officially* first by the Royal Canadian Mounted Police, RCMP: and RCMP is used here unless it is important to differentiate from the Canadian Counterintelligence (CI) Branch or the Intelligence (I) Branch. However, the rescue of the key figure was the work of Intrepid's wartime British Security Coordination (BSC). Neither the organization nor the man could be acknowledged, and Stephenson was known as WSS. Without him, there would have been no case.

Terms in use at the time the case began included:

A B C: America, Britain, and Canada; as in "the ABC secret warfare conference. . . ."

CD: Head of Special Operations Executive (British).

CSS: Head of Secret Intelligence Services (British).

FCC: SSS: U.S. Federal Communications Commission: Signals-Security Service.

---

*It was accorded fleeting recognition in 1976 with publication of *Secrets, Spies and Scholars* (Washington, D.C.: Acropolis Books) by former CIA director Ray S. Cline, when the OPC was included in Cline's list of the CIA's 1948 acquisitions of paramilitary groups.

FIS: U.S. Foreign Information Service of Coordinator of Information (preceding OSS).

FOURTH ARM: A separate ABC fighting force, equal in status to the three conventional armed services, dedicated to secret-warfare methods.

GCCS: Sometimes known as the Golf, Chess, and Cheese Society, the British Government Code and Cipher School responsible for ULTRA, etc.

G-2: U.S. War Department military intelligence.

MEW: Ministry of Economic Warfare (British).

ONI: U.S. Office of Naval Intelligence.

OPG or OP20-G: Communications intelligence branch of U.S. Office of Naval Communications.

OSS: U.S. Office of Strategic Services.

PWE: Political Warfare Department (British).

RSS: Radio Security Service (British).

SFE: U.S. Survey of Foreign Experts.

SIS: Secret Intelligence Service, used in 1982 to cover all British secret services, including MI5 (counterintelligence) and MI6 (foreign intelligence).

SOE: Special Operations Executive (British).

SSA: Signals Security Agency, U.S. War Department.

WEC: Wireless Experimental Center (an ABC project).

In the West, secret agencies now operate systems designed to prevent a spymaster or spycatcher from designating another as his successor . . . to prevent a Soviet mole at the top from replacing himself with another mole. Nothing fogs Western vision more than to have intelligence officers glancing over their shoulders for fear of being spied upon by their own colleagues. Clumsy and annoying loyalty tests were introduced to stop Super-Mole I from replacing himself with Super-Mole II, and so on down the line. Nobody knew how to monitor the committees monitoring the spies. In America, Britain, and Canada—the ABC nations of wartime intelligence triumphs—such committees in the early 1980s investigated the allegations set forth below. One security commission reported in May 1982 that at least the British government was now "moleproof" but then warned that hostile infiltration of the secret-intelligence and diplomatic services was still a danger. Commentators concluded that moleproofing was not yet possible—and meanwhile seventy thousand government workers had undergone a tiresome, even humiliating examination that was now to become a seasonal mole-hunt.

The word *mole*, in the sense of a burrowing, long-term secret agent sent over by the other side, seems to have originated with a speech by Karl Marx in London in 1865: "The old mole that can work in the earth so fast, that worthy pioneer of the Revolution." The word became as familiar as Washington's "Toy Factory," or London's "The Circus," or "The Neighbors" of Moscow Center. But the source of the word *mole*, like that of other secret-warfare terms, is always in dispute.

Muddiness is a cultivated art in the spy business, whereas the atomic glossary is precise, as befits scientific inquiry. The basic expressions used later are:

EXPOSURE DOSE: Amount of radiation to which a body is exposed. The unit of measure is the *roentgen*.

FALLOUT: Radioactive substances scattered over Earth from the atmosphere after a surface explosion. Fine particles in the upper atmosphere may take about twelve days to circle Earth; fine particles in the stratosphere may take years to reach Earth.

NUCLEAR FISSION: Splitting of nuclei of heavy atoms like plutonium or uranium. An atom bomb is a fission device.

NUCLEAR FUSION: Light atomic nuclei, like those of hydrogen, combining to form heavier nuclei. A hydrogen bomb uses a fission bomb wrapped in hydrogenized material to trigger a fusion reaction.

PROTECTION FACTOR (PF): U.S. scale representing degree of protection from fallout. An efficient shelter shields against all but 1 or 2 percent of the fallout gamma radiation.

RADIATION PRODUCTS: Types of radioactive isotopes formed from the material of a bomb and the interaction of neutrons with ground or interactions with earth and debris sucked up into the fireball. This causes fallout.

Contemporary U.S. intelligence agencies are the National Security Agency (NSA), the National Reconnaissance Office (NRO) and the Defense Intelligence Agency (DIA). Nominally coordinated by the CIA director, these are quasi-independent. The NSA keeps electronic watch outside the United States by extracting billions of words daily out of the ether, decoding, sifting, and translating from a bedlam of dialects. NRO's satellites and spy-planes try to picture anything on earth. NSA eavesdrops, NRA scans, and the DIA stores the information.

A four-nation signal intelligence (SIGINT) pact is the result of secret agreements dating back to the 1940s. A senior partner is Britain's Government Communications Headquarters (GCHQ), notionally part of the Foreign Office, but actually answering to a secret intelligence committee of top civil servants, its funds "laundered" through defense and other budgets. GCHQ and the American NSA work with Australia's Defence Signals Division (DSD) and Canada's Communications Branch of the National Research Council (CBNRC).

Between them, they give some assurance of warning against nuclear attack and other possible Soviet mischief. There is no known protection against the misuse of these agencies except the ethics of the society in which we live. This is why responsible intelligence chiefs argue that our protective agencies must reflect the moral values of the societies they defend. The philosophical arguments grew bitter in the wake of Gouzenko's defection. The dangers of immense and secret power were not so well understood in 1945, which may explain the grotesqueries of Intrepid's last case.

CONTENTS

C O N T E N T S

INTREPID'S LAST CASE IS REVIVED

ONE

THE CASE THAT
WON'T BE CLOSED

A shadow fell over the eighty-seventh birthday celebrations of the man called Intrepid, Sir William Samuel Stephenson, on that otherwise sunny Tuesday in January 1983. Seated in a special corner of his Bermuda library, he read: "The man who organized American secret intelligence was a German-Soviet mole."

The bald accusation was given the prominence of a front-page review in the *New York Times Book Review* for the following Sunday. An advance copy arrived, ironically, in the same mail as a letter of congratulation from Nancy and Ronald Reagan.

Stephenson reacted quickly. The charge was leveled against his wartime aide Charles "Dick" Ellis of the British Secret Intelligence Service. Already, Ellis had been accused, posthumously, of suppressing parts of a Russian defector's evidence, supposedly to protect himself and other alleged Soviet moles. Stephenson had "brought in" that defector in 1945: Igor Gouzenko of the Russian Intelligence Services.

The Gouzenko case had been revived after a gala dinner given in 1981 by veterans of the U.S. Office of Strategic Services, the legendary World War II intelligence organization that grew from the partnership between Stephenson and General "Wild Bill" Donovan. As the book review was now pointing out, Dick Ellis had assisted Donovan in the creation of the OSS "and was in a perfect position to expose and compromise every secret agent, operation and modus operandi of the agency" during World War II.

Did Ellis commit gross acts of treachery?

Stephenson had returned to the Gouzenko case to learn how the Russians had "burned" the defector in the hope of preventing further detection of agents of the Russian Intelligence Service, the RIS. Gouzenko had submitted documentary proof of extensive Soviet infiltration. Russian disinformation had successfully forced public attention to concentrate only on charges of atomic espionage. When parts of Gouzenko's evidence were released, it was made to appear that some traitors who provided the RIS with atomic secrets and government papers were acting out of a muddle-headed loyalty to the wartime alliance against Hitler. Stalin, alarmed by news of the West's atomic bomb, had called together Russian physicists: "A single demand I have. Provide us with atomic weapons in the shortest possible time. . . . Remove a great danger from us." The scientist in charge, Igor Kurchatov, soon discovered, from the traitors in the West, which of several possible paths to follow.

The real issue was Gouzenko's frustrated attempts to expose Russian agents recruited from the West's own public servants—even inside our own intelligence services.

Now it was being said that Stephenson's hand-picked intelligence expert, Ellis, was such a Russian agent, recruited because his pro-Nazi activities made him vulnerable to blackmail. Ellis, it was said, used his power to help the Russians silence Gouzenko.

The cases of Gouzenko and Ellis were thus inextricably linked. Ellis died suddenly just before the allegations against him were made public. Gouzenko died just as unexpectedly in 1982, in circumstances that dramatized the strangeness of both these men's lives. Gouzenko was buried secretly under the name of "Mr. Brown who came to us from Prague." A circumspect funeral oration was delivered by an anonymous preacher of an unidentified faith in a place merely described as "somewhere in North America."

Stephenson ended his birthday celebrations on a much happier note. He was asked to accept the General William J. Donovan Award for outstanding service to the cause of freedom. This gave symmetry to the review of Intrepid's last case. The award had previously been made to Britain's Prime Minister Margaret Thatcher at that earlier gala OSS dinner of 1981, to which Stephenson had asked me to go, hoping to pick up more clues to the Gouzenko-Ellis mystery.

"Reformed experts in skulduggery." The description was delivered by William Casey, newly appointed director of the CIA, when he hosted the 1981 gathering of OSS veterans in New York. He spoke in tones of genuine admiration, for he found much to admire as he surveyed the guests in the Waldorf-Astoria's Grand Ballroom. Nearly a thousand strong, resplendent in evening clothes glittering with diamonds and military decorations, Casey's old World War II comrades presented an inspiring spectacle.

Survivors from America's first foreign-intelligence agency, they seemed to confirm Johnny Shaheen's retrospective assessment: "We got the best." Shaheen was chairman of the Donovan Award Committee, and was squiring Prime Minister Thatcher. Born in the same farm hamlet as President Ronald Reagan, at Tampico, Illinois, Shaheen had been wartime chief of OSS Special Projects. He had worked behind enemy lines to retrieve secret weapons. He had secretly negotiated the surrender of an entire enemy fleet. Now an oil millionaire welcome in the White House, he could identify around him dozens of distinguished figures who had made their mark in quite a different way some forty years earlier, plunging into secret warfare in the service of democracy.

My host was a law secretary to New York's Mayor Fiorello LaGuardia and a member of President Franklin D. Roosevelt's "brain trust," Ernest Cuneo. A peppy, all-American athlete and patriot, Cuneo had received the highest British secret-intelligence award for his work of liaison between the White House, OSS, the FBI and Stephenson, and for settling the basis of anti-Nazi Resistance operations. Cuneo had brought along his old friend Arthur Goldberg, the former Supreme Court Justice, who managed the wartime infiltration of the anti-Nazi labor movement in Europe.

Around us sat ex-CIA chief Bill Colby, who had parachuted behind Nazi lines and was almost killed on a sabotage operation; the Countess of Romanones (formerly Aline Griffith of Pearl River, N.Y.), who escaped a Nazi trap by leaping from a speeding car. James Angleton became the CIA's most notorious spycatcher after learning the trade among Anglo-American codebreakers. Travel writer Temple Fielding smuggled devices stinking of human excrement into Nazi-occupied territory "for their psychologically disturbing impact." Michael Burke fought with the Resistance, later organized guerrilla forces, then became a CBS-TV executive and president of the New York Yankees and of Madison Square Garden. TV chef Julia Child traveled the world on OSS business. Beverly Woodner, a prewar Hollywood set designer, became an OSS expert on deception and visual aids. So many had been drawn from the Social Register that the OSS became known as the Oh-So-Social—a misnomer, because many others had been recruited among new immigrants to America, and still others (conspicuous by their absence on this night) came from the ranks of safecrackers and cat burglars, counterfeiters and confidence tricksters.

The group, assembled this final night of February 1981, symbolized the spirit of American-British-Canadian coordination that attended the creation of the OSS in 1942. They had invited Canadian ambassador Ken Taylor for his clandestine support in Iran during the long hostage ordeal. When host Casey presented the Donovan Award to Britain's Iron Lady, there was no trace of the Artful Mumble by which he was known to baffle eavesdroppers. Instead, he announced proudly the purpose of the award, "to foster a tradition and spirit of the kind of service to country and the cause of freedom Bill Donovan rendered for the world's security and safety."

"Little Bill" Stephenson had coached Donovan in Britain's secret arts. They had become a legend as "The Two Bills—Big and Little," after Stephenson cabled the Secret Intelligence Service in London, "OUR MAN IS IN POSITION," on June 18, 1941. A year later, Donovan had set up the basis of the OSS with administrative guidance from Dick Ellis. Without Ellis, wrote one of Donovan's intelligence chiefs, David Bruce, "American intelligence could not have gotten off the ground."[*]

Stephenson would have appreciated, no less than Casey, this revival of ABC unity. The term ABC, used loosely to describe the American-British-Canadian teamwork, arose from a 1941 "review of strategy" *before the United States had yet entered the war.*[**] The ground had been prepared by British Security Coordination in America, established by Stephenson using the codename Intrepid. The combined efforts of the three countries had won an unpublicized race to build the atom bomb. There were ABC agreements during United States neutrality that resulted in the sabotage of Nazi-held sources of exotic materials for nuclear ex-

---

[*] See Part One, "Groundwork with the Americans," of the unpublished BSC history, *Top Secret*, p. 22.

[**] The ABC grouping became known as ARCADIA, after the secret Washington war conference following Pearl Harbor in December 1941. But since ABC better conveys the sense of Atlantic unity, I have kept to it, though purists may prefer ARCADIA.

periments, and in the rescue (some would say the kidnapping) of physicists from Nazi territories. British experts were secretly moved to the American continent. Canada's vast hinterland concealed experimental projects, and in World War II was the free world's only source of certain raw materials needed to create an atomic bomb that for a time seemed to be made mostly from the cobwebs of fantasy.

Another ABC creation would prove of utmost concern to Stalin: a Fourth Arm of subversive operations to rank alongside the army, navy, and air force as an arm of the regular defense services. The Fourth Arm had been conceived as the means by which Nazi despots would be overthrown in Europe by local patriots, led by trained guerrillas, aided by saboteurs and other experts in insurrection. A Fourth Arm, if it persisted in the postwar years, would be used against other tyrants, of whom the most obvious was Stalin. And Stalin had been obsessed, even in the worst moments of Hitler's war against Russia, with the danger of internal revolt—especially with the danger of uprisings fomented by that archvillain among anti-Bolsheviks, Winston Churchill, and his American friends.

The violent reaction of Stalin to the Fourth Arm theory of subversion was best known to Dick Ellis, whose first secret-intelligence work during the Russian revolution had earned him Stalin's personal hatred as a British spy fomenting "counterrevolutionary forces." The part played by Ellis in Fourth Arm operations after the first ABC talks revived the Soviet dictator's hostility to Stephenson's deputy.

Having known Ellis, I could well imagine his response to the 1981 reminder that ABC ties still prevailed. The New York *Sunday News* headlined its report on the OSS dinner: THATCHER BACKS PREZ IN FIGHT TO CURB SOVIET. Ellis would have said this new celebration of solidarity must attract the attention of Moscow Center, that the principals at the dinner were sitting ducks for KGB character assassins. "Sowing suspicion is the classic KGB tactic," he had told me. "They've got a name for it, *dezinformatsiya*, and a department to direct it."

DISINFORMATION
AT WORK

Within weeks of the OSS dinner Bill Casey was under attack as unfit to direct the CIA. It took many months for him to survive scrutiny by the U.S. Senate Intelligence Committee. *Time* magazine commented: "The character and judgment of America's top spymasters are being questioned around the world."

The London *Daily Mail* set off a series of scandals with the front-page flare: MI5 CHIEF WAS RUSSIAN SPY SUSPECT. The new upsurge of "spy-fever" in Britain had begun with serialization of veteran correspondent Chapman Pincher's *Their Trade Was Treachery* during the week of March 26. An earnest investigator, Pincher claimed to have uncovered more instances of Soviet espionage than were known to a public convinced that the notorious Kim Philby represented the most serious case of Soviet penetration. Pincher pointed to Sir Roger Hollis, onetime director general of MI5, as having twice been investigated—with results sufficiently inconclusive that Prime Minister Thatcher was later moved to attest that it was impossible to prove Hollis a spy.

So on the morning of Friday, March 27, 1981, Russian defector Igor Gouzenko was rousted out to appear on Canadian television. Hooded, out of what some reporters openly suggested was an irrational fear of Soviet reprisals, Gouzenko claimed that his evidence of treachery at the highest levels of British intelligence had never been acted upon—indeed, had been willfully suppressed.

As a friend of Gouzenko, I sat in the studio, surprised by his vehement statements. He seemed especially vulnerable because his credibility had been eroded by thirty-five years of subtle backstabbing. It was ironic that this man who had told me, "Stephenson saved my life," was now exposing himself to danger once more. He was a man of rare courage—some would say recklessly brave, for he had set out to challenge the agents of Soviet revenge so many times. Few remembered now that, soon after his defection, he had authored a remarkable novel of Tolstoyan quality that revealed his intimate understanding of the methods by which Stalin controlled thoughts as well as actions within his Soviet empire. It was the work of someone better educated and more knowledgeable about the internal workings of the Russian secret police than his attackers wished to admit. They dismissed him consistently as a mere "cipher clerk."

Stephenson, using his own resources, now believed it vital to reopen the case. One of the reasons the case had been juggled away out of his hands in 1946 was his insistence on the Russian's right to testify in public. Had Gouzenko been allowed to speak out earlier, to present all his evidence of moles and super-moles in our democratic institutions, the disaster of McCarthyism might have been avoided. Instead, the frenzied response to Gouzenko by hidden bureaucrats left a vacuum that McCarthy's demagogic and ultimately counterproductive hysteria filled all too nicely, as far as the Kremlin was concerned. The search for Soviet spies degenerated into a decade of witch-hunting.

Stephenson would be up against character assassins again: Gouzenko had already been libeled as a drunk, a spendthrift, and worse. His revelations of secret Soviet successes were distorted and neutralized. Stephenson himself had come under attack. And the reputation of Dick Ellis, his trusted aide, was especially vulnerable. Ellis had suffered interrogation in the sixties, during an earlier outbreak of spy-fever. Even now, Chapman Pincher was saying he could prove Ellis confessed to spying for both Nazis and Russians. Ellis was entitled to have someone spring to his defense. His maverick ways, the distrust he shared with Stephenson of bureaucrats who cultivated an air of infallibility, had shadowed his career. The charges against him were predictable, but Stephenson knew what he knew: the unobtrusive Australian who started out to be a musician had been a brilliant linguist, a tough soldier, and, as he moved undercover between the wars, tracing the tangled threads of Soviet-Nazi collaboration, the very model of eccentric creativity essential to any successful intelligence service.

"I must insist on Ellis's innocence until, and if, I hear the tape of his alleged confession," Stephenson cabled the Australian prime minister, whose own security service was now said to have been compromised by

Ellis, a founding father. And to the commissioners of a fullblown British investigation into the charges of KGB penetration, he wrote: "The authors of the allegations against Ellis must be made to reveal their sources."

Stephenson was on his way to shaking out the truth of the Gouzenko case. He had the contacts. I had the mobility. We resumed an old working relationship. Through the spring and summer of 1981, while the public was treated to the spectacle of Western security agencies being forced once more into self-purification that seemed only to damage their effectiveness, we began our own investigation. Stephenson had been concerned that all through the years, traitors had made use of "official secrecy" to disguise their own activities inside the bureaucracies. "The best defense against that kind of treachery," he had long argued, "is public disclosure. It then becomes the best safeguard against KGB misrepresentation, the best antidote to the dottiness lurking in the corners of the institutions of intelligence."

We met obstacles at each turn in attempting to reassemble the facts behind the Gouzenko case. There seemed to be greater interest in guarding the myths of institutional infallibility than in placing the facts before the public. "The public is allowed to see only the tip of the iceberg, and it's little wonder," Gouzenko told us. "The iceberg is one on which the armada of Western intelligence has been ripping itself apart since the wartime alliance with Stalin."

Suddenly, smelling more scandal, journalists in North America and Western Europe extended their own spy hunts. The *Washington Post* quoted a London editor as saying, "There's nothing so jolly." Other investigators made use of the Freedom of Information Act to try to turn Washington archives inside out. The partial declassification of government papers in Britain and Canada led to the stunning conclusion that official and secret records had been silently "weeded" by unknown hands. Vital sections of CIA, FBI, and SIS files on Gouzenko could not be traced.

"Mountains of stuff were missing," according to Professor J. L. Granatstein, an eminent historian writing the biography of Norman Robertson, the Canadian undersecretary of foreign affairs involved in the Gouzenko case. Gouzenko-related files were empty or contained useless, single sheets of paper. Minutes of the committee coordinating the Gouzenko case and developing methods to combat Soviet espionage: *gone*. Communications about Gouzenko with Washington and London: *gone*. Reports from Gouzenko's interrogators: *gone*. Policy advisories: *gone*. To the professional historian of integrity, such tampering with the files rendered all documents useless.

Then top-level notes on the Gouzenko case, written by Canadian Prime Minister Mackenzie King, were officially said to have disappeared. They represented a crucial section of the diaries King kept all his life, affording insight into a significant piece of North American history. Those diaries were guarded as national treasures. They filled fifty-three boxes in Canada's National Archives, amid physical safeguards that always excited the envy of other governments. King's diary entries on Gouzenko were meticulous. Anyone could read them *up to the first ten days of November 1945*, following a confidential meeting in London between King and the Soviet's highest-ranking NKVD representative abroad. The missing section of King's daily notes extended to the beginning of 1946, the year the case was forced into the public domain. It was, historian Granatstein said, "inexplicable for one volume of his diaries simply to vanish."

Next, security files on Gouzenko were found to have been injected with poisonous character assessments. These lies were repeated in Anglo-American counterintelligence records. The proof came unexpectedly from an Ottawa-appointed commission investigating the Royal Canadian Mounted Police and general counterintelligence problems. Its 1981 report, *Freedom and Security Under the Law*, criticized an unknown official who had "editorialized" on Gouzenko's character, inserting into his dossier remarks about his personality that destroyed his credibility. Gouzenko had been the victim of a deliberate campaign of character assassination. He had been increasingly ignored by the authorities after the dossier on him was compiled in 1946, and expanded covertly later. Because it was secret, neither he nor anyone who knew him well had been in a position to correct the false witness.

The KGB had developed new ways to neutralize its enemies. Defectors, under Soviet law, could be condemned to death in their absence. Execution of the sentence had in wartime been the work of SMERSH assassination teams. But the threat to the Soviet Union could also be lifted by tampering with files, an easier procedure. How damaging this could be, General Michael Dare, then chief of Canadian security services, had indicated to a 1979 parliamentary inquiry into secret-intelligence practices. Dare divulged that his country's top spycatcher, James Bennett, had been interrogated for several days as the result of "overall concern in the Western community as to the possibility of penetrations at high level" consequent to disclosures of alleged KGB defectors. Bennett had been relieved of his duties "on medical grounds," in 1972. Something had been happening about which the public was kept in the dark. Reputations had been damaged, careers ruined, possibly in some cases because skilled KGB operators exploited the very secrecy on which secret intelligence is based. The agencies had been investigating themselves, behind closed doors, accepting evidence that sometimes came from professional liars.

Bits of paper had replaced the old violence. Stalin had struck across frontiers with ice picks and bullets. A modern version of SMERSH had pursued the Russian defector who survived Stalin's assassins and "eliminated" him with paper and pen.

But there was one record of the Corby Case that had not been violated. Stephenson had never been part of the establishment and had kept his own records, resisting the blandishments of successive rulers of intelligence. He had preserved the secret section of the Corby Case report, anticipating the likelihood of later distortion. It contradicted the rewriters of history. As a gifted amateur whose patriotism was beyond doubt, Stephenson was his own boss and he kept his own bits of paper. The official history of British Security Coordination had been secretly produced "to provide a record available for reference should future need arise for the secret activities and security measures of the kind it describes." Now it survived as an independent account, free from second thoughts and bureaucratic "improvement," safe from the paper-handlers.

Because of this, Stephenson himself became a target not only of the KGB but also of those Western mandarins who had used secrecy to squelch whatever they disapproved. Some talked of him as an old man whose memory was impaired and whose wartime SIS aide had been a spy for the enemy. And an official CIA history, after six years under a secrecy ban, unwittingly provoked more sniping. The public could read about U.S. State Department worries that Stephenson's BSC operations had "constituted a full-size secret police and intelligence agency . . . run by the British on American soil." More provocative still was the mysterious appearance of an appendix, said to come from Stephenson's still-secret files on Gouzenko. This proposed a continuation of the wartime BSC-OSS partnership with provisions for "influencing American opinion by covert means." Stephenson had never written it.

A MOLE CALLED ELLI

By the first week of November 1981, what had once seemed like an open-and-shut case was proving to be still full of unsolved mysteries. Gouzenko insisted that in 1946 he gave evidence of two Soviet agents codenamed ELLI. One in Canada, Kathleen Willsher, had been caught and punished. The other, in England, had escaped; there had been *no* pursuit of this ELLI by counterintelligence; Gouzenko's evidence had been suppressed; all further inquiries had been terminated by Soviet agents.

Suddenly breaking its own oath of secrecy, Pierre Trudeau's Liberal government in Canada succumbed to pressure from opposition Conservatives; and this late in 1981, Ottawa now declassified six thousand pages of Gouzenko's testimony, given before the 1946 commission. Among these pages were two passages concerning the existence of a super-mole high inside the Secret Intelligence Service during the crucial period of the last years of World War II and on into the Cold War.

The relevant exchanges between Gouzenko and the royal commissioners were now reported by the *Times* of London, apparently with official British approval, thus:

Q: Do you know if ELLI was used as the nickname or cover for any person other than Miss Willsher?
GOUZENKO: Yes, there is some agent under the same name in Great Britain.

Later:

> Q: There is a Kay Willscher [sic] who is known under the cover name
> of ELLI?
> GOUZENKO: That is right.
> Q: Would that be the same person?
> GOUZENKO: No.

Evidence that Gouzenko had been on secret record all this time as affirming in 1946 the existence of the second ELLI caused an uproar. Why had this part of his testimony been suppressed? What national security was served? Clearly, nothing had been done to pursue his declaration under oath. Had the security services suppressed evidence that would prove he told the truth? In London, Chapman Pincher again called for parliamentary answers to the questions thus revived, and quoted Gouzenko to support the allegations against Dick Ellis.

Gouzenko had told the commission in 1946 that the second ELLI had been identified in England. Gouzenko was sure action had been taken on his confidential disclosures to the Secret Intelligence Service. He was kept in ignorance of the outcome of these disclosures, just as the public had been. He thought this natural, and assumed the London ELLI had been quietly arrested. It was a fair assumption. It would have seemed lunatic of the security authorities to neglect further action, and in those days Gouzenko had never thought they were lunatics.

But by that fall of 1981, nobody suffered from such illusions. During the preceding decades, the public had become educated about Soviet moles. Nobody was therefore too surprised when it turned out that the "secret" testimony released by Ottawa was *not* in fact the classified material demanded earlier in Parliament. It had been fed as a sop to those who called for the fullest investigation of the Gouzenko story. A bureaucrat had spent many months combing through the material to remove anything of potential embarrassment. What was left did *not* include a thousand pages of direct evidence, which remained instead under the total secrecy ban. The telltale exchanges between Gouzenko and his questioners regarding ELLI had been buried in a mountain of otherwise familiar testimony, evading the secret censor's eye. When this embarrassing slip was spotted, the revealing exchanges were removed from a government summary of the new material.

"The government picked over the 'secret' testimony," wrote the Toronto *Sun*'s editor-in-chief, Peter Worthington, "and found nothing damning there, so released it five years ahead of an extended secrecy ban. The *real* story was hidden in supporting evidence they held back, the direct evidence from the Soviet embassy. Nonetheless, the questions about ELLI finally confirmed that Gouzenko did not invent his story later, as his enemies suggested."

The ruling Liberal party of Canada had been intent on protecting its political position, and tossed forth the "secret" testimony to divert those in Ottawa's parliament who demanded a full-scale investigation. "We know of some clear cases of espionage around the Gouzenko case," said Prime Minister Pierre Elliot Trudeau. "Presumably espionage has been going on, and will go on. . . . I fail to see how an investigation by some public body will turn up names of spies that should not have been turned up by other methods."

But of course it had been the failure of "other methods" that led to demands for the investigation.

More crucial papers dealing with Gouzenko were found missing by the Toronto *Globe and Mail*, whose editors concluded that "the lying and deception and evasion which is part of spying itself spills over into the policy of continuing concealment."

The London *Times* commented that the new Gouzenko papers, though not yet fully disclosed, "confirm the existence of a mole very high in the British intelligence service in 1945." At this point, Gouzenko expanded on another of his claims: that in the summer of 1946 he had been visited by "a gentleman from England" who personally guaranteed that the information on the London ELLI would be pursued right through to the end. Asked the identity of this "gentleman from England," Gouzenko replied that it could very well be Sir Roger Hollis, who was at the time employed by the British Secret Intelligence Service as a London-based spycatcher. Hollis had now been accused of serving the Russian Intelligence Services.

Stephenson remembered very clearly an attempt by SIS to have Hollis interrogate Gouzenko just after the defection, but he'd always supposed himself successful in turning the SIS man back in New York to avoid what he had sensed, even then, was a potential danger. Would I question Gouzenko again? This I did.

Gouzenko said he had learned about the super-mole in 1942 while working at Moscow Center in the main cipher room of GRU military intelligence. Forty cipher experts worked in the center, he said, and one day a lieutenant passed over a telegram just deciphered from London, originating "from one of ours, right inside British counterintelligence." The spy was in such a prominent position that he could only be contacted through *duboks*, secret hiding places for pickups. His codename was ELLI.

Then Gouzenko asked me: Was Dick Ellis married to a Russian? Did he serve inside Russia? Was he in Paris before the Hitler war? These questions arose from what Gouzenko had heard in Moscow about a Soviet agent in British service. The answers were all affirmative. Gouzenko said: "Then it's possible ELLI was Ellis."

Later, I quoted this to a prominent member of Anglo-American secret intelligence. He spread his hands. "Married a Russian . . . worked in Russia . . . was in Paris—There can't be any doubt then, can there?"

This readiness to jump to conclusions was as unsettling as the earlier rejection of everything Gouzenko had tried to say in warning. One faction inside the intelligence community proclaimed Ellis's innocence as fiercely as another his guilt. And to confuse matters, there was the exasperating mystery of Sir Roger Hollis, whose name could be mistaken so readily for that of Ellis!

Dick Ellis, awarded the U.S. Legion of Merit by President Truman for "the development of certain of our intelligence organizations and methods," was now said to have spied for the Nazis and for the Soviets. Ellis, whose "superior foresight and diplomacy," according to President Truman, "were responsible for the success of highly important operations," appeared to be the prime suspect for Gouzenko's ELLI. Ellis, personally selected by Intrepid to serve him during the war years, and later Number 3 in the SIS hierarchy, controller of British intelligence operations in the Western Hemisphere and in the Far East, was alleged to have betrayed everything to the enemies of Western democracy.

Stephenson lived quietly nowadays at the hub of an informal network of old, well-placed colleagues. His Bermuda home saw a steady stream of visitors, of whom the most welcome were the young. He kept in touch daily with friends abroad by Telex and telephone; and he responded with the quick elasticity of the lightweight boxer he'd once been to requests for comment on international news. He was frequently well ahead of us in discerning new trends in diplomacy and politics. When the youngsters came to see him, it was not from a sense of obligation to an elder, but out of a feeling that he was one of themselves, and able to talk sympathetically about their problems.

Out for a spin in his car, along the North Shore, Stephenson could glimpse between oleander and fruit trees and the perennially blossoming hedgerows his typically Bermudan home, high on Camden Hill. He had planned it, down to the lover's moongate in the white stone wall, with his wife Mary, who now lay buried close by. A small handful of us had attended Lady Mary's funeral. "A spymaster's kind of funeral," a friend had mused, "straight out of James Bond." He meant, I suppose, the tight-lipped self-control and the simplicity of the service. The speaker had recalled that Bond's creator, Ian Fleming, once wrote: "Stephenson worked himself almost to death carrying out undercover operations and often dangerous assignments that can only be hinted at."

The austere assembly in the cold stone church did convey something of the style of intelligence when Stephenson and Dick Ellis were close partners. The preacher had been asked to stick to the bare bones of the funeral service. Behind the coffin, Stephenson walked unaided, a triumph of will power. His air-crash injuries from the First World War, accidents in the Second, and a crippling series of more recent illnesses had sentenced him to restrictions against which he rebelled. Nobody among the few mourners who followed him through the quiet country churchyard would dare offer him assistance.

Until her death, Lady Mary Stephenson had been tirelessly on guard against those who might bear him a grudge. She shared his dislike of ostentation. They had planned their own funerals together, being practical folk. Then came the slanders against Dick Ellis, attacks on Intrepid himself, and a revived effort to discredit Gouzenko. Suddenly there was unfinished business Lady Mary would have wished him to complete, and unanswered questions she would have wished him to pursue.

In the past, as General Gubbins of Special Operations Executive had observed, those with problems beat a path to Stephenson's door "as if drawn by an unseen thread." In 1981 Stephenson was instead often seen tapping with his cane along corridors of distant hotels, or consulting with groups of elderly men and women in hotel suites. The writer Roald Dahl, vacationing that summer at Martha's Vineyard with his wife, Patricia

Neal, said he would not have been surprised to see his old chief once again "striking the fear of God in me, bouncing along on the balls of his feet like a boxer springing from his corner, such a small man with such a silent blazing stare."

None of the spiritual bounce had gone. Just the way Gubbins had remembered it, callers beat a path to his door from all over the world, perturbed by a sense that Western intelligence agencies had been turned into Soviet puppets. Gubbins had said long ago, about the manipulation of German intelligence by British agents, that "if one nation penetrates the security and intelligence of another, it pulls the strings." Some war-time Soviet infiltrators had learned that lesson well.

The Russians had acquired experience before World War II by milking the German intelligence services. This was where Dick Ellis had become involved first with both Nazis and Soviets. He had worked alone in the field, dealing with agents from both sides and reporting back to London. Intrepid was convinced that by doing this, Ellis had left himself open to an attack on his reputation. But why was such an attack launched now?

On a day when Stephenson had withdrawn to his library in Bermuda, we discussed the question. I was conscious of plunging back into territory where nothing is firm, no depth of field measurable. No perception was so solid that it would not dissolve into its opposite in this land of chiaroscuro. An expert navigator through such territory was this man, whose features were not those of infirmity. The nose was thin, precisely chiseled like an eagle's bill; the skin taut over finely wrought facial bones. His eyes reflected the steel-gray Bermuda sky, brightening with the sun's first rays, for he still rose at the crack of dawn. He had the old fighter-pilot's breadth of vision, taking in a small pajamaed child of the household in one doorway and also, on the other side of the library, the big picture window overlooking terraced gardens sloping toward the mist-laden sea.

He might have been a Scottish laird, or a proud crofter, beside the open fireplace, with shelves of books and personal photographs within easy reach. His cane hung from the arm of a chair. At his elbow were the radios and recorders with which he had been monitoring the world's daily chatter for many years. Within his hearing were the Telex machines whose sudden clatter would bring anticipation to his eyes. Old colleagues persisted in cabling him INTREPID BERMUDA, and his critics sniped at him for continuing to use the Churchillian codename, but this was not by his wish. An understanding cable station routed such telecoms to his registered cable address: INTER. The cable authorities had not forgotten Stephenson's contributions to the development of communications, sparked by his first explorations as a small boy on the Canadian prairies, tapping out Morse signals to wireless operators on the ships of the Great Lakes. That old Morse key now occupied space on the desk beside his central teletype machine.

Stephenson reached up for a recent book by former MI6 officer H. Montgomery Hyde, author of *The Atom Bomb Spies*. It chronicled the consequences of Gouzenko's defection, the execution of Ethel and Julius Rosenberg. If the Rosenbergs had confessed to stealing atomic secrets, their lives would have been spared. They had refused. They had died as martyrs in the eyes of many. Ethel Rosenberg's suffering was illustrated in Hyde's book by the photograph of an unidentified woman at the moment of agony in the electric chair: a secret camera had recorded a woman's body bursting against the leather restraints, the obscene helmet straining, a blurred eye bulging toward the hidden lens. Something like that image of explosive violence had inflamed public opinion, which in general held that the Rosenbergs were unjustly slaughtered in a Salem-style witch-hunt.

The public had not been told that evidence against the Rosenbergs came from decoded Soviet intelligence traffic. The facts had been withheld from the courtroom because the Russians would have switched their codes once they realized these had been compromised. The work started by Western intelligence in wartime had been continued under operational codenames such as BRIDE, VANOSA, and others.

Stephenson shifted his attention away from his notepads and studied the distant surf creaming along the coral reefs, the sunshine dancing on a peaceful, twinkling sea. Deception was a two-edged sword. Secret power was dangerous power, inviting arbitrary decisions that cut across the system of justice in democratic societies. The Soviets understood this, and exploited it, knowing the handicaps under which counterintelligence labored, so that even if the execution of the Rosenbergs had been justified in the minds of those Americans able to study the Moscow Center traffic in 1953, the public could see only the apparent injustice.

He glanced through advance proofs of *Mole*, a book by William Hood, a former CIA executive, who wrote:

Like war, spying is a dirty business. Shed of its alleged glory, a soldier's job is to kill. Peel away the claptrap of espionage and the spy's job is to betray trust. The only justification a soldier or a spy can have is the moral worth of the cause. . . . When an ordinary man puts his life at stake for a political cause, and has an impact on history, the story is worth telling. . . .

Gouzenko had made such an impact. But the story, it was now clear, had never been fully told; it illustrated the terrible temptation of secret power, the seductive quality of hidden authority over the fortunes of those trapped in a secret war. Dick Ellis had also made an impact—as the ordinary man who unwittingly dramatizes the temptations of secret power. Ellis had long ago staked his life on a cause, and Stephenson had accepted him as a patriot with the professional standing to be privy to British Security Coordination secrets.

Stephenson, staring at the distant sea, might be thought to be suffering great inner anguish. If he was, he gave no sign. I had learned after many years that he directed attention away from his own feelings. He was an enigma to those who seemed closest to him. If an oldtime colleague was in need of cheering up, Stephenson acted with an almost boyish readiness that had something to do with the camaraderie within fighter squadrons of 1914–18. "It's like finding yourself in one of those old schoolboy magazines where chaps buck each other up," Ian Fleming once said.

Stephenson wished Bill Donovan could be here, to see how matters had turned out since their high hopes for Atlantic unity. They'd dreamed of a peacetime intelligence system based on joint war experiences, and this had been finally achieved. They had not foreseen the confused loyalties, the inversion of set values, the routine of betrayal. But Stephenson was never a doomsayer. The democracies had the enormous strength of versatility and a willingness to test new ideas. Gouzenko, who had dreamed of a new life, was rewarded with British citizenship by King George VI, and this had meant a great deal to the Russian.

"Stephenson always looked for the sparkle of gold in the dross," Fleming used to insist. He had consulted Stephenson on spy paraphernalia for the James Bond novels. He did not acknowledge this in public, explaining later, "The joke was, Stephenson's wartime guise remained the biggest secret of all." Stephenson's close involvement with the FBI and the forerunners of the CIA was never fully understood in Gouzenko's lifetime. Just before the former Russian intelligence officer died in the summer of 1982, he remembered Stephenson as the man known, among his personal security guards, as Mister Whoosis.

THE BSC IN
TIME OF WAR

What some would later call Stephenson's Secret Occupation of Manhattan began in 1940, after British forces were rescued from Nazi-dominated Europe and before the Battle of Britain began. By 1941, J. Edgar Hoover of the FBI was complaining that the Rockefeller Center headquarters of British Security Coordination controlled an army of British secret agents; and Assistant Secretary of State Adolf Berle was protesting in a confidential memo that BSC covered the British Secret Intelligence Service, Special Operations Executive, and a Fourth Arm building up rebel armies, as well as British counterintelligence, codes and ciphers, secret communications . . . and that Stephenson directed nine secret and distinct agencies of British intelligence, with bureaus in most large American cities. Hoover objected at one stage that Stephenson often acted first and told the FBI afterwards—and sometimes forgot to tell at all. To this, U.S. Attorney General Francis Biddle answered that there was "an unfathomable contradiction" if Hoover pretended to know no details of Stephenson's activities because "the FBI sends out two or three hundred messages a week in secret code from British intelligence here to British intelligence in London. The truth is," Biddle had said in despair, "nobody knows anything about what Stephenson does."*

*Thomas Troy, Donovan And The CIA: History of the Establishment of the CIA (CIA, 1981).

Except, he could have added, President Franklin D. Roosevelt and Winston Churchill.

"One shadowy figure (Stephenson), through undercover operations . . . exercised on the fate of the Western world an influence indispensable to its survival," David Bruce, as permanent U.S. representative on the North Atlantic Council, later wrote. "This modest, almost anonymous, figure endowed with determined will and singular charisma, whom Churchill cherished, succeeded not in dominating but in persuading Churchill and Roosevelt into a communality of views on most security affairs which made his own position unique."

The two wartime leaders had formed, in effect, a secret alliance two years before Pearl Harbor. In the period when Britain, alone in Europe, defied the Nazis, and the United States remained neutral, certain preparations had been made against the possible conquest of Britain by Hitler. Underground resistance would be coordinated from overseas. Plans for new secret weapons were transferred to the United States for further development and manufacture. As the danger of German invasion diminished, Stephenson turned more to Churchill's major assignment: "Bring the Americans into the war, I don't care how." Greater emphasis was placed on the undeclared American war at sea. Ways were found to drive huge quantities of military equipment through the U.S. neutrality laws and into British hands. As part of the British Security Coordination, Stephenson built his own security division to protect such supplies against sabotage, and he built another group to sabotage Axis shipping. "BSC committed more acts of sabotage than the whole of the German-born colony in the United States," reported a Russian Intelligence Services general whose identity would become vitally important when the Gouzenko-Ellis connection was finally explored.

This is what the Soviet intelligence report had to say:

Stephenson devoted his best efforts [to] persuading the Americans that it was high time they created an intelligence service of their own. . . . It would be better for the British to get in on the ground floor [in 1940–42] and, by offering all help in the early stages, [to] earn the right to receive in return the intelligence that might be expected to flow from deployment of the greater resources of the United States. [Stephenson's] achievement was to stimulate the interest of Roosevelt himself, and to make quite sure that the president knew that Stephenson and his backers, among whom were SOE and MI5 as well as SIS, had a lot to offer. Thus when the OSS was born with General "Wild Bill" Donovan at its head the closest cooperation with the British was already assumed at the highest level.

In other words, Stalin was being advised: If you want to use American strength, American inventiveness, and America's huge resources of space, manpower and natural wealth, you cannot do better than copy Stephenson's methods of placing well-disposed friends in positions of secret influence.

"Stephenson," concluded the Russian report, "is a friend of Churchill's and wields more real political power than any other British intelligence officer."

By the end of the war, Stephenson had maintained his guise in New York as a reclusive Canadian who had succeeded in "some sort of business having to do with communications and electricity." Friends like Gene Tunney knew him as a former world-class boxer whose speed in the ring won the nickname "Machinegun Billy." He still had the energy of an athlete. He was forty-nine, and living at 450 East Fifty-Second Street. He had been married to Mary for over twenty years. Together they were known in society as a jolly, middle-aged couple with friends from a variety of occupations. Mary French Simmons came from Springfield, Tennessee. Her demeanor, that of a soft-spoken southern belle, disguised an iron will. She had helped Stephenson build up, from English bases, a small empire in radio, movies, aviation, electronics, and the automobile industry. She had done a lot of wartime entertaining by herself—deftly turning aside questions when her husband was off on some mysterious excursion. She knew the war-winning need to keep his friends secret: they often gave their services free, and not always wittingly, for they ranged from film stars to shipping magnates, publishers, and transatlantic cable operators. She understood the strange demands her husband had to make: on Hollywood for masters in makeup and other forms of deception, on bankers to meet urgent demands for huge sums in foreign currency to be parachuted to the secret armies, on boatbuilders for high-speed gunrunners. BSC amateurs came from walks of life where they had learned tricks that came in handy for war. Safecrackers were released from jail to invade enemy coderooms. Gold experts schemed to snatch away Nazi loot. A fortuneteller fed his fans around the world with doctored predictions, using a syndicated newspaper column (quietly sponsored by the British Security Coordination) to mislead superstitious Hitlerites.

Now, as summer edged toward fall in 1945, Mary looked forward to a busy season with her husband at her side. The allies had triumphed: Germany had surrendered on May 8, and Japan—two of its cities decimated by weapons of unparalleled destructiveness—gave up on August 14. Most of the world was prepared to celebrate. New York was no exception. A dinner for Al Jolson was in the works to raise money for army welfare. Parties were planned in connection with Walter Winchell's Damon Runyon Memorial Cancer Fund and Ed Sullivan's Heart Fund. Clare Booth Luce had excused herself from Congress to play Candida on Broadway. Clare and her husband, Henry Luce of *Time*, were good friends of the Stephensons and had helped Mary find quarters in the city when BSC was first launched. Some of their friends understood why a knighthood had been awarded Sir William. They were (in the prevailing jargon of intelligence) "fully conscious." One such was Nelson Rockefeller, who had made room for BSC at Rockefeller Center and who provided cover for its communications staff. Another was Noel Coward, who would later disclose his own involvement.* These friends began to sense, during this warm September, that the Intrepid days were not ended. Again there were the missed engagements; again the lame excuses about ill health.

*Talking with me, shortly before he died, Sir Noel Coward discussed for the first and last time his wartime work with Intrepid. "I was never much good as a spy," he said. "Never terribly good at wearing a jewel in my navel like Mata Hari. . . . Churchill, I think, had issued a forbiddance and Little Bill met me with the news in New York. He told me to go off and do my stuff, anyway. . . . If Bill was with you, he was with you until the last shot." Coward described courses of action he took that illustrate Stephenson's use of contacts in the entertainment industry: "I was the perfect silly ass," said Coward. "Nobody in South America or among other neutrals—you see, I spoke Spanish among other things—considered I had a sensible thought in my head, and they would say all kinds of things I'd pass along to Bill."

Prior to making world tours during the war, Coward had been stationed in pre-Nazi Paris, where his London-directed clandestine work proved intensely frustrating. "We invented silly ideas like propaganda postage stamps which, if you dropped them from an airplane over Berlin, would stick to the pavements—provided it rained—and madden the Berliners into rioting against Hitler." Coward could not resist ridiculing what he called the "House of Lords," a secret intelligence department packed with English peers who thought up these wheezes. Churchill, according to Coward, had a bizarre discussion with him about this. It seemed in the end to prejudice Churchill against Coward, whose services have never been officially acknowledged.

The immediate crisis was a rescue operation. The Soviet intelligence officer codenamed by Moscow Center KLARK, and known to Stephenson as Igor Gouzenko, was in very great peril. He had trustingly come into the Western fold, only to be shunned by the very government he thought would protect him. Stephenson was intervening on his own, defying the political powers of the resurgent peacetime security agencies, to save Gouzenko.

THE BIRTH OF THE BOMB

The crisis grew out of a complex background. It began with the decision to build an atomic bomb. The first steps had been taken before the United States entered the war, and at the same time the secret ABC strategic talks of 1941 heard the British argument for a Fourth Arm.

Russian intelligence had been alarmed by the proposals for spreading revolt against tyranny in Europe. Allied use of "dirty tricks" could threaten Stalin's authority and seemed ultimately a more formidable danger than theoretical bombs, "each no bigger than a pineapple," Stalin had been informed, "capable of devastating an entire city."

There was by 1942 a British Central Scientific Office, BCSO, in Washington. It performed the duties of a clearinghouse. Two houses, in fact: one on the Fifteenth Street side of McPherson Square, and the other at Seventeenth Street and Massachusetts Avenue, N.W. The FBI recorded at least three Nazi-directed attempts to siphon off information concerning Tube Alloys, codename for the British contribution to the bomb. Nobody spotted Soviet attacks against the same target, although RIS questionnaires, not deciphered until later, revealed that Moscow was even more interested in skullduggery than in the bomb.

The testing of the bomb took place near Professor Robert Oppenheimer's prewar family retreat, a ranch high in the Pecos wilderness of northern New Mexico. The difficulty of keeping the work secret was illustrated by pupils at Los Alamos Boys' School, thirty miles northwest of Santa Fe. "These two characters showed up," one boy said later. "The man in the porkpie hat called himself Mr. Smith. The other with a tiny fedora said he was Mr. Jones. We'd seen their pictures in our physics books. One was chief of a famous lab, the other the best theoretical physicist of his time. We knew whatever they were doing here, playing spooks, it must be important." One was Oppenheimer, who, in that year of 1942, estimated he could build the bomb with a core of thirty scientists. Two years later, on the grounds of the boys' school, he ruled a walled city of six thousand, with its own radio station (minus call sign), dance bands, soda fountains—and a cyclotron to trigger, in a millionth of a second, a violent chain reaction powerful enough to destroy a whole city.

Yet, partly because of a miraculous American sense of purpose and unity by that period in the war, loyal Americans collaborated to keep the secret. The secrecy reached back in time and ranged over many lands. Key scientists had been smuggled into the American desert from Nazi-held Europe. Saboteurs blew up Nazi-controlled research centers and destroyed material for atomic experiments. Resistance armies moved on orders from clandestine radio transmitters to cover the escape of men needed on the Manhattan Project. In England, a professor was mystified by the disappearance of one closemouthed colleague after another for destinations unknown. Then he was himself sworn to secrecy and told he must get ready for a sudden transfer to Canada. He consulted his local library for information on life in Canada, and only then discovered where his missing colleagues had gone—each at some time had signed out the same books on Canada! The country possessed the huge hydropower resources needed then to smash the atom; and the Canadians and British for a time had considered going it alone.

Then the main effort was taken over by the United States. Soon a Princeton stationmaster was puzzled by the one-way tickets he was selling to a whistle-stop outside Santa Fe. In Denmark an anti-Nazi secret-army chief wondered why he was risking agents to deliver antique keys to a long-haired academic, unaware that the keys contained instructions for escaping to help the allies build the bomb. And in New Mexico, rancher Dave MacDonald bristled when smiling gentlemen from Washington insisted that he must make way for an air-to-ground gunnery range.

"Pretty soon," MacDonald said later, "some six or seven hundred people were living in and around my house and I was darned if ever I saw a shot fired in anger until the night of the earthquake."

The earthquake resulted from the first 1945 test in "the Journey of Death," the Spaniards' original name for the region. An unmarked truck came to the test site at Alamogordo, two hundred miles south of Los Alamos, carrying a steel shell. Another rancher, Holt Bursom, was reminded of an old *Time* cover showing an atom breaker. "When they shipped this thing in, if I didn't think I was crazy or something, I'd say they was fooling around with bustin' atoms."

Robert Oppenheimer had been given cover as Coordinator of Rapid Rupture, a title that seemed to disclose more than it concealed. But when the project began, nobody could have associated "rapid rupture" with atom-busting. There was scarcely enough plutonium in the world to cover the head of a pin, and very little U-235, needed to fuel the test bomb. To produce U-235, an enormous plant had been constructed at Oak Ridge, Tennessee. Giant reactors labored in other parts of the country to bring forth precious ounces of plutonium. On July 11, 1945, the world's entire known supply of plutonium—ten pounds—was delivered to the conscripted ranch. The receipt valued it at a billion dollars. It might as well have read a thousand billion, since nobody knew its true worth. All Oppenheimer knew was what it had cost to produce.

The locals accepted the need for secrecy and the teams of FBI agents swarming through their territory. In Santa Fe, they joked that it was a submarine base to make windshield wipers for periscopes, or an air-force base producing skyhooks for hanging up bombers.

There was a storm on the night when the five-ton sphere called Fat Man was to be exploded at the place the soldiers and scientists called Trinity Site. In those early hours of July 16, 1945, Fat Man lay cradled atop a tower so tall that it seemed certain to attract lightning from the storms sweeping the desert. At the core of Fat Man were two machined hemispheres containing plutonium, a substance that seemed to those who touched it eerily warm, and deadly. Suppose a thunderbolt destroyed their work? There would be an end to the current test program. Perhaps an end to the whole notion of atom bombs. Scientists in the command post, five miles away, bet on the probable devastation to follow the explosion, planned or accidental. Technicians were aghast to overhear a distinguished physicist wager on the probable incineration of all New Mexico.

The flashes of lightning around Fat Man's tower made any prophecy of doom seem far from extreme. But there was no accident.

"I just never expected so much heat from the explosion when we triggered it," said Frank Oppenheimer, brother of Robert and himself a physicist. "The thunder from the blast bounced on the rocks around us, going back and forth in that Journey of Death. An ominous cloud hung over us, so brilliant purple, with all the radioactivity glowing, hanging, it seemed, forever above our heads."

A local businesswoman, Elizabeth Ingram, had been driving her sister back to school when she saw a great flash. "My sister said what was it, lit up the whole prairie around us? That was a strange thing for my sister to say because she was, you see, blind."

Three weeks later, some locals guessed what the secrecy was all about when they made the connection with the destruction of Hiroshima. On August 6, that Japanese city was atomized. It had been among those listed for some time as out-of-bounds for U.S. bombers. The air force had wanted a virgin city. It was the only way the scientists could measure the destructive effect. In about nine seconds, in a flash some said would have been visible from another planet, the first bomb to be delivered had obliterated nearly eighty thousand people, leaving many more to die lingering deaths from a new kind of illness: radiation.

Then the ranchers around the Journey of Death understood. They talked about cattle with hair turning white like frost. "Where the fallout touched a herd," said Bursom many years after, "if a cow was lying on her left side, well, the right side got burned, and the hair instead of coming back red like it should in, say, a Hereford, it come back white like in saddle-burn on a black horse. There was a black cat that old man Mac Smith had up at the store. That cat was black as the ace of spades until the bomb. Then it come out white spots all over. He sold it to tourists eventually for five bucks."

"The secret was kept from the enemy because, as Americans, we knew what patriotism meant," commented a local rancher later. "It was a good time to be American. The whole country was pulling together. People knew that everything we meant by civilization could come to an end in a war that, if we lost, could lead to a thousand years of Dark Ages."

The secret had been kept by the ordinary people of the community wherein it grew. There were those present at the creation of the bomb, however, who set themselves above their fellows, and believed they had the right to share the knowledge of its construction with the Soviet Union.

THE SEARCH FOR PROOF OR TANGIBLE EVIDENCE

PART TWO

WANTED:
ONE DEFECTOR

A secret war directed by the Soviet Union against World War II allies seemed unthinkable. Evidence of hostile operations by the Russian Intelligence Services had been retrieved by Western experts searching through captured Nazi files. RIS penetration affected every Western institution. German intelligence had known about this in detail. Traffic from Soviet diplomatic radio stations in North America confirmed these RIS activities.

But none of this was generally known, and the prevailing political innocence of 1945 was reinforced by Soviet sympathizers and "agents of influence." They had succeeded in covering up, for instance, the discovery of microfilms in the Reich Foreign Ministry confirming that Hitler had concluded a "Secret Additional Protocol" with Stalin just days before the Nazi invasion of Poland in September 1939; and that this addendum to the notorious German-Soviet agreements carved up Europe between the Soviets and the Nazis, making the Russians as guilty of waging aggressive war as the Germans.

It would take the ingenuity of a lawyer defending one of the Nazi war criminals at Nuremberg, more than a year later, to shock the West with proof of Stalin's cynical deal. In the immediate aftermath of Hitler's defeat in 1945, however, the West was more concerned with coaxing Stalin into cooperating in the birth of the United Nations. Nothing must be done to annoy Stalin—who, meanwhile, extended his power by a mixture of promises and brute force until he would soon govern the very same territories specified in his secret pact with the Nazis.

Stephenson faced another problem. British Security Coordination had set up secret bases in Canada, before the United States entered the war, where Americans recruited for covert operations in Nazi Europe could be trained and provided with forged documents. After Pearl Harbor, the BSC base called Camp X, on Lake Ontario opposite Rochester, New York, expanded its activities and now included powerful radio facilities codenamed HYDRA, partially buried underground. Above the bunkers rose

HYDRA's tall towers, and these had to be passed off as part of the expansion program of the government-financed Canadian Broadcasting Corporation. In fact, HYDRA was another vital link in the response to Soviet intelligence operations. It provided highly secret liaison between radio interceptors and cryptanalysts working on illegal Soviet transmissions from American, Canadian, and British territories.

The coded traffic out of the Soviet embassy in Ottawa was scrutinized by teams working under the vague title of Examination Units, under the even vaguer title of the National Research Council. These teams had directed attention against illegal operations by Nazi and Japanese spies and sympathizers until the war drew to a close. They had first become aware of clandestine Soviet activities by accident, and then they had slowly assembled fragmentary retrievals.

Enough became known to reinforce the suspicions of Stephenson, the Royal Canadian Mounted Police, and the FBI that the Russians were running agents at the very heart of atomic research. But how could suspicion be turned into hard fact? Nothing less would galvanize the West. Stephenson had bitter memories of the reluctance to understand and act on the warning signals preparatory to Pearl Harbor.

Stephenson suspected that 1945 marked the end of the age of the great heroes. America had taken pride in Roosevelt's elegant courage, his grace under pressure. He had been replaced by Harry Truman, who inspired no great excitement but offered instead the comfortable assurance of what Norman Mailer later called a storekeeper's salty common sense. The British had expelled their great hero, Churchill, "the man who mobilized the English language and sent it to war," and put in his place a seemingly bloodless socialist, Clement Attlee, described as "a modest little man with a great deal to be modest about" by Churchill, and as "a dead fish who has not yet stiffened" by George Orwell. In Canada, Mackenzie King clung to power, a political animal who saw that returning soldiers everywhere were infected by dreams of a new social order and that, in the popular imagination, the Soviet Union had proved a brave ally. If any hero of historical dimensions still governed, most would say it was Stalin.

The continuing activities of BSC and offshoots like Camp X would come under fire. Stephenson could not go to Mackenzie King with speculation based on intercepts: King believed Stalin was an honest man who would be outraged if he thought his private correspondence was being read. Indeed, King's salient characteristic had been summed up by his foremost critic: "King has a marvelous command of the feminine argot." News of Soviet perfidy, without documentary proof, would give King the vapors. Besides, the intimate relationship between BSC and Canadian security men was being questioned by Canadian External Affairs, infected by the U.S. State Department view that Stephenson's operations had no legal basis, and should have ended with the war.

Hoover of the FBI had no greater hope of receiving a sympathetic hearing at the White House. Truman "had no time for that shit" when confronted with counterintelligence reports. He was still in the stage of regarding Stalin as "straightforward."

In London, the jealousy of peacetime professionals for the wartime amateurs was being exploited by those intent upon breaking up allied defenses. The career chiefs of the Secret Intelligence Service had always treated Stephenson with caution. When he saw a need for action, he refused to waste time going through bureaucratic channels. Now he was treating the SIS men with reserve, for the rather more grave reason that he distrusted their political motives.

What Stephenson needed was tangible evidence that could not be ignored. If someone came in from the other side, such a defector might be given a hearing. If he brought with him documents, his personal testimony would be hard to discredit. There would be no risk whatsoever of losing a precious window into Soviet intelligence—for there would then be no need to submit intercepted Russian Intelligence Services traffic to a public inquiry, which would have alerted the Russians to the existence of the interceptors.

There had been an unnerving demonstration of the dangers surrounding the analysis of Soviet intelligence traffic. The U.S. State Department had ordered Donovan and the OSS to return to the Soviets four coding systems stolen from Russian intelligence, together with several hundred secret RIS documents. This extraordinary order was said to have been issued by President Roosevelt shortly before his death. By the middle of February 1945, the codebooks had been returned. Miraculously, Moscow Center did not switch ciphers affecting Canadian cryptanalysis. But Stephenson sensed that the urge to treat the Soviets as intimate friends was shared among the presidential advisers who had survived Roosevelt's death and who had placed upon the dying president the responsibility for an order tantamount to betraying a major American intelligence coup. Stephenson thought it best to keep the monitoring of Soviet traffic secret, even from our own side, rather than risk a political decision to stop the analysis of RIS signals. This work, however, would be pointless if the information retrieved could not be acted upon. Hence the need for a defector, someone who could legitimately produce the information and disguise the fact that some of it had been derived already from another source.

Soviet missions were scrutinized for prospects. A young embassy man already spotted by the RCMP in Ottawa was Igor Gouzenko. He lived apart from his countrymen, among Canadians, with his wife and small son. Neighbors noticed his apparent disillusionment with the Soviet Union, his shocked response to talk among coworkers of a third world war in which the Soviets would defeat their onetime allies. He had resisted one recall to Moscow. Evidently he did not look forward to returning.

But as to how he would defect, there seemed no safe road between openly collecting him and leaving him to blunder as best he could through Ottawa's bureaucracy. An open move was out of the question: Communists and their sympathizers would campaign to prove incitement and enmity toward the Soviet Union; inquiries would be held, endangering the top-secret status of the BSC. As for the politicians, they would be disposed to heed embassy complaints that the man had committed some crime under Soviet law and must therefore be returned to Soviet justice.

No matter how things were handled, there would be a terrifying interval during which Gouzenko and his family would be exposed to mortal danger. Somehow they must secure protection from the local police. Until that time they would be like soldiers crossing no-man's-land, targets for either side, groping through an unknown minefield.

SEVEN

ENTER
IGOR GOUZENKO

Igor Sergeievitch Gouzenko of the Red Army's GRU intelligence directorate had arrived at the Ottawa embassy two years before, in the summer
of 1943. A full-fledged Soviet specialist in every aspect of secret communications, he had flown into Canada under diplomatic cover as a
translator and secretary. With him on the plane was spymaster Colonel
Nikolai Zabotin, traveling as a Soviet military attaché. Svetlana, Gouzenko's wife, had not been allowed to make the trip: she was pregnant,
and in any case Moscow Center was inclined to hold on to "hostages"—
family members of those who might be tempted to defect. Only when
the NKVD had located the numerous relatives who could be jailed if
the Gouzenkos misbehaved was it agreed that she might follow her husband later in the year.

Gouzenko was captivated by the dashing Colonel Zabotin from the
moment they met, shortly before embarking on their four-day flight.
Unaccustomed to his own cover as a civilian, he had instinctively saluted
his new superior—a dead giveaway that he was not the civilian described
in his papers. When he shrank with embarrassment, Zabotin roared with
laughter. Gouzenko had better get rid of that habit, he said. A real civilian
would never show respect for a mere colonel!

But Gouzenko knew there was more to Zabotin than his charm. The
colonel's aristocratic background, which ordinarily would have meant his
eclipse, had been overlooked by party purists when he proved to be a
brilliant officer. As director of GRU intelligence in Mongolia, he had
conducted long-range operations inside China, where the political soil
was being prepared for the postwar Communist takeover. He had a good
scientific mind, and he had spent the previous months mastering the
rudiments of nuclear physics. Now, traveling on a diplomatic passport,
he was on his way to North America to fulfill his latest assignments: the
supervision of Soviet-run atom spies, already positioned at crucial points
from the uranium mines in Canada all the way to Santa Fe, New Mexico.

◆   ◆   ◆

Zabotin had more than a general sense of the secret progress made by the Atlantic allies to win the race with the Nazis and the Soviets to build a bomb. Far more work had been done inside Russia than was generally known, and there was no intention to reveal this to Russia's "allies." Europe's first cyclotron, or "atom smasher," had been built by the Soviet Laboratory for Measuring Instruments under Igor Kurchatov. Further research had been conducted into what the Academy of Sciences called "the uranium problem."

Zabotin knew that uranium was the essential element in accomplishing an atomic explosion. Heavy water was thought to be vital to moderate the process. In 1943, Canada was the free world's only source of both. In that year, British agents and Norwegian saboteurs attacked, and eventually destroyed at heavy cost in lives, the source of heavy water in Nazi-occupied Norway.

Zabotin's own GRU service had been involved in the cloak-and-dagger side of work on the bomb, and he knew how the British had smuggled Professor Niels Bohr out of occupied Denmark to join the U.S. program. The extent of German research was reported from Stockholm by Lise Meitner, a coworker of the Berlin physicists who had first demonstrated, in 1938, that atoms of the radioactive element uranium would split when bombarded by neutrons. Moreover, Lise Meitner was the scientist who had correctly interpreted the chain reaction: and Nick Zabotin was well aware that she had been helped, as a Jew, to escape the Nazi purges by his service.*

The Nazis' counterpart in research was called the Uranium Club. As reported by Dr. Meitner, the German work languished from the self-indulgence of scientists protected by the state and under no critical scrutiny. Meanwhile, French scientists had shown that heavy water could moderate neutrons released by splitting the atom, permitting a chain reaction to be sustained in a lump of uranium. In the year preceding the Nazi conquest of France, there had been a fantastic race between the Gestapo and French physicists to acquire all known stocks of heavy water.

Zabotin was familiar with that bit of cloak-and-dagger. During the "phony war"—in the first winter of the Nazi push in Europe, before either France or Norway fell—both German and French physicists sought

---

*Albert Einstein later wrote that Lise Meitner "put the information in the hands of Niels Bohr." But this was only part of the story.

heavy water from the only commercial producer, Norwegian Hydro. The French bought up all the Hydro stock through secret agent Jacques Allier. Pursued by the Germans, he shook them off by switching at the last moment from a Paris-bound airliner to a flight headed for Great Britain. The heavy water eventually reached the Paris laboratories, only to be threatened with capture again when the German army took the city. The heavy containers were smuggled into a bank vault in the provinces, then hidden in the condemned cell at Clermont-Ferrand. Finally, they were moved by secret agents and stored in one of the homes of England's rulers, Windsor Castle.

"A sinister term, eerie, unnatural," Churchill said of *heavy water*. "Undoubtedly, the human race is crawling nearer to the point where it will be able to destroy itself completely." In October 1941, he had set up a British Secret Directorate under the codename Tube Alloys to try and build the bomb with the United States. He had been convinced that Britain alone could not fight Hitler and also finish her own bomb-building project, disguised as the MAUD Committee. Instead he dispatched to the Americans the secret MAUD report, "The Use of Uranium for a Bomb."

President Roosevelt had already formed the Uranium Committee after receiving a letter through Wall Street financier Alexander Sachs from Einstein. Einstein had written in the summer of 1939 that "uranium may be turned into an important source of energy . . . a single bomb of this type . . . might destroy" an entire city. Then he drew Roosevelt's attention to the ominous signs of Nazi progress.

A sense of shamefaced urgency seemed to invade all those touched by rumors of the bomb. Even Einstein's circuitous route for his message to the president had a sheepish quality. Everyone realized they were talking about a method for self-destruction so awful it amounted to blasphemy. But "we could not run the mortal risk of being outstripped in this awful sphere," said Churchill in June 1942 when he met with Roosevelt at Hyde Park. Together they reached the historic decision that the American-British-Canadian alliance should pool national efforts, pay whatever price was necessary, to develop the bomb.

Now, in 1943, it would be Zabotin's job to convince the ABC alliance, with open diplomacy and clandestine help, that Russia deserved a share in these atomic secrets. American resources had overwhelmed the British contribution, and the multibillion-dollar Manhattan Engineering District Project was under way.

Zabotin had a great deal of help awaiting him, including RIS disinformation already at work among those associated with the project. Lenin himself had provided general guidelines for disinformation, the art of chiaroscuro, the arrangement of light and dark to deceive the people if necessary into believing black was white. When Felix Dzerzhinsky, the fanatical founder of the Russian secret police, realized how many enthusiastic amateurs he had running around loose in the West during the Bolshevik revolution, Lenin advised: "Tell them to tell the West what the West wants to believe about us." Since what the West wanted to believe in those days was that the Communist regime was collapsing, this is what Dzerzhinsky's agents fed Western intelligence. The West ended up misjudging the situation and intervened in self-defeating ways.

In Moscow Center, it was said that the revolution had been saved by disinformation. A quarter of a century later, it fell to Zabotin to use the same weapon against the Western scientists who desperately wished to believe that Stalin would be a trusting peacetime friend if the Soviets were let into the alliance. Overlooking Russia's draconian secrecy rules protecting Soviet research, many in the Manhattan Project were willing to share their knowledge to prevent the alternative: a suicidal arms race. Zabotin already knew this from the work of his RIS colleagues. And Zabotin, in the phrase of another Soviet defector, was "only three places away from Stalin."

Once in Ottawa, Zabotin set up shop with Lieutenant Gouzenko as his expert cipher clerk. From a residence in genteel Range Road, Number 14, several blocks from the embassy, Colonel Nikolai Zabotin took command of the spy networks and prepared to intensify the campaign of Soviet disinformation.

Since he reported directly to Zabotin, Gouzenko divided his working hours between the colonel's residence and the embassy. Located at 285 Charlotte Street, the Soviet embassy was housed in a three-story building that reflected the shabbiness of Ottawa's middle-class neighborhoods after five years of wartime shortages. The secret cipher branch, on the second floor, was separated from the other sections by a big steel door behind a thick velvet curtain. Beyond this door, manned by the NKVD, was an even heavier door that opened on a corridor of small rooms with still more steel doors. This was the Trusted Unit, where the secret files were kept and where the diplomatic radio service maintained contact with Moscow—with the Ministry of Foreign Affairs, the Directorate of Military Intelligence, and the NKVD. Gouzenko's office, Room 12, was at the back of the building, its window glass painted white and protected by steel bars and steel shutters that were closed at sundown. In this claustrophobic atmosphere, Gouzenko enciphered and deciphered telegrams while radios blared at full volume to prevent eavesdropping. He had absolute control over who came into this room. It was his exclusive domain.

Periodically, he attended "commissions for burning" in another room at the end of the corridor, where, page by page, documents slated for destruction were burned in an incinerator under the supervision of the NKVD. Next door was another incinerator, much more powerful— accessible only to Alex Ouspensky, then chief of the secret cipher branch in Ottawa and later sent to Washington in the same capacity. Here, in case of emergency, documents could be consigned to the flames in wholesale quantities. NKVD chief Vitali Pavlov, who designed the second incinerator, had described it as "big enough to consume the body of a man."

Gouzenko was no stranger, of course, to the ways of the NKVD. He was wary of a Soviet spy system that stemmed from a centuries-old heritage one of his favorite authors, Chekhov, had described as "weighing down on every Russian like a rock." Even as a boy he knew enough to hold his tongue in their presence. And later, when he was first admitted to Moscow Center for training, he had been warned that anyone entrusted with state secrets was both precious and dangerous: NKVD watchdogs would be after him day and night. At Moscow Center he had also learned about the NKVD's ruthless sweep through Soviet-occupied Poland,* in the bizarre period of the Hitler-Stalin pact before the Nazis invaded Russia. Under General Ivan Serov, the NKVD had cooperated with the

---

*It was later estimated that Stalin's "liberating" of Poland was proportionately comparable to a Soviet occupation of the United States in which 13 million Americans were sent to Siberia.

Gestapo in the winter of 1940, running down political enemies and "liberating" Poland through mass deportation.

The NKVD was determined to dominate foreign-intelligence operations. On every level it competed with the GRU in an intense rivalry that threatened the effectiveness of the Russian Intelligence Services. The GRU had grown out of the Registry Section within the Cheka,* later known as OGPU, then as the NKVD (the KGB emerged later). After the Bolsheviks seized central power in 1917, it was the Cheka's responsibility to quell whatever smacked of counterrevolution. Six years later, fifty thousand Russians had been killed and three times that number had died in Chekist concentration camps. Cheka officers controlled the population, censored the press, guarded the party elite, oversaw communications and transport, suppressed religion, regulated prisons, and ran special forces and border guards whose chief task was to keep people in. The Registry Section, which provided cover for foreign intelligence, was transferred to the Red Army in 1920 and renamed the Directorate of Intelligence (GRU). When its agents abroad began feeding intelligence to Moscow, overriding the less-well-informed Cheka, an internal struggle began that was still unresolved.

In Ottawa, the rivalry was all too evident. Zabotin of the GRU and Pavlov of the NKVD seemed to be fighting a duel to the death. Zabotin refused to let the NKVD apply the customary security checks in his quarters on Range Road. Pavlov was bent on demonstrating his superior power. When Zabotin's chauffeur, in reality a Red Army intelligence captain, damaged an embassy car in an accident, he tried to pay for its repair from his own pocket rather than be punished for his carelessness. Pavlov found out, and the next day Moscow recalled the chauffeur. Pavlov took care that unauthorized employees "accidentally" saw the summons home as evidence of NKVD power.

Gouzenko already knew, from the messages he handled, that Moscow Center responded swiftly and cruelly whenever the NKVD reported a misdemeanor by a member of the staff. As with the chauffeur, it usually meant an immediate recall, then silence. A telegram would arrive containing the ominous phrase "he is required for other work." It was no

---

*Cheka is the transliteration of the Cyrillic acronym of the Russian name for Extraordinary Commission. The KGB still calls its officers Chekists.

secret that "other work" could mean a punishment post or penal servitude in Siberia. It occurred to Gouzenko that Moscow might save itself trouble in extreme cases by disposing of bodies in Pavlov's huge incinerator. The Canadian authorities need never know about it.

Behind the barred windows of the Soviet missions, Gouzenko moved as unobtrusively and silently as he could, sickened by the claustrophobia of conspiracy. Outside this world full of unknown pitfalls stretched Canada, its wide open spaces reflected in the character of its free-spirited people, who combined American openness with a more European reserve. Behind the embassy's iron bars, Gouzenko lived on sufferance. Outside, he felt free.

Gouzenko's life in Ottawa's suburban Somerset Street was tranquil and filled with simple pleasures. His wife, whom he called Anna, short for Svetlana, had arrived by sea in October and had given birth to their first child, Andrei. Their apartment was in a building next to a greengrocer, an immigrant from Lithuania, whose frank and outspoken criticism of officialdom and the government at first shocked them. The Lithuanian laughed when they cautioned him against being reported for disloyalty. It took the Gouzenkos a while to understand that "the Greens," the codename used by Moscow Center for Western counterespionage, did not care about the views of private citizens.

The long nights of that first winter, the deep snow, the plummeting temperatures were all reminiscent of Moscow. The great granite Gothic arches and towers and walls of Parliament Hill were comfortable reminders of home, but minus the ominous suggestion of things concealed. Canadians skated on the frozen waterways or plodded out to the nearby hills to ski, much in the way of Muscovites; but these citizens were friendly to strangers, welcomed the Gouzenkos into their homes, threw neighborhood parties, and a baby shower for the infant Andrei.

Summer unveiled a countryside lush and prosperous. The Ottawa valley burst with the produce of individual farms. There was an abundance of fruit, meat, and vegetables that even in peacetime Russia had never been known to the Gouzenkos. Instead, they remembered the famines and the mass slaughter of peasants in the name of Communist planning. Gouzenko had an insider's knowledge of how the mismanagement occurred: through secret police suppression of dissent. All the miseries of totalitarian rule were offered in microcosm by his embassy, a world he reentered each day with growing reluctance.

What was known to the local NKVD contingent as "the Soviet Colony" came under strict discipline. But, just as in Moscow, there were exceptions made for such elitists as the ambassador's wife. Gouzenko was enraged to discover she was among those who purchased luxury Canadian goods for shipment back to the Soviet Union, to be distributed among privileged relatives or sold. The cost was concealed in department budgets. Gouzenko's salary had risen from $200 a month to $275 plus the 10 percent payable for the first two years of foreign-intelligence operations. The bonus would rise to 20 percent for the third year. A large part of the Soviet staff seemed to be drawing these intelligence bonuses. Gouzenko understood why, after Zabotin told him, "Canada, with thirteen million people, is penetrated by nine separate Soviet intelligence networks reporting directly to Moscow, and quite by accident I've just discovered another Soviet network here in Ottawa under army intelligence headquarters in Moscow."

Then a Canadian public investigation, into charges that the provincial government of Ontario had been running a gestapolike police unit, revealed that the Soviet embassy was financing the Canadian Communist party. Gouzenko was astonished when his ambassador warned all the staff to do nothing that might confirm this. The local Communists were codenamed CORPORATORS, and it was important to conceal their Moscow links. There was no justification, in Gouzenko's mind, for subverting a free country whose citizens had shown all Russians a trusting hospitality.

By now, Gouzenko was creating in his head a novel based on what he knew about conditions inside Russia. He did not dare commit any of it to paper. He created an imaginary writer whose fame protected him against NKVD interference, but whose days were numbered because he was surrounded by sycophants and party bureaucrats who placed personal ambition above conscience. Gouzenko's fictional hero would be betrayed in the end by those who professed to be his friends.

This mental fiction ran side by side with his enjoyment of the free society in which he took refuge when he went home. He drew a contrast between the generosity and contentment of his neighbors, and reports reaching him from newly arrived colleagues of conditions in Moscow. He learned that none of his many parcels of food and other gifts had ever reached his mother, who was living in wretched circumstances. This at a time when the commercial counselor at the Soviet embassy was shipping bicycles to party bigwigs at their request, and paying for them out of office expenses checked only by Politburo lackeys. Gouzenko's small gifts to his mother, paid for from his tight budget, were being siphoned off upon arrival.

Gouzenko wanted very much to be a writer. And it was dawning upon him that the novel he wanted to write would expose the Soviet system's use of spies to protect the privileges of the party elite.

The threat of recall darkened his days. Major Romanov, who had flown out with him, was so disturbed by his own sudden recall to Moscow that he drank embassy vodka night and day until his departure. He was convinced, he told Gouzenko, that he would never leave alive—or else he would arrive dead.

Then, one afternoon in September 1944, Gouzenko was ordered into Colonel Zabotin's office. "For reasons unstated," said Zabotin, "the immediate recall of you and your family has been ordered by the director."

Gouzenko told his wife when he got home that night. She sank to her knees on the floor, not crying, but staring in silence at the wall. Finally, she voiced the question they both dreaded: Were they being punished? They knew of too many cases of returnees who had disappeared because they were presumed to have picked up disloyal ideas.

Down the hallway from their apartment, a party was going on. They could hear laughter above the dance music from the radio. Gouzenko's wife looked at baby Andrei, and said, "I wanted him to grow up in this country."

Gouzenko went back to Zabotin with an argument that he was more useful in Ottawa, that he had other skills qualifying him for a different post if Moscow had earmarked someone to replace him. Surprisingly, Moscow agreed. He realized he was not under a cloud. But Anna saw it only as a reprieve. "Some day," she pointed out, "we'll have to face the crisis."

At that moment, Gouzenko made the fateful decision. It was to prove hair-raising. It would mean another year in which he must prepare for his defection.

It was not a painless decision. Gouzenko had strong loyalties to the

Russia of his ancestors. Soviet indoctrination had taught him to identify that patriotism with communism. Once he rejected the party line about the inferiority of Western life, he began to wonder why his homeland was denied the truth. Why was it necessary to "protect" the populace from non-Communist influence? What right had the NKVD to consume such a fortune in operating costs, such an army of able-bodied youths, merely to imprison people's minds? Gouzenko had experienced the hardship of the collectives when government funding ran short, while the local NKVD multiplied. He had an exceptionally clear picture of the extent and complexity of Soviet espionage. Why did Stalin spy on wartime allies? Why spy on his own people?

Gouzenko began a systematic search of Zabotin's journals and the separate GRU files, for material that would be most useful to the Western cause. Working steadily on into the summer of 1945, he made copies of secret correspondence, discovered lists of Zabotin's agents and contacts in North America, and carefully earmarked only those files that were likely not to be incinerated: he could not risk an investigation resulting from a marked file being seen by Pavlov during a commission for burning. He looked at everything now as if he had already defected. It was from this viewpoint that Gouzenko first saw the report to Moscow of an atom spy codenamed ALEK:

> . . . secret test of atomic bomb took place over New Mexico. . . . Bomb for Hiroshima made of Uranium 235. . . .

The great secret had been kept from Germany and Japan, the known enemies during World War II. But, on the evidence of ALEK's message of August 1945, Gouzenko knew that the secret had been given away to the Soviet Union.

He shivered. Not even in his wildest moments of mental fiction-writing had he imagined a situation like this. He had heard talk inside the embassy of preparations by the Soviet Union for a third world war, a war that really mattered, a war against ideological enemies in the West. Suddenly he was confronted with proof that the West was living in a fool's paradise, smugly confident that the United States had a monopoly on the weapon that made war unthinkable.

Now he had more reason than ever to escape. The fear of recall went with a dread of becoming part of a Soviet war machine in some future conflict, of seeing his children swallowed up as ciphers in a tyranny unchallengeable from outside. He used the plural, *children*. Young Andrei would soon be joined by a sibling, for Anna was pregnant again— another compelling reason why they must get away soon.

... IF SUICIDE SHOULD TAKE PLACE ...

On the evening of Wednesday, September 5, 1945, Gouzenko left his apartment after supper and headed for Range Street. The final, dreaded summons had reached Zabotin's desk, and this time there was no countering Moscow's demand: a ship was sailing from the West Coast for Vladivostok, and Gouzenko had better be on it. He was to spend his last weeks training the replacement who would take over from him.

As he walked through the sweltering city, he felt both fear and gratitude. His life was in danger. Anna and the baby could be shipped back to Moscow alone, where he would have no control over their fate. But he was full of confidence in Anna. She would back him all the way as he crossed the gulf between the "Soviet Colony" and freedom. He had been made aware, in recent weeks, that men of some indistinct authority but obvious goodwill were in his vicinity: one, indeed, had become a neighbor. To nobody, though, had he yet entrusted the compromising RIS telegrams he had quietly concealed in the apartment, in Anna's pots and under her dishes on the kitchen shelves. Two telegrams were so clearly important that, fearing these might be missed, he had copied them out— and then put the copies back into the secret embassy files, bringing the originals home. That last undertaking had been especially risky. One

telegram demanded specific atomic-bomb information; the other was an
assurance to Moscow Center that an agent had been elected to the Canadian federal Parliament and would continue his secret Soviet activities.
If anything should happen to Igor Gouzenko in the next few hours, these
telegrams could help Anna secure asylum for herself and Andrei. If the
NKVD broke into the apartment, she could burn them rather than let
them fall into Pavlov's hands.

The Range Street residence was guarded that night by Captain Galkin,
one of Zabotin's intelligence men, registered with the Canadian government as a civilian. When Gouzenko told him he had work to do in the
photographic labs, Galkin suggested he come along afterwards to see a
movie with some of the officers.

"Okay, give me five minutes," Gouzenko said, seizing the chance to
leave early instead of lingering under the pretext of having business there.
He made a quick round of the labs, checked that his replacement was
on duty, and joined the others in the main hallway. Hidden in a solid
group of bored Russian military men, he walked to the neighborhood
cinema, then slapped his side in exasperation. He had already seen the
main feature, he claimed, and would go downtown to another movie
house.

At this point, Galkin's friendliness became a hazard. "I'll keep you
company," he said.

Gouzenko brushed aside the offer. When Galkin looked hurt, he added
hastily that he might just return home to his wife. This was understand-
able. Galkin knew that Anna was five months pregnant with their second
child. Gouzenko was able to break free and make his way to the embassy.

There, sitting in the foyer, was NKVD chief Vitali Pavlov. Forcing
himself to move calmly, fortified by the fact that it was normal for him
to bring Zabotin's duty diaries and reports at this time of night, Gouzenko
began the complicated procedure of entering the Trusted Unit. He pressed
the bell concealed in the staircase, walked up to the second floor and
put his face before the opening in the steel door. Apparently Pavlov had
noticed nothing out of the ordinary, and he was allowed to pass through.

Once in his office, Gouzenko moved with quick precision. There were
now more than one hundred earmarked documents in the secret files:
the only way to get them safely out of the embassy was to hide them in

his clothes. For the first time, he appreciated the baggy pants he wore, issued at Moscow Center's supply depot. He stuffed the documents under his shirt, around his waist, and added some current telegrams he had set aside that day. Then he passed again through the steel doors, descended the stairs and walked casually across the reception room to the front door. Pavlov had vanished.

"This is out of our field." The night editor of the Ottawa *Journal* was clearly not interested in the stolen documents Gouzenko laid on his desk. He suggested that the minister of justice was the man to see, and waved aside Gouzenko's fear of pursuit by the NKVD.

It was almost midnight when Gouzenko arrived at the ministry on Wellington Street. The policeman on guard said he should try again next morning. He had no choice but to return to the apartment, where he spent the rest of the night whispering with Anna while he rocked their two-year-old son in his arms and wondered about his family's future.

He could go back to the embassy in the morning, resume his routine, slip the stolen papers back in place, and perhaps thank his lucky stars that he had discovered early enough the incompetence, and the lack of interest in Soviet conspiracy, among the institutions of the West. He was, for the moment, a man in limbo, suspended between his diplomatic status and defection. But he had already made up his mind: if he returned to the embassy, it would be only as a prisoner or a corpse.

"I'll go first thing to the Ministry of Justice building again," he said. "They can't refuse my request for asylum."

"We shall all go," Anna said. "I'll carry the papers in a shopping bag. If the NKVD tries to take you, I'll get away with the documents."

"What about the baby?"

"I'll have him in my arms. Pavlov wouldn't dare hurt a pregnant woman *and* a baby in public."

It was not quite true, and they both knew it. Pavlov would have killed the baby, too, if necessary.

The next day saw the opening of Parliament in Ottawa after the summer recess—its first peacetime session since September 1939, when Canada had joined Britain in declaring war on Nazi Germany. Only a month had passed since Hiroshima. Officialdom was caught up in the aftermath. Politicians were under pressure from their constituencies to turn attention to the backlog of neglected domestic problems. Nevertheless, this was not enough to explain the reception Gouzenko received. With Anna and the baby he turned up at the Justice building at eight in the morning, insisting that he speak only with the minister. A secretary said the minister was at his other office in the Parliament building. The Gouzenkos walked over to Parliament Hill, where another secretary heard the story, talked at length in French to someone on the phone, hung up, and directed the Gouzenkos back to the first office. There followed a wait of two precious hours. Then an official told Gouzenko, "The minister cannot see you."

The Soviet embassy's daytime routine had started five hours before, time enough to learn of Gouzenko's actions. The only recourse was to return to the *Journal*'s offices. Back at the newspaper, they were fobbed off with the remark: "Nobody wants to say anything but nice things about Stalin these days."

They had now walked back and forth through Ottawa for more than half the day, juggling between them the shopping bag of documents, and the baby. In what Gouzenko later called, with masterly understatement, "a state of utter despair," they made their way yet again to the Justice building, this time to plead for "naturalization." Each journey was increasingly dangerous, the chances growing that embassy watchdogs were now on their trail.

On their third try that day, Justice referred Gouzenko to the crown attorney's office. This meant another journey of several blocks. There, they were told that the "person in charge of naturalization is still at lunch." Andrei was now showing the strain, and it was decided they would have to risk taking a streetcar to Somerset Street and leaving him with a neighbor. At the crown attorney's office, the Gouzenkos filled out application forms before being instructed to come back the following day to begin further proceedings. How long, asked Igor Gouzenko, trustingly but with concealed edginess, were "proceedings" likely to take? Why, several months, came the reply.

All their hopes sank under what they took to be the dead weight of bureaucracy. It did not then occur to them that the delays were calculated. They were both very frightened, though each tried to hide it from the other. Once again, they went home. They collected the baby and cautiously entered the apartment. The windows had been locked shut all day. The air inside was stifling. Reluctantly, Gouzenko opened one window a crack and immediately saw two men sitting in the park opposite. There was no doubt they were watching his apartment. Gouzenko knew the signs: they were waiting for darkness. It was now just after seven o'clock.

Suddenly there was a knock on the door. Then more knocking as Gouzenko and Anna held their breath.

"Gouzenko!" rasped a voice from the hall. It was one of Zabotin's men. "*Gouzenko!*"

After a moment, heavy footsteps receded down the corridor. Opening the door to the rear balcony, Gouzenko found his next-door neighbor seated on the other side of the railing.

"Right," said Air Force Sergeant Harry Maine. "Pass the child over to me. Anna and you shelter here while I call the cops." The sergeant was one of the Gouzenkos' newer, and exceptionally friendly, neighbors.

During the night they heard more banging on their apartment door. From across the hall, sheltering with another good neighbor, Gouzenko could see clearly through the keyhole: Vitali Pavlov was standing just outside with three other members of the NKVD. Another door opened, and Sergeant Maine approached the Russians. The Gouzenkos were not at home, he said. Pavlov and his men descended the stairs, only to return moments later with a crowbar. They had barely forced their way into the apartment when Gouzenko saw two city policemen follow them inside. Finally an inspector arrived on the scene, and Pavlov was allowed to leave the premises with his thugs after they claimed diplomatic immunity.

There were no further commotions during that long sleepless night. Only once more, toward four in the morning, did Gouzenko hear a sound in the hall. Peeking through the keyhole for the last time, he saw a man he could not identify: a rather small man who walked carefully away.

The stranger was Bill Stephenson. All night he had argued for the end of secrecy, for he already knew the value of the documents brought out by Gouzenko. "This is the most important opportunity we'll ever have," Stephenson insisted, "to find out the extent of Soviet operations against us, and to get public support for counteraction."

Opposing him was the Canadian prime minister, Mackenzie King, who had been told within half an hour of Gouzenko's first plea to the Ministry of Justice that the Soviet spy was seeking asylum, that his return "would mean certain death," that he carried documents proving the existence of Soviet spy rings throughout North America. It was "a most terrible thing," King later wrote in his diary. "It was like a bomb." While Gouzenko walked in trusting suspense between the Justice building and Parliament Hill, Minister of Justice Louis St. Laurent instructed his staff to make absolutely certain that the Russian see no one in authority. Told Gouzenko might kill himself, the minister replied that good relations with the Soviet Union were more important.

Prime Minister King was in favor of letting the NKVD settle the issue in its own way. "If suicide takes place," he told his diary, "let the city police take charge and secure whatever there is in the way of documents, but on no account for us to take the initiative." In any case, King wrote, Gouzenko was "a political hot potato, too hot to handle."

Mackenzie King was seventy years old. He had stayed Canada's prime minister for more than eighteen years by carefully cultivating the prejudices and domestic obsessions of his fellow countrymen. He believed passionately in always being "right behind" Canada's allies in foreign policy, never getting out in front. Now, some miserable little Russian, nothing more than an underpaid clerk, was asking the great man to stick his neck out. That was something King had trained himself never to do.

Behind the prime minister was Norman Robertson, the permanent undersecretary of state for external affairs, an Ottawa mandarin of immense influence, steeped in King's cautious philosophy. Robertson was the key to unlocking King's mind. Stephenson had motored over from his hideout at the Seignory Club, an exclusive retreat in the countryside around Ottawa, to beard the mandarin in his own home that Thursday evening. During the three-hour drive, he reviewed what he knew already about the stolen documents. These included evidence against pro-Soviet informants and agents among Robertson's external-affairs staff, and among the prime minister's small group of senior public servants, who were regarded as exceptionally gifted.

Stephenson knew that Robertson could be self-righteously stubborn. The undersecretary shared with King a great sensitivity to Canada's image as a dominion dependent on Britain—indeed, as a colony of Britain. Nobody, least of all the director of a secret British organization with U.S.

affiliations, was going to pull hidden strings in the old imperial manner. The fact that Stephenson was a Canadian who had accepted a British knighthood only made matters worse.

Thus Robertson's objections came as no surprise when Stephenson proposed that the Royal Canadian Mounted Police Intelligence Branch should take over Gouzenko. Fortunately, Stephenson had by this time received a summary of what Gouzenko could offer. Stephenson pointed out that if Gouzenko had gone for help from the local police in some criminal incident, the RCMP would have handled the case. But, said Robertson, no laws had been broken in this instance. Well, responded Stephenson, the same might be said about the three hundred Canadian names listed by Gouzenko as Soviet spies and suspects, of which many were public servants appointed by the Liberal government. This concentrated Robertson's mind most wonderfully. Then Stephenson mentioned that Gouzenko's apartment had been broken into.

"Ah, well then!" said Robertson. "Gouzenko has been seen to be threatened and justice must be seen to be done, eh?"

There was no need for further arm-twisting. In the dry language of the unpublished, confidential BSC report: "The Under-Secretary of State for External Affairs telephoned the RCMP officer who had been secretly in charge, to inform him privately that the Department of External Affairs would be prepared to modify its previously expressed injunction against proceeding with the case."

The case required a codename. In early discussions, Stephenson and his colleagues endured long night sessions with the help of Corby's Canadian rye whisky. The empty boxes from which the bottles were taken were later refilled with the top-secret files on the case. The codename suggested itself: CORBY.

The Corby Case became the concern of "Slim" Cliff Harvison, chief of the I-Branch intelligence department within the Royal Canadian Mounted Police. Slim Harvison was highly sensitive to the Gouzenkos' plight and wanted to take them into protective custody at once. He was also keenly aware of the need to avoid political and international complications. All the good work of netting Gouzenko would be destroyed if parliamentary critics accused Harvison or Stephenson of acting in flagrant disregard of the law. There had been a salutory reminder of the public's concern for the legalities in the allegations of a provincial "gestapo." Slim Harvison had come up through the RCMP the hard way, like all mounties. He had served in remote regions, keeping law and order, for which he had a great respect. He had run Nazi defectors as double agents during the war. He was well aware of the dangers implicit in the sort of swift action he preferred. Described in the secret BSC report as "knowing a considerable amount about Vitali Pavlov of the NKVD . . . well aware that these men would not stop at murder to obtain the documents," Harvison had had his men accompany the Gouzenkos "at a discreet distance" throughout the day—a circumstance never made known to Gouzenko himself.

Harvison had learned a lesson early in the war when he had made a Nazi spy play back his radio transmitter. Unaware that the spy's contact was in North America, and being under great pressure to act swiftly, Harvison boosted the spy transmitter so that its signals reached German intelligence headquarters in Hamburg. It was a fatal error. The Germans guessed that the spy was now transmitting under Allied control, and acted accordingly. Now, Harvison did not want to burn out this new case of espionage through overhasty action. In the end, it was the Russian intelligence officer hammering on the door that gave the RCMP the chance to intervene. Suddenly the situation had turned into a simple disturbance of the peace—a matter for the local police. Nobody from the higher political levels could accuse the RCMP of adopting gestapo tactics, or of blundering into a delicate question of diplomacy. The British Security Coordination report quotes the RCMP watchers in the park:

> "We watched the City Police leave [and] settled down to wait. . . . We did not have to wait long. The Soviet embassy car arrived shortly after 11 o'clock in the evening. Four men got out and disappeared into the house. A few minutes later the city police patrol car drew up and two constables followed them inside after a discreet interval. . . ."

The BSC report continues:

> Presumably most foreign diplomats would be somewhat embarrassed at having to explain to the police their presence at night in an empty apartment which does not belong to them. They had already broken open the door with a crowbar. The Soviet embassy's second secretary

did not appear to be in the least put out, and had the moral support of the assistant military attaché, Vassili Rogov, who was in uniform, and of Pavel Angelov, the air attaché. They were all, of course, NKVD agents, of whom only one was out of uniform: Alexander Farafantov.

The Russians became immediately aggressive. . . . The constables' report set out the situation with admirable simplicity: "*We found the four men scattered through the apartment. They stated they had permission from the owner as he had lost his key. . . . They would make no statement regarding their presence and resented our interference. . . . They said they were from the Russian legation and could do nothing wrong so far as the Ministry of Justice was concerned. . . .*"

At ten-thirty on the morning of Friday, September 7, Igor Gouzenko could at long last sit down with the chief of the RCMP I-Branch, Slim Harvison, and explain some of the secrets he had been hauling around Ottawa night and day.

"A preliminary survey of these made it evident that the Soviet Union was conducting espionage on a large scale," says the BSC report.

Gouzenko's story first seemed so fantastic that it was difficult to believe until he *began to produce the documents*. . . . Agents operated inside government departments including the Canadian Department of External Affairs. . . .

In charge of networks were Colonel Zabotin, assisted by Lt.-Col. Motinov, Major Sokolov, staff of the Commercial Counsellor in Ottawa, secretaries and other staff of the military mission. . . .

It was inopportune to press for details, for Gouzenko was now near to collapse. It was decided to move him to the hideout, where it would be possible to interrogate him at leisure without fear of detection by Pavlov and his agents.

That afternoon, with Anna and the boy, Gouzenko was taken to Camp X in an unmarked RCMP sedan.* The choice of this secure hideout was

---

*Camp X was in the province of Ontario, which was governed by Conservatives. The local premier was politically opposed to Mackenzie King, and had never disguised his contempt for King's "shilly-shallying" support of Allied causes. To prevent King from interfering in wartime secret warfare, he had arranged for the clandestine purchase of farmland on which the camp stood.

dictated by more than the fear of the Russian NKVD. There was also the danger of direct intervention by politicians and mandarins, not necessarily aware of serving Moscow's cause. The RCMP I-Branch was always on guard against parliamentary denunciations of secret-police tactics and disregard for civil rights. As Gouzenko himself had noted, when the Ontario government was accused publicly of using police investigators as a "gestapo," the Soviet embassy had encouraged local Communists to play up the suggestion of Fascist tactics. Stephenson and the BSC were in a worse plight: they had no legal standing at all as a police force.

Stephenson had stage-managed an intelligence coup without upsetting the elected federal government. He would have to continue to maneuver behind the scenes. Robertson had recovered well from the shock of discovering his department to be under suspicion. He was again fretting about the political repercussions for the Liberals in federal power—specifically, for Mackenzie King.

Robertson had been told about the curious behavior that Thursday night of Soviet ambassador Georgi Zarubin. Everyone knew Ambassador Zarubin, bluff and hearty, the very soul of Russian goodwill toward her allies. Mackenzie King, as self-appointed architect of an *independent* Canadian foreign policy, had spent many happy hours with Zarubin discussing postwar cooperation between the Arctic neighbors. Ambassador Zarubin caught the fancy of the senior mandarins of external affairs, who suffered from the inverted snobbery of what would later be called "radical chic." He was the living refutation of the myth that diplomacy was the exclusive province of the privileged. A factory hand at the age of thirteen—or so his RIS-approved legend proclaimed—he seemed destined for high office when he returned to Moscow.* If ever a Russian seemed unlikely to engage in the shabby business of espionage, it was jolly, vodka-drinking, backslapping Georgi Zarubin.

Nonetheless, Ambassador Zarubin had been observed in the middle of the night with NKVD chief Pavlov, hunting along the banks of the canal and the river. What were they searching for? The RCMP and monitors of NKVD traffic concluded that someone outside the Soviet embassy had informed the ambassador of the report given Mackenzie King and his justice minister that Gouzenko might commit suicide. They were looking for his body.

*Ambassador Zarubin later became a Soviet deputy foreign minister.

To Robertson, this sounded farfetched. Then why not, he was asked, watch Zarubin's reaction when asked about last night? The Russian ambassador was scheduled to go to the British high commissioner's garden party later that Friday afternoon.

Spymaster Nick Zabotin was also scheduled to attend. Stephenson arranged for watchers to stand by, just in case the colonel chose this opportunity to plead for asylum. The day before, when a frantic search of the Soviet embassy files had confirmed that Gouzenko's failure to report for work was not an innocent case of oversleeping, Colonel Zabotin had tried to conduct his own investigation. But Pavlov had already spoken with Gouzenko's replacement, who related several inconsistencies. Taken separately, they might have seemed unimportant; together, they were damning. Gouzenko had stopped at Colonel Zabotin's residence, poked around the labs, then left for a movie with friends. On arriving at the theater, he claimed to have seen the film already—though it had only just opened. Then he said he was going, after all, to rejoin Anna at home; instead he had been seen entering the embassy by Pavlov himself.

Pavlov pulled political rank. In cases involving suspected Communist backsliding and anti-Soviet operations, the NKVD took precedence over the GRU. Colonel Zabotin must have known, at this precise moment, that his own goose was cooked. The ultimate responsibility was his: recall and punishment were only a matter of time. He made several phone calls to friends outside—not to his Canadian agents, but to acquaintances who had displayed a human warmth toward him. One of these was Malcolm MacDonald, the British high commissioner, but a secretary took Zabotin's call. The commissioner was at a meeting, she said. Was there a message? Zabotin replied that he'd like MacDonald to call back; then, conscious of Pavlov's long ears, he added that it was in connection with the next day's garden party.

Shortly after this call, Pavlov appeared in Zabotin's Range Road office. The colonel, said the NKVD chief, could forget the garden party.

Did Nikolai Zabotin have his own plans to defect? Those who knew him had always stressed his unfeigned delight in Western ways. His dossier showed him to be, from a Communist viewpoint, politically unreliable because of his aristocratic background. He was a professional in intelligence, playing the game for its own sake. He had more in common with the intelligence chiefs among his nominal enemies than he had with many of his own colleagues at headquarters. There was mutual respect stemming from shared danger and experience in the esoteric arts. There was the gamesmanship of outwitting an opponent suffering the same skull-splitting headaches from the same dilemmas.

Buf if Zabotin or others on his staff considered changing sides to escape Moscow's vengeance, steps had been taken on the Canadian side to make such moves difficult. The news about Gouzenko's escape was confined to the handful of political leaders in Ottawa who wanted to avoid, at almost any cost, a breach in relations with the Soviets.

Britain's high commissioner, Malcolm MacDonald, plumed and braided in red, white and gold, received the long line of guests while a military band thumped and blared under the Union Jack, and white-gloved waiters scurried across the manicured lawns high above the Ottawa River. The mood was light.

Suddenly Ambassador Zarubin stood before the commissioner. Beside him was Pavlov, going through the motions of being an interpreter. Though MacDonald knew perfectly well that Zarubin could manage on his own, the delay was welcome: it provided an opportunity to study Zarubin's reaction, for by this time the Soviet ambassador's nocturnal activities were known to the British representatives too.

"You look as if you've been fishing all night," MacDonald said finally.

It was Pavlov's head that came up with a jerk. Zarubin simply turned red in the face.

"Have any birds whispered little secrets to you lately?" responded Zarubin after a long pause.

"No," said MacDonald. "No more than you've caught any big fish these last few days."

The Russians moved on to make way for the next guests. There was nothing in the exchange to cause offense. Zarubin was notoriously fond of fishing; MacDonald was famous for birdwatching.

Then Mackenzie King strolled across the greensward. The Canadian prime minister was still in shock. The Soviet ambassador, on the other hand, had recovered his poise and was now on the attack. There was a good deal of theatrical bear-hugging and comradely grunts of goodwill, and then Georgi Zarubin asked for King's close attention. Stalin had a proposal to make. It seemed to the Soviet Union's great leader that Canada's immense contribution to the war had been obscured by her two larger allies, Britain and America. Therefore, the great leader would like King to know that the Soviet Union was prepared to pay tribute to a great Canadian. Stalin, in short, would like to cement their undying friendship by conferring the highest honors. . . .

The great Canadian that Stalin had in mind was later identified as a general who had held command in Europe. But observers saw the incident as a blatant attempt to play upon King's vanity. Even King later commented that while Ambassador Zarubin talked, his face betrayed anxiety. Whatever the ploy, it was only the opening of the Soviet game. King was associated with Canadian nationalism; and the RIS had recruited agents by appealing to both Communist and intensely nationalist feelings in Canada.

King left in haste, afraid of being compromised. The garden party continued. The British high commissioner was suddenly called to the phone. When he returned he was no longer his usual bouncy little self: a figure sometimes reminding others of Charlie Chaplin, with a smile full of protruding teeth and an inclination to destroy the gravity of the social hour by doing handstands. Malcolm MacDonald had just caught the first whiff of scandal in his own office.

"HAND HIM OVER FOR DEPORTATION"

On Saturday morning, the Soviet ambassador demanded that External Affairs should "seek and arrest I. Gouzenko and hand him over for deportation as a capital criminal who has stolen money belonging to the embassy."

This was the test. Stephenson waited. There was nothing more, officially, that he could do to stiffen the backbone of Mackenzie King. The prime minister was regarded in many quarters as a bag of wind and pomposity, a spiritualist who consulted his dead mother more conscientiously than his cabinet, a compulsive diarist who recorded each day's events as if chronicling the adventures of Queen Victoria.

Ambassador Zarubin and the NKVD had every reason to suppose they could cajole or even blackmail King into giving Gouzenko up. The NKVD was well aware of the disrepute into which the counterintelligence and police agencies of the West had fallen; they had launched disinformation campaigns for that very purpose. They had seen politicians paralyzed by the threat of Soviet hostility to the formation of the United Nations. They had used the fears of diplomats to pressure great soldiers like Field Marshal Alexander, Supreme Allied Commander in the Mediterranean, whose surrender to NKVD demands was relevant to Gouzenko's situation.

Gouzenko had heard part of the frightful story from a new NKVD arrival at the embassy. This man had previously served at SMERSH headquarters in Vienna when, in May 1945, Stalin had called for the execution of six White Russian generals and thousands of other Russians held by the British in Austria. The NKVD presented the British with a proposal for moving them all into Soviet custody with the least fuss. But British military commanders identified the majority as "displaced persons of nationalities other than Soviet." Their leaders had shepherded these flocks of men, women, and children into what seemed the safety of British camps, on the assumption that they were to be dealt with as displaced persons. The Foreign Office in London, however, instructed Field Marshal Alexander that this entire group of Russians should be forcibly "repatriated," in keeping with the Yalta Agreement signed three months earlier. This agreement in itself was iniquitous: the Soviets claimed that Balts, Poles, and Rumanians—whose homelands Hitler granted to Stalin in 1939—were therefore "Soviet citizens"; that millions of White Russian emigrés were also "citizens"; and that all such "citizens" must be repatriated—by force if necessary.

One of the doomed Cossack generals, Semon Krasnov, had fought with Alexander against the Communists during the Russian Revolution. As a young British army officer in 1919, Alexander had been attached to the anti-Bolshevik forces, and in 1945 he still wore a medal awarded him by the general. Now Krasnov appealed to Alexander, "drawing attention to the special position of the Cossack host."

The political judgment from London prevailed. The "Cossack host" would be delivered into Soviet hands. The NKVD anticipated the difficulties of such a forced repatriation, in which many Russians would attempt suicide, and advised the British to pretend to be taking the leaders to a conference with Field Marshal Alexander. This the British did, coaxing the men into wagons that were then hastily rushed into the NKVD camps, where the wire cages awaited them. Even so, hundreds of Russian men and their families put up a struggle. British soldiers found themselves clubbing Russians at prayer in their improvised churches. Some Russian women later flung themselves against electrified wire in a violent attempt at mass suicide.

Political expediency won. General Semon Krasnov was not even legally "returnable"; nor were another four out of the five remaining generals. They had acquired, before the war, other European nationalities. But Stalin had instructed the NKVD's SMERSH brigade to stretch the word *citizens* to cover "undesirable witnesses against communism and the Soviet system."* SMERSH squads actually took possession of the surrendered Cossacks. The U.S. State Department and the British Foreign Office cooperated. This attempt to mollify Stalin only increased his contempt. Exactly what SMERSH thought of British diplomats was recorded by General Krasnov's grandson Nikolai. By some miracle, Nikolai had escaped the fate of the six generals—all executed in Moscow—and after a long spell in Siberian prison camps returned to the West, having finally won Soviet acceptance of the fact that he was in reality a citizen of Yugoslavia. Nikolai described the meeting in Moscow on June 4, 1945, between his grandfather, himself, and one of the NKVD's three bosses, V. N. Merkulov, who said, "For twenty-five years we have waited for this happy meeting." General Krasnov and the rest of the anti-Bolsheviks would be killed or sent to Siberia. They had been fools to put their trust in British shopkeepers, and especially "in the British Foreign Office, which is a brothel, headed by a diplomatic madam . . . trading in foreign lives."**

*See A. I. Romanov, *SMERSH from the Inside*, London, 1972.

**The betrayal was kept secret from the general public until the 1970s, when researchers found many relevant documents had been abstracted from official files. Count Nikolai Tolstoy, heir to the senior line of the Tolstoys of Russia, obtained the facts from original sources to write the revelatory *Victims of Yalta*.

The fate of the anti-Communist Cossacks was not one Stephenson intended should befall Gouzenko. The more outsiders there were who knew about Gouzenko's existence, he calculated, the less danger there was of a secret deal to remove the Gouzenko family's embarrassing presence from the world into which it had stumbled.

The day after the Soviet demand, Stephenson met with Mackenzie King, Malcolm MacDonald, and Norman Robertson—only to find that the first item on the agenda was a proposal "to hush everything up." Lacking any constitutional authority, Stephenson nevertheless had now woven Robertson into his web, and together they won agreement to take another course—one appealing to King's vanity. King should call the shots, since the Gouzenko case had begun on Canadian soil. King's government would confer with the heads of the U.S. and British governments while investigations continued. Then King should go personally to brief the leaders in Washington and London.

"It is all very terrible and frightening," King later wrote in his diary.

For the Gouzenkos at Camp X, the situation was no less frightening. They clung together, feeling cut off from the familiar things that uphold morale in a strange land. They had only the faintest notion of where they were. Great secrecy surrounded the heavily guarded base. This was not merely a holdover from its wartime functions. A new role had been developing, so secret that in Washington more than a year earlier there had been cautious reference to "the need for new legislation against unauthorized disclosure of communication intelligence," providing the groundwork for the complex system that later wedded America's National Security Agency with the British Government Communications headquarters and Canadian monitoring stations. Their joint task was to eavesdrop on Soviet radio traffic and both decode and analyze it. In Stephenson's BSC labs in Manhattan, a battery of new high-speed enciphering and transmitting machines (Rockex-1 had been named after the Radio City Rockettes nearby, and there were others with less exotic names) helped speed this new combined effort.

Gouzenko and his family could not be permitted any knowledge of these secret matters. They were virtually prisoners. They were prevented from moving freely in or out of the camp. It consisted of wooden barrackslike huts, long bunkers enclosed within more fencing, and patches of empty wasteland that still bore traces of gunfire and explosions. Along the southern edge was Lake Ontario, black and uninviting.

The select few who knew about the Gouzenkos' escape had been told they had been whisked *north* of Ottawa. It was clear to Igor that the camp was *south*. He accepted the assurance that the deceptions guaranteed his safety from assassins. Still, he could not help regarding his guardians as having something in common with the NKVD guards of the vast labor camps inside Russia, from which there was no escape. The NKVD did as it liked to the internees. Gouzenko had heard that such camps were answerable to no known laws. Here, he felt isolated and vulnerable. Nobody knew he was here with his small family, except his interrogators.

He had discovered already that the authorities regarded him as an infernal nuisance. Even the sturdy RCMP intelligence men seemed to have reservations; and at an early stage in his debriefing, they seemed to wonder if he was being both disloyal and selfish by virtue of putting in jeopardy the lives of relatives in Russia. Possibly Gouzenko misconstrued the questions. Cliff Harvison had gathered Russian-speaking men who sympathized with any true defector, but who were at this point on guard against agents-provocateurs and plants. They were making sure Gouzenko was not a double agent.

Unaware of these lingering suspicions, Gouzenko felt that the watchdogs shared the popular view that Stalin must not be provoked—indeed, that a Russian owed his first loyalty to the leader who had led Soviet resistance to the Nazis. It struck Gouzenko that few in the West now remembered Stalin's pact with Hitler. Stalin had been perfectly comfortable in bed with Hitler, even a week before the first Nazi blitzkrieg launched World War II. It was then Stalin had toasted "the Führer whom I know everyone loves" while Nazi swastikas decorated the Kremlin walls to celebrate the Nazi-Soviet treaty of August 23, 1939. Gouzenko knew about the secret protocol providing for the division of Europe between German and Russian interests—a division still regarded by Stalin with supreme effrontery as valid today. The treaty had allowed both the Soviets and the Nazis to slash through Poland like a dividing sword.

No record existed of the Soviet-Nazi celebration after Hitler invaded Russia. Gouzenko and his wife had discovered that, when they were studying in Moscow's Lenin Library. They had first met at the architectural institute, and quickly learned that newspapers were "purified" to remove events contradicted by later Soviet postures.* They were warned against Jewish "antisocial traits" and later, when Gouzenko went to work at Moscow Center, he was told that Stalin favored Hitler's extermination program because "the more manpower the Germans waste on death camps, the fewer troops to send against Russia." A military intelligence study, following Hitler's invasion of Russia, claimed that only 260,000 German soldiers were fighting on the Russian front out of a total of 8.3 million troops in uniform. A large proportion was involved in Hitler's "final solution to the Jewish problem." Railroad traffic to the camps diverted rolling stock from the front lines.

That was one of the practical considerations leading Stalin to share Nazi views about Jews, and it was apparent to Gouzenko that the Soviet leaders were far more uneasy within the Western alliance forced upon them by Hitler's later treachery. The codenames he had seen at Moscow Center involved literally thousands of Soviet-run agents in Britain, Canada, and the United States and were clear evidence that, even while at war with Germany, Soviet preoccupation was with the West.

Now Ottawa's leaders wanted to placate Stalin by sending a Russian defector back to Moscow—and certain death. Suppose a trap had been set so they could still avoid public embarrassment? Suppose the rulers of intelligence on both sides had decided on a settlement of their own? Gouzenko, whose adult life had been spent in what he called "a kingdom of intrigue," knew such secret agreements were possible. He saw himself being bundled onto a Soviet plane in the greatest secrecy, an inconvenient corpse.

He turned his mind to his dream of becoming a writer and decided that, rather than endure nameless fears, he should shape his novel of a great writer's struggle against Stalin. Such a writer would need to be a titan to match the great dictator. Again, nothing he could imagine was

---

*In Ottawa, Gouzenko had studied a commentary in the British left-wing journal *Tribune* by George Orwell (November 17, 1944) on Communist rewriting of history. "One way of falsifying history," wrote Orwell, "is by omission." He quoted a French Communist leader who had deserted from the French army and altered the records to make it appear that he had *not* been disenchanted by the Nazi-Soviet pact. Tampering with the records, wrote Orwell, was irresistible to top bureaucrats everywhere. He had already divined the "weeding," censoring and emendation of secret records. "It doesn't much matter," he added, "so long as we all keep our eyes open and see to it that the lies do not creep . . . into the history books."

equal to what was happening to him now. He was told he would be seen by someone new.

Gouzenko had no knowledge yet of Stephenson or the BSC; spymaster Zabotin had never been briefed on them because the chiefs of Russian intelligence were only just now getting fully briefed themselves. The man he was taken to meet that Sunday night, in a wooden hut set apart from the other buildings, was known only as Mr. Whoosis: a man who at first gave the impression of a certain ruthlessness associated with NKVD interrogators. His steel-gray eyes, the hooded lids drawn down at the corners, gave away nothing but signs of extreme fatigue. Yet somehow this composure was reassuring. Accustomed to the awesomeness of authority, Gouzenko had begun to despair of finding anyone big enough to act upon his warnings to the West. Now he felt encouraged by this man who faced him with the confident stare of someone holding great power.

"Nobody's going to kill you here," Stephenson said.

"My wife is pregnant," said Gouzenko. "We have one son already born here. They need protection, no matter what happens to me."

"In this place," Stephenson replied softly, "I'm in charge. If I say you'll be safe, you'll be safe. All of you."

Gouzenko studied the hawklike face, the hooded eyes, and felt relief. Prompted by the slight softening of this austere stranger's grim expression, Gouzenko reached that moment, known to interrogators, when a man crosses the lines to find a kindred spirit, and so begins to open his heart. The Russian began to describe a nightmare in which terror reflected the mentality of the masters he had now abandoned, a terror he believed would threaten the tranquillity of the world he had tried so desperately to enter.

What passed between them was never made public. Each man, spy and spymaster, had moved too long in the underworld where in moments of great danger there is no alternative to total trust and total silence.

Gouzenko went back to his family, to the quarters Anna had already turned into home. In this land of chiaroscuro he was still bewildered by the change in shadows, by the sense that he was trapped inside a picture where black could suddenly become white. But of one thing he now felt certain: his family was no longer personally friendless.

THE
END
OF
INNOCENCE

TEN

WILLIAM STEPHENSON
HANGS ON

William Stephenson entered St. Patrick's Cathedral on Fifth Avenue and approached the altar. He was not known to be a religious man: in his heyday as an industrialist, his critics said he negotiated with God on equal terms; at nineteen, fighting in the trenches and then as a combat pilot, he had disliked the expedient eve-of-death prayers forced out between chattering teeth in moments of peril. But he had always felt guilty about surviving. Now he bent his head in a gesture of respect for those who died in battle. Their sacrifices would be wasted if freedom was again in danger because the battle-fatigued democracies insisted on trusting Stalin.

The war just ended was beginning to reveal itself as the ugliest in man's history. By mid-September 1945, the Holocaust in Europe had given up its foul secrets, leaving decent people sick with horror. The meaning of the atom bomb had sunk in. It was difficult now to see the bomb as Churchill's miraculous deliverance. Men capable of World War II atrocities might just as easily launch a final war of annihilation. "Tomorrow we die!" proclaimed the first antinuclear demonstrators.

Leading scientists were proposing, as a gesture of good faith, to give Moscow the material that Stephenson knew had already been delivered through the spy rings. Some American newspapers reprinted a cartoon from the Russian satirical magazine *Krokodil*—Mr. Uncle Sam and Mrs. John Bull were shown wheeling a pram labeled *A-Bomb* and telling inquirers they planned to raise the infant in a private school.

The only hope for restraint seemed to be that other infant: the United Nations. Many Westerners were prepared to sacrifice a great deal to make certain the Soviet Union supported the UN, since a boycott might have the same catastrophic result as the U.S. refusal to join the old League of Nations. "That's how Stalin blackmails us," warned Churchill. But Churchill was no longer in power. Holding the reins were men like Mackenzie King, whose calculated inaction had almost silenced Gouzenko forever. Every assembly with influence over the future of the UN was watched with nervous concern. In London, the Council of Foreign Ministers was meeting to discuss peace settlements. Preparations were in hand for the first meeting of the Security Council in the United States. Meanwhile, as if deals with Hitler still had validity, the Soviets were calmly implementing their agreement with Nazi Germany of 1939 to hold on to half of Europe, while preparing also to take over all of Poland. And to keep the West quiet, Stalin cynically guaranteed prompt and free elections with a parliamentary system like that of prewar Belgium, knowing full well that the Communist party would never permit Poland to indulge in such an extravaganza.

Stalin and his agents were taking full advantage of the prevailing mood among allied military forces. Stalin was much admired, was known as "Uncle Joe," and became the subject of fond and ribald jokes. "Joe for King" was the popular, tongue-in-cheek slogan of the day. Only a fraction of the American veterans in Europe had been ferried home by September. The War Department had promised a faster rate of demobilization, but though the Queen Mary and 843 troop carriers and combat vessels scuttled back and forth across the Atlantic, only 700,000 Americans had been mustered out. The groundwork was being laid for the "Wanna-Go-Home" riots that would shake many cities in Europe and Asia, challenging the view of the liberated nations that Americans fought with extraordinary discipline. And so they had. Their anger now was directed at "fumbling, bumbling politicians" on their own side. Even General George C. Marshall caught some of the flak: it was Marshall who promised an equitable procedure by which those with two years' service (a long time in a war where men's expectations of life shrank to a few weeks) could be home by the coming first Christmas of peace.

Clearly, the promise could not be kept. Less obviously, General Marshall was in fact anticipating the new conflicts ahead. He was among those who feared that a third, secret world war had been born.

Stephenson walked out through the wide cathedral doors and looked across the way at the figure of Atlas outside his Rockefeller Center office. Albert Einstein had pointed out that the sphere weighing down on Atlas resembled an atomic scientist's dream of dancing atoms. Now it seemed a working symbol of atom spies and the penetration of Western security. Stephenson was far from confident that Gouzenko would be permitted to play his part in meeting the Soviet threat. And yet the visit to Camp X had convinced him of Gouzenko's integrity, to Stephenson the greatest of all virtues. He was certain the Russian would cling stubbornly to his

resolve to expose Stalin's intentions against the West. Bearing this out
was the thick file entitled *I. Corby: His Life and Times.* . . .

From the start of the crisis, Gouzenko had been disguised as Corby. His
dossier,* even then being compiled from random information gathered
about Gouzenko and his Soviet handlers, included the false Moscow
Center biography turned over to the Canadian Passport Office. The Russians knew what they were doing when they provided their agents with
such legends. Long ago the British had discovered a rich source of intelligence on individuals could be quarried from the forms filled out by
applicants for passports and visas. Passport Control Officer was, at this
time, still the traditional cover for British "legal" agents abroad. Indeed,
this was the cloak for Stephenson's initial period in New York as Intrepid.

The Soviet embassy was demanding the return of the family it now
called "Gusenko," and sent to the Canadian government this description:

IGOR
Born January 13, 1919. Arrived to Canada July 20, 1943. Height—
5'6" Weight—145–150 pounds. Color of hair—brown. Color of eyes—
gray. Nose—straight. Sometimes wears spectacles.

SVETLANA
Born December 12, 1919. Arrived to Canada July 20, 1943. Height—
5'7" Weight—140 pounds. Color of hair—light brown. Color of eyes—
blue. Figure—slender. Nose—straight.

Have a son—Andrei.

A somewhat different picture emerged from the BSC researchers: "The
man known to Canadian officialdom as Igor Sergeievitch Gouzenko was
born, not in Gorky, but in Rogochen, a village near Moscow, in
1919. . . . His wife is, in fact, Svetlana Borisovna Gouzenka, and she

---

*Gouzenko's dossier was a proso-profile, from the art of prosopography, described by one of
Stephenson's men, Professor Gilbert Highet: "It's a skill developed by historians to make the best
use of limited information about a remote elite. . . . You can identify known figures, study their
personalities, their contacts, their behavior patterns. We did this successfully with Hitler's gang.
One reason for Russian secretiveness is to prevent such a proso-profile on Stalin's thugs, but it's
surprising how well the method works despite all the secrecy."

did *not* arrive in Canada on the date stated here." Igor Gouzenko's father died after fighting with the Red Army at Petrograd. Raised by his maternal grandmother, Ekaterina Andreievna Filkova, a devout member of the Russian Orthodox Church, he rejoined his mother while she was teaching children from collective farms in the Central Black Earth District. He went to the Maxim Gorky School in a workers' district of Moscow and from there to the capital's architectural institute. His training as an architect developed his considerable talent as an artist. Earmarked by the NKVD for training in military intelligence, he was enrolled in the Kubishev Military Academy, on his way to Moscow Center's secret world of ciphers.

Now that Gouzenko had crossed over, he was in urgent need of protection—not only from Russian vengeance squads, but from pro-Soviet sympathizers in the allied bureaucracies. Gouzenko had already lifted a corner of the veil concealing active Communists holding positions of trust and influence. They knew how to play on the fears of other politicians and bureaucrats who were convinced the Soviet Union must be handled with kid gloves, and who therefore wished to suppress Gouzenko's evidence or silence him, rather than worsen relations with Moscow. Furthermore, Gouzenko was assembling the documents to prove his assertions that Soviet agents existed among senior officials in the West, some of whom were in a position to tamper with his testimony. Not only was he in personal danger: what he had to say was vulnerable to official distortion.

In a formal diplomatic note (note no. 35 of September 7), the Soviet embassy demanded Gouzenko's deportation as a *capital criminal.*

BSC took immediate and unprecedented precautions to secure the confidentiality of the Corby Case signals flying between the Atlantic allies. The secret BSC history states: "Security considerations were of such paramount importance that even the necessary clerical work had to be done by the handful of operational directors. . . . *There was evidence already that other allied ciphers had been compromised,* and it was agreed that only BSC channels through the New York office, and via Telekrypton lines to Canada, should be used. . . . Secretarial staff were prevented from handling papers dealing with the case."

So far, knowledge of the Corby Case outside Canada had been limited to Hoover in Washington and the Secret Intelligence Service in London; all material had been dispatched over protected landlines, using BSC's own encoding system. NKVD chief Pavlov had been informed that Canada's RCMP would investigate Gouzenko's whereabouts.

"As part of the RCMP's coverup," the BSC file recorded, "a number of constables all over the country spent some considerable time pretending to look for Gouzenko." Also as part of this coverup, the FBI had issued a continentwide alert for the defector. The police of both countries were not ruling out the possibility of pro-Soviet informers within their ranks who would pass all this along to Moscow's bloodhounds, hoping they would reach Gouzenko first. The impression was deliberately fostered of the defector's roaming unprotected somewhere in North America.

This would, it was hoped, help delay a strong official Soviet protest from Moscow, which would intimidate Mackenzie King. It diverted attention from the Gouzenko family, and postponed the moment when the NKVD might start another operation to reach the defector before he revealed too much. Camp X was physically safe from outside penetration. But what about infiltrators already planted within the security agencies? The possibility, in that period of relative innocence, seemed outrageous. Men like Hoover and Stephenson risked ridicule by suggesting it. Events would prove they were right. Gouzenko was "like a sheep among the wolves, though he was kept with his small family in comfort and security," wrote a BSC historian later. "In the kingdom of spies, a commoner has no rights."

And because Camp X was so secure, any fate could befall an inmate without public notice. Dick Ellis would later testify that during the war just ended, "We sometimes 'lost' individual enemies of Britain we picked up in the United States and smuggled into Canada. Sometimes the FBI would reproach us, or Hoover would demand explanations, and I could only say, 'Sorry, we seem to have "lost" the chap.' We had *disposed of the body under protection of the Crown*, to use the SIS phrase."

Nobody was going to lose Gouzenko if Stephenson could help it. He sensed problems for Gouzenko from SIS men whose previous lack of response had aroused his suspicions: men in London who in the past had failed to give the FBI information concerning Communist subversives in the United States. There was the additional hazard of inexperienced "intelligence officers" now scavenging Europe as members of competing units spawned in the aftermath of the war, all fighting to win permanent establishment. He had telegraphed SIS/London that he would take charge of the case. Stewart Menzies, the director-general, responded by sending out Roger Hollis, the future counterintelligence chief, to conduct the most confidential part of Gouzenko's interrogation. Stephenson did not want a stranger walking through the gates of Camp X. He wired London: "Sending back your man by next available transport." He would assign trusted SIS men of his own: men tested by himself on wartime assignments, who could be depended upon to steer Gouzenko through the weeks of detailed debriefing.

For the moment, he had done all he could to keep Gouzenko safe from intruders. Anna would be hospitalized under an assumed name when her time came to give birth. Toys were bought for Andrei to brighten his days spent in barracks behind wire. The RCMP traced the outlines of the family's feet in order to shop for winter boots. The small luxuries were purchased by Stephenson in New York, then sent to the camp in military vehicles to minimize the risk of Gouzenko's location leaking out. They were given new cover names and biographies. The way was open for them to become subjects of the United Kingdom.

Now Stephenson could return to the troubles of his BSC organization. Its headquarters in New York came under fire almost daily, yet he was hampered by secrecy from defending what he considered to be a vital concept. The Gouzenko case was confirming the need for speedy and secure communications between the Atlantic powers. New York was proving itself the best clearing center. But Stephenson thought too much in practical terms for the taste of his rivals. One of his staff, Roald Dahl,* the writer, would say later: "No postwar politician wanted him to come within a mile, because he cut through red tape and got things done without regard for men with tiny minds. And in that postwar world, even the intelligence bureaucrats were playing politics."

Stephenson believed passionately in the Atlantic alliance and the need to defend it along the front lines of intelligence. So much experience

*Dahl had been seriously injured as a Royal Air Force fighter-pilot. He was posted to Washington as an air attaché, a role he loathed in wartime. He fell foul of senior officers but Stephenson intervened. "You'll work for me," said the BSC chief, and not even the air chiefs dared interfere.

had been built up during the war. It had never been easy to maintain goodwill between secret-intelligence agencies run by passionate patriots of varying nationalities, but Stephenson and General Donovan had learned the tricks. The coordination of intelligence had become an art in itself. If BSC dissolved itself too fast, it would take years to rebuild. Stephenson was perfectly prepared to change its name from British Security Coordination to American Security Coordination, so long as the practicalities remained. It was the *coordination* that mattered—simple in concept, hard to achieve among quarrelsome and competitive departments within different governments.

The case of Gouzenko ought to demonstrate how coordinated American-British-Canadian intelligence could meet the Soviet challenge. Gouzenko had more than a story of atom spies. He wanted to impress on the West that its security agencies were being penetrated by his old RIS masters.

He had not discussed with Stephenson the existence of two ELLIs. One had been indicated earlier as Kathleen Willsher, a confidential secretary to the British high commissioner, Malcolm MacDonald. She reported to her Soviet control through Fred Rose, national organizer of the Labor-Progressive party, and through a Bank of Canada official.

The other ELLI was something Gouzenko wanted to discuss in utter confidence. He was unaware that he would not see Stephenson again. It was only with someone of such stature that Gouzenko felt safe. He thought the second ELLI, and certain other Soviet-run agents, had been recruited among local nationals and inserted into Western security agencies. He could not risk alerting a Russian mole who could strike back at him and also destroy his evidence. The only secure course for Gouzenko was to discuss this with someone totally trustworthy who would not distribute the information even inside the security services. Inadvertently, Gouzenko played into the hands of the double agent he feared.

WILLIAM DONOVAN
TRIES TO
SAVE THE <u>OSS</u>

Events outside were moving fast. Churchill, brooding over the English Channel after the successful invasion of Hitler's Europe, had said, "The eagles depart. Now the vultures gather." The vultures now spread propaganda to divide the American-British-Canadian alliance. Donovan and his wartime Office of Strategic Services had been made unpalatable to President Truman. A faction in OSS accepted the view that Britain was intent on restoring her empire. Other OSS officers prepared to transfer to a State Department intelligence organization kept totally secret. Coordination between ABC intelligence agencies would be impossible in peacetime, it was said, because each country had quite different aims: Canada wanted to display complete independence from Mother England and Big Brother America; the United States was seen by propagandists as embarking on a schizophrenic crusade for the independence of what would be called Third World countries, while enriching herself by a new form of economic colonialism; and the British were preoccupied with their loss of an empire and their need to find a new role in the changed world.

The State Department had become a new contender in the postwar rush to grab a lion's share of new intelligence operations. Indeed, President Truman was now drafting a request to Secretary of State James Byrnes for a plan "for coverage of the foreign intelligence field." On September 20, 1945, the OSS would cease to exist and Truman would finally see the last of General Donovan, a man for whom he "had no use."*

Donovan himself had outlined the concept for "a modern centralized foreign intelligence agency, free from the bias of any single Department, run by a director appointed by the president, and in sole charge of

---

*Thomas Troy, *Donovan And The CIA: History of the Establishment of the CIA* (CIA, 1981).

espionage and foreign counterintelligence . . . designed to anticipate and counter penetration and subversion of our national security by enemy action." Confronting Truman's fears of a "gestapo-like agency," he had advised that the new agency "should be prohibited from carrying on clandestine activities within the United States."

Donovan was too pushy to suit the tastes of his rivals in the conventional armed services. His proposal sounded to them like a prolongation of the Fourth Arm, competing for limited defense money and threatening to perpetuate the notion that terrorism, sabotage, and guerrilla warfare could overthrow hostile governments. This alarm was shared in Moscow, whose Western friends in high places added their voices to the well-intentioned objections of military men. The Russians were keenly conscious of Donovan's work in liberated Europe, picking the brains of captured Nazi chieftains, supervising ambitious studies of wartime campaigns, and utilizing all sources of intelligence on the Soviet Union. If Donovan ever headed a peacetime version of ABC intelligence and Fourth Arm, Stalin's nightmare would be realized: an assembly of forces capable of encouraging dissent within his vast empire held together by fear.

Working in the Russians' favor was the West's obsession with keeping on the right side of Stalin. This had been illustrated for Stephenson by the inability of the OSS to take legal action in the case of a magazine now defunct, in whose offices three hundred stolen secret documents had been found—including reports filched from Stephenson's BSC headquarters and labeled A-*Bomb*.

The chief of OSS security had told Stephenson he was "shocked almost speechless" by the discovery. The magazine, on investigation, proved to be in constant contact with Soviet secret agencies. When the OSS case had been ready for the grand jury in the summer of 1945, the Justice Department was instructed to withhold prosecutions until the end of the preliminary conference to create the UN, for fear of antagonizing the Soviets.

To keep Donovan occupied, the Truman administration would eventually earmark him as deputy to Judge Robert Jackson for the international trial of Nazi war criminals. Now, he spent a great deal of time in Europe explaining U.S. war-crimes policy. But Donovan found that, while the U.S. government rounded up war criminals, new covert-action groups were also scooping up ex-Nazi confidence tricksters for U.S. employment against the Soviets. It seemed evident that the concept of *coordination* of intelligence had been replaced by rivalry between competing agencies whose policies often contradicted one another. Soviet brutality, he feared, was just beginning in the territories under Stalin's domination. The panic response, however, was desperately wrong. The Soviets had the advantage: their party central committee ruled Communist agencies with an iron hand. The coordination that worked so well for the West in wartime had, by contrast, fallen apart. It appeared likely that the OSS would be divided up between the armed forces and the State Department, throwing away a lot of hard-won experience.

Before the threat to the OSS turned into the certainty of its demise, Donovan had proposed setting up CROWCASS, a Central Registry of War Criminals and Security Suspects, to be based in Paris. By drawing on the resources of the FBI and Scotland Yard as well as security services in Western Europe, it would ensure the identification of Nazi criminals— not only Germans, but other nationals who had taken part in war crimes.

But Donovan was butting his head against various forms of resistance. His rivals in intelligence, more intent on securing information than justice, were now asking hundreds of Nazis, including war criminals, to cooperate with the United States in return for a safe future as U.S. citizens. General Reinhard Gehlen,* Hitler's reputed expert on Soviet intelligence, had already successfully bargained for immunity from legal prosecution with what he claimed were thousands of microfilms detailing Soviet Russian operations. A congressman would say, many decades later, "We seemed to have had more intelligence agencies than there were countries to spy on."** And these, multiplying in the wake of the Nazi defeat, were under no centralized control. Each sought spectacular results in the new clandestine warfare against a new enemy, hoping to ensure postwar favor.

In those first two weeks of Gouzenko's defection, as a last-ditch effort to save the OSS concept and to present the general theme of coordinated intelligence among the Atlantic allies, Donovan let loose a barrage of news leaks.

---

*For Gehlen's account to the author of how he negotiated his transition from a Nazi to an American spycatcher, see *The Bormann Brotherhood.*

**Congressman Barney Frank, a Massachusetts Democrat, House Sub-Committee on Immigration, in 1982.

OSS: CAPITAL AX FALLING ON OUR PRICELESS SPY SYSTEM blazed the Chicago *Daily News* in a series whose headlines must have left the Russians in no doubt that at least some Americans believed in a peacetime foreign-intelligence agency of their own: SAVAGE FIGHT LOOMS FOR CONTROL OF OSS. . . . MATA HARI'S OKAY BUT SPYING'S DONE BY LONGHAIRS NOW. . . . IF OSS DIDN'T EXIST IT WOULD HAVE TO BE INVENTED. But the truth was that General Donovan had been involved in a losing struggle since President Roosevelt's death in April. "Donovan," Drew Pearson wrote at the time, "will miss Roosevelt terribly. [He] gave Donovan full free reign, including grandiose plans for a postwar espionage service. . . . Truman does not like peacetime espionage and will not be so lenient."*

Stephenson had watched Donovan's rearguard action to save the OSS. Now, as the papers carried stories of OSS men decorated for heroism in wartime exploits, he knew this latest campaign meant no more than a brief delay. The days when he could lean heavily on Donovan were over; it was time to turn to his original allies, Hoover and the FBI.

J. EDGAR HOOVER
SUSPECTS
SUBVERSIVES

J. Edgar Hoover was equally worried by the "freebooting" agencies that seemed to spring up everywhere. His own bid to extend the FBI's operations in South America into a worldwide intelligence agency had been rejected by Truman, who blamed it on overweening ambition. Yet Hoo-

*Quoted in Troy's *Donovan And The CIA: History of the Establishment of the CIA.*

ver was a patriotic American, concerned by what he had seen already of Soviet actions and the chaos of competing American and British agencies. Only Moscow Center seemed to benefit.

The FBI director had been in on the Corby Case from the very start. To counterbalance pussyfooting by London or Ottawa, Stephenson had secured his support—as he had done since the dark days of 1940, when "a secret marriage" between the FBI and SIS had been blessed by Roosevelt despite U.S. neutrality. The key had always been to demonstrate how Hoover needed him and thus to moderate the power of this man who tried to get his way by hoarding confidential dossiers on those who might clip his wings. Now Hoover saw the value of Gouzenko in promoting his "Plan for a Worldwide American SIS."

But from the moment he took office, Truman had made it clear that he wanted Hoover to stay at arm's length. A little scene summed up the relationship: Calling in General Harry Vaughan, his military aide who had responsibility for the army, for vets, and for the FBI, Truman had introduced him to Hoover and said, "Anything I want to give Mr. Hoover, you'll deliver to him direct, and anything Mr. Hoover has for me, he'll call you and you'll bring it over to me."

A spy scandal would prove Hoover's own claim that Soviet subversion was widespread. Even before the defection, he had suspected what Gouzenko would confirm: the existence of RIS agents close to the White House; support bases in half a dozen U.S. cities for RIS spy rings; penetration of the Manhattan Project. He had already been prepared to burn the secret files of FBI agents serving in South America rather than allow confidential material to get into the hands of dubious successors.

Some of his suspicions were confirmed by the capture of Gestapo records. Unlike the allied services, the Gestapo had been ruthless in its interrogation and torture of Russian spies. After the D-day invasion in mid-1944, both the Soviets and the West realized that these Gestapo records might contain valuable intelligence on RIS operations in Europe. A race began. Soviet special task squads grabbed up much of the compromising evidence; some Russian-led teams operated inside territory liberated by the Western allies. American counter-squads were hurriedly improvised to snatch up whatever remained. For months, the skirmishes continued. American and British specialists scavenged through the relatively few pertinent Gestapo files they were able to recover.

Now, in September 1945, it had become known to Hoover that Britain had asked U.S. Army counterintelligence to disclose nothing concerning secret Soviet operations in Britain. *Why?*

Hoover feared that Soviet intelligence ha penetrated the West's own security agencies under cover of war. But the FBI lacked specialists in RIS operations. The pattern of these operations was emerging from the study of the captured Gestapo records, from the limping analysis of recovered RIS radio traffic, and from the disclosures, of certain other Russian defectors. It seemed that, at the outbreak of Germany's war on Russia, the British had taken over the anti-Nazi intelligence networks that the Soviets already had functioning inside Britain.

The existence of these Russian networks had never been admitted by London. Once, when Hoover had requested routine information, there had been so many delays that finally Stephenson had to reprimand the chief of SIS in London: "If I am not to be accused once again [by Hoover] of withholding relevant material from London on Communist activities, it will be essential that you personally instruct that I should be promptly supplied with all available documentation so I may implement our promises." To this protest, there had been no response for seven weeks; then came nothing more than a promise that action would be taken, followed by further silence.*

This particular incident had occurred in 1943, when SIS knew more about Soviet activities than the FBI. The real enlightenment came for the FBI with the first captured Gestapo documents to reveal the existence of what the Nazis had dubbed *die Rote Kapelle*, the Red Orchestra, their own cryptonym for the networks discovered in Europe and extending into Britain. German interrogators had pieced together the history from Russian intelligence officers who belonged to the Red Orchestra and were caught after the 1941 invasion of Russia. It was clear now that the first nets were created as early as 1935; that the main targets had been Britain and the United States; and that the highest priority was given to the penetration of U.S. and British intelligence. The most brilliant of Moscow Center's espionage experts had been employed in recruiting native-born Communists in the target countries. They had enjoyed a considerable success in England. After the German attack on Russia, these pro-Soviet residents of Britain had been mobilized by SIS/London.

---

*Reading this now, in the previously secret BCS report, it is apparent that Hoover was correct in suspecting that London was not cooperating in the investigation of many Soviet activities because of an agreement with Moscow.

The versatility of Soviet espionage was illustrated by just one intercepted exchange between Moscow Center and a Communist underground leader, Tito, codenamed WALTER. On April 26, 1943, Tito sent from his Yugoslav Communist army headquarters a signal to his Soviet control: "PLEASE URGENTLY VERIFY THROUGH THE COMMUNIST PARTY OF CANADA, YUGOSLAV SECTION, IF P——, S——, A——, AND E—— HAVE BEEN SENT AS PART OF BRITISH MISSION HERE." The names were those of Camp X graduates, Yugoslav-born recruits to SOE. Tito had wished to guard against the possibility of infiltrators. His messages indicated active political support from pro-Soviet agents within SOE. These were later thought to be responsible for directing the Cairo-based SIS reinforcement of Tito's guerrillas, with the accompanying sacrifice of those anti-Nazi partisans who were also anti-Soviet.

Such startling facts were coming out only now, as analysts went through the backlog of wartime intercepts. To Hoover, at least, these explained a number of mysteries. The barely perceptible shift in London's policy, for example: nothing more definite than the creak of a stair, a soft adjustment of weight from one leg to another. The men running the new peacetime SIS in London, under Foreign Office supervision, were quietly reducing their links with the FBI and building up relations with those Americans expected to replace OSS with a new centralized intelligence agency. This appeared to Hoover to be part of a design to break wartime ties between the ABC spycatchers. The irony was that opponents of a centralized Western intelligence system were far from being Soviet sympathizers. Admiral Ernest J. King had told Navy Secretary James Forrestal that he "questioned whether such an agency would be consistent with our ideas of government." President Truman said repeatedly (with the FBI more in mind) that "this country wants no Gestapo, under any guise or for any reason."

The value of Gouzenko, in the minds of both Hoover and Stephenson, was that he could force a return to sanity in the postwar competition between the services. President Truman's native suspicion of a centralized agency might change if Gouzenko's evidence could be properly dramatized. All the chiefs of espionage, with varying degrees of concern or approval, became aware of this as news of the Russian's defection seeped into the international intelligence network—the converted prison cells and tsarist lecture halls of Moscow Center, the rabbit warrens from Broadway to Piccadilly of "the firm" in London, the RCMP I-Branch, an embryo external-affairs security force in Ottawa, and the rival intelligence services in Washington.

In a throwback to their 1940 collaboration, Hoover now suggested, in the words of the secret BSC history, "reviving the regular meetings between himself and Stephenson that accomplished so much during the war." Hoover "made clear his conviction that Intelligence is the only defense against the atom bomb, and that there should be the closest collaboration (to use Hoover's own forceful expression) 'in the interests of civilization.' "

They would short-circuit the bureaucracies. They would limit those who saw the Gouzenko material, thus reducing the chance of leaks to Moscow. Hoover would put FBI resources at Stephenson's disposal; Stephenson would continue to give Hoover whatever emerged from Gouzenko so the FBI could move swiftly against suspects in the United States.

That earlier 1940 collaboration had to be kept hidden too. As the BSC history notes: "The fact that it was kept secret from the State Department provides striking illustration of the strength of American neutrality."

The obstacle to their renewed cooperation was President Roosevelt's open 1940 directive giving the FBI control of investigations into espionage and "violations of neutrality." In 1945, with the war over, this original directive could be regarded as effectively overriding the secret, Roosevelt-approved alliance with Stephenson. Hoover should now be studying BSC's "violations" with an eye to demanding its departure. The American occupation of Germany and Japan had begun. The British occupation of Manhattan should be ending.

Hoover did not overlook the reality, however, that he and Stephenson still could help one another against a host of enemies. Both men shared the same uneasiness about the arguments for suspending suspicion of Soviet intentions. Hoover had many faults, and pro-Soviet observers were quick to point them out, feeding the legitimate reservations of his critics.

But he was also effective in blocking Russian aims in some situations. Hoover had personally prevented President Roosevelt from granting Moscow's wartime request to base official NKVD and GRU missions in Washington.

A similar request had been granted in London on a political level, despite Stephenson's opposition. London thus tolerated a large NKVD representation, reinforcing the presence of some of the most experienced GRU officers. The NKVD had infiltrated Soviet agents into Europe with

British help, in accordance with a secret Anglo-Soviet agreement to co-ordinate clandestine operations. General Donovan's OSS had exchanged intelligence data with the NKVD and GRU. Now, the odd situation was developing in which Anglo-American coordination was imperilled while Anglo-Soviet exchanges continued. When Stephenson questioned this, wondering if counter-subversive actions against the Soviets were in fact threatened, he was told not to worry. SIS counterintelligence specialists had everything under control.

The test of this SIS claim would be how swiftly and efficiently SIS/London dealt with the suspected atom spy Professor Alan Nunn May.

THIRTEEN

MACKENZIE KING
SAVES THE
CHRISTIAN WORLD

The first hasty translations of Gouzenko's stolen documents had yielded the name and codename of a Soviet-run British scientist at work in Canada. Camp X had transmitted a summary to the SIS chief in London:

> The most urgent concern is the spy codenamed ALEK. He is British nuclear physicist Alan Nunn May, now working here in Canada, due to fly back to England in ten days' time, and under orders to make contact with London-based Soviet controllers.

The scientist-spy known to Moscow Center as ALEK, renamed PRIMROSE by BSC, was to leave for England on Sunday, September 16, supposedly to take up his old job as lecturer in physics at King's College, University of London, but also to rendezvous on October 7 with a Soviet contact.

Whether or not he should be permitted to return home as scheduled had become the center of controversy during the week following Gouzenko's defection. The chiefs of British diplomatic, military, and scientific missions in Washington opposed Professor May's return on the grounds that there was too great a danger of "diversion or capture." This opposition sounded to Stephenson more like a way to make sure May would never lead investigators to the Soviet contacts in London whose identities were still unknown. Did someone want to protect the Soviets, while pretending to keep Professor May under Western control? The only clear-cut way to convict May of espionage was to catch him passing information to his London handlers.

Stephenson agreed that May must not be given the slightest chance of falling into Russian hands, but this was very different from keeping him in Canada. To break the deadlock, he put his own arguments to Sir Alexander Cadogan, permanent undersecretary and effective chief of the British Foreign Office. Using the direct, guarded BSC channel, he reviewed the advantages of keeping PRIMROSE under constant surveillance while the spy continued unsuspectingly to follow Moscow's orders. It was best to let Professor May go his merry way, blissfully unconscious of leading his pursuers to the Soviet spy networks in Britain.

Cadogan agreed but pointed out that there were political hazards. Canada must handle an affair that began in Canada. Though other countries were involved, each government had its own political concerns. Later publicity might lead to damaging criticism of the politicians who permitted such a situation to arise. Also, spy rings were difficult to break up. People in a democracy became uneasy over secret-police inquiries. In Canada, the prime minister could obtain a secret order-in-council restricting knowledge of it to three or four cabinet ministers, and get away with it. Stephenson could almost hear Cadogan clear his throat across four thousand miles, and recognized the diplomatic stutter, the slight hiccup before a bureaucratic delay.

All these considerations, Stephenson replied, would be cleared up at an urgent conference Mackenzie King would arrange within the next week or two with President Truman and the British prime minister. It was more important now to keep the Russians from getting wind of counteraction. Some hint of the Corby Case must have leaked out in Washington, where there was evidence that unauthorized officials knew about it and were trying to stop any behavior on the part of Professor

May that would reveal more information on Soviet operations. It was vital, Stephenson insisted, that May follow Soviet instructions about meeting the London contacts. May had been advised that if the October 7 rendezvous fell through, he should try again ten days later; if that failed, then ten days later still. The details were in a message from Moscow Center:

> Place: In front of the British Museum, on Great Russell Street, at the opposite side, about Museum Street, from the side of Tottenham Court Road. . . . ALEK shall have under his left arm the newspaper *Times*, the contact man will have in his left hand the magazine *Picture Post*. . . . In the beginning of the conversation ALEK says, "Best regards from Mikel."

Professor John Cockcroft, the Englishman who first bombarded and split the lithium atom, had been contacted in his Montreal research center and warned to travel by night to Ottawa. The scientist had just been secretly named as director of the new Canadian atomic-power plant at Chalk River, near Ottawa. Now he would have to give a verbal assessment of what Professor May could have betrayed to his Soviet masters. He was to do nothing that might seem out of the ordinary: his journey must be kept secret.

It was obvious to Cockcroft, after studying the decoded telegrams produced by Gouzenko, that Professor May had betrayed many of the secrets of the American bomb. Cockcroft and May had helped in the Los Alamos preparations and shared the Journey of Death celebrations of success. May was "almost second in knowledge [of] the atomic bomb," Cockcroft reported to Stephenson, and knew "practically all about the current state of nuclear-weapons research." May had already delivered to spymaster Zabotin samples of atomic fuel and "might have had access unofficially to uranium metal irradiated in the X pile and containing plutonium in quantities of a milligram. . . . Such samples would be of great value." The X pile was the new experimental plant to produce power and new atom-bomb ingredients. Professor May had "complete knowledge of the design of the Canadian heavy-water pile and knowledge of the construction of the U.S. graphite pile. . . . He knew the methods for separating plutonium and U-233 and he could probably guess the relative role of uranium 235 and 239 in U.S. bombs."

John Cockcroft was asked to continue to advise Mackenzie King's unofficial committee. The Canadian prime minister had formed the committee hastily, with the purpose of studying all the political and diplomatic consequences of any public action. Cockcroft's news forced King to consider having a special order-in-council passed, the secret procedure that would enable Canadian police to watch May and arrest him if he should try to contact his Soviet colleagues in Canada again.

Cockcroft was sent back to the laboratories with the uncomfortable task of rubbing shoulders with an atom spy and behaving as though nothing had happened.

Mackenzie King was now gripped by the melodrama and its possibilities for self-aggrandizement. Atomic spies still at large! A famous atomic scientist, appearing out of the dark night like a magician in a puff of smoke! The secret Soviet world, laid bare by Gouzenko's disclosure of Moscow Center's lexicon, was a thrilling confirmation of Soviet efficiency. LESOVIA was the codename for Canada. ("Sounds too close to Ruritania for comfort!" clucked the little prime minister.) METRO stood for RIS headquarters in Ottawa. The Neighbor was the NKVD, supplying a "roof" for illegal operations and "shoes" in the form of fake passports for frontier dodgers. Canada was the most popular supplier of such passports: there was even someone called the Executioner in a Canadian government department who issued these passports. Someone else known as the Doctor made the alterations. GRANT was the Soviet cryptonym for Zabotin and the spy center in Ottawa feeding back North American secrets to GISEL, which was Moscow Center.

"It can be honestly said that few more courageous acts have ever been performed . . . than my own in the Russian intrigues against the Christian world," gushed King's diary. He revealed, however, ambivalence. At one time he seemed to admire Russian technique; the next moment he gathered up courage to act against Canadian-born agents. In the latter mood, he considered the political risks if he should be accused later of "Star Chamber methods." The Star Chamber, his critics frequently reminded him, had been abolished in 1641 in England, where it had formerly investigated cases involving national security. But such a cloak of secrecy had surrounded King's wartime actions that newspapers had almost lost the habit of prying into government matters. The war had provided some handy excuses for high-handed actions, and King was not above using these emergency powers now.

Paradoxically, security had not been served by this routine secrecy, which simply made it easier for Moscow Center to work with subverted government employees. Their secretiveness could always be explained away by reference to "matters of national security." Public servants could remove documents, covering their actions with a shrewd wink and words like, "It's confidential for upstairs." *That* was all apparent now from the Gouzenko papers. And it was that aspect Mackenzie King needed to obscure: at first, by having Gouzenko silenced; and when that became impossible, by making some show of dramatic intervention.

King was looking for political advantage. The situation could bring down his government. He made no bones about this. Stephenson saw hope in the prime minister's insistence that Washington and London keep this foremost in their minds. So when King wanted to have Professor May arrested at once, on Canadian soil, Stephenson pointed out that the general applause would be much greater if May became the means of uncovering spy networks across America and Britain. King would be seen as a leader of great subtlety and patience. Besides, if the Canadian prime minister were to rush off to Washington and London, to brief President Truman and Prime Minister Attlee personally, how much more effective this would seem if in the meantime the Soviets were kept entirely in the dark. No arrests. No public statements.

If King could be coaxed into the role of dragon-slayer, this might cut out interference from London's intelligence bureaucrats. They would be careful not to offend Canadian pride. The fact that King had allowed the delays of the recent past, out of fear for his political future, need not disqualify him as a source of help. As for public statements, Stephenson would see that these were made only if they helped his own cause.

PRIMROSE was now vital to the plans of Stephenson and Hoover to break Stalin's spell. The Soviet dictator's reputation for being difficult had the effect of "making almost any concession to Stalin's demands seem necessary," wrote a BSC political analyst. "The furtherance of good relations with the Soviet Union has become all-consuming. Any concession is possible, no matter how base or cruel, if it doesn't dramatically affect strategic or political interests." There was the political tendency in London, as in Washington and Ottawa, to brush under the carpet anything embarrassing to Stalin. But exposure of spy rings run by Moscow throughout the Atlantic alliance was not going to be so easily concealed.

Pro-Gouzenko security men were anxious to take action on his warnings that Soviet intelligence had long-range aims involving the placement of "agents of influence." Gouzenko was swept in this direction. He really wanted to convey, in utmost secrecy, his reasons for believing that the Soviets had penetrated Western security itself. He was carried along, away from this most devastating disclosure, by the well-intentioned security men who were startled by his evidence that there were pro-Soviet agents who might not be activated for many years, sleepers and sympathizers whose presence at a decisive conference could tilt policies—military, strategic, technological, geopolitical—in the direction Moscow desired. Gouzenko had delivered the list of these pro-Soviet agents. The names were many. Stephenson's men had already spent several hours checking through them with I-Branch chiefs. The British Security Coordination file notes:

> The telephone directory of dominion [federal] government officials became a useful reference book. The GRANT networks spread through the country, concentrating on centers of political and commercial life. . . . What was alarming was the degree of vital penetration into Canadian government offices . . . : Naval and Air Intelligence, Ministry of Munitions and Supplies (covering atomic research and all military developments), external affairs . . . Parliament. . . . Some agents were themselves charged with the duty of safeguarding the very information they were passing to the Soviet Union [and] nearly all had access to Top Secret documents (often relating to the most highly secret matters in the United States and Britain). . . . The standards demanded from these agents were extremely high, and evidence of the network's success is shown in a copy of GRANT's mailing list to Moscow of January 5th, 1945, containing over one hundred official documents from Canadian Government offices . . . including sensitive papers such as letters from the Canadian ambassador in Moscow to Mackenzie King.

From such lists, it was estimated that more than two hundred secret government documents had been dispatched from GRANT to GISEL in the first five days of 1945. This suggested an incredible volume of traffic over the year. "The measures taken to protect both the security and identity of agents were remarkable," the BSC file notes. "Methods of contacting were meticulously careful. . . . The authorities were faced with the problem of how to liquidate a widespread and brilliantly contrived espionage organization threatening us. Once a Professor May decision was made, we realized the organization could not be broken by direct action without the most serious consequences to relations with Russia."

Again Mackenzie King revealed the pressures on him from his foreign-policy advisers. Torn between saving "the Christian world" and saving his domestic political skin, King let Stephenson know he would now favor a direct and secret approach to the Soviets "as the basis on which to build better relations," adding: "To make [Soviet espionage] known to the world would prove as disastrous as no action at all."

King had become a mass of contradictions. He wanted to eat his cake and have it too. He wanted to sound the alarm in the White House and at Number 10 Downing Street. He would be the dragon-slayer who caught Stalin's spies red-handed. But then he would persuade Stalin to become more cooperative with the West! His view, set out in the Corby Case file and otherwise unrecorded, was that "a frank talk with Moscow . . . might help induce a change of heart in the Russians. If it were linked with the adoption of some helpful policy about the secret of the atom bomb, these two factors [a threat to reduce Soviet missions and to cut down Western loans] might influence the Russians considerably."

Someone had put this idea in King's head. It appealed to him because it would put him on the same level as the Big Three at Yalta. He had not been invited and had never concealed his chagrin at letting Roosevelt, Churchill, and Stalin make decisions without consulting Canada, whose contributions to the war had been disproportionately large. It would go down well with the Canadian public, too, when the story of his secret diplomacy trickled out, for Canadians vaguely resented the way their part in the war was buried in the overall "British" effort. The alternative, a scandal about spies in government, might unseat his ruling Liberal party, which, according to a BSC profile of King, he regarded as "the fount of all his powers and glories, and a much more important thing than the Canadian nation." Putting Gouzenko before a public tribunal could seriously harm the party, since he would name the Soviet agents who had burrowed into government departments built up and manned by

Liberals. If King diverted attention from these agents, and pulled off some seeming diplomatic coup with the Russians, it would suit King—and it would suit Moscow just as well.

But what kind of coup? A promise from the Soviets to curtail espionage in return for Canada's offer to cooperate with the Soviet Union in the field of atomic energy?* It seemed impossible that King was such an innocent. A biographer had written: "No man in Canada leads a more solitary social life except perhaps a few celibate keepers of lonely light-houses. . . . He is infinitely more suited to the occupancy of a pulpit or a professorial chair."** Yet he was a cunning political animal. He kept would-be senators and judges in suspense, making them pay homage at the foot of his throne by doling out sinecures in exchange for unquestioning loyalty. In his seventieth year he still consulted the spirit of his dead mother, believing he got guidance from "across the Great Divide." He was dangerously naive about Communists and thought they claimed Christ as their first teacher. His favorite way of entertaining guests was to read them Gray's "Elegy in a Country Churchyard."

With King flip-flopping all over the place, there was a real danger that Professor May might be stopped from sticking to his normal plans. Stephenson had overcome the opposition, and in Washington and London there was no further open resistance to May's being left to follow Soviet instructions. But King's nervous dithering could jeopardize plans to have May unwittingly expose the British end of the Soviet spy networks.

*Astonishing disclosures were made a week after Hiroshima in *Atomic Energy for Military Purposes*, by Professor Henry De Wolf Smyth of Princeton University, written and published on the insistence of the Manhattan Project's managers. Helpful to bomb-makers everywhere, it showed that a plutonium bomb was possible and that U-235 could be produced by gaseous diffusion. The first chairman of the U.S. Atomic Energy Commission, David Lilienthal, called it "the principal breach of security since the beginning of the atomic energy project." The Soviets said that they had no need to steal atom secrets: everything was in the book.

**The biographer happened to be one of Stephenson's favorite political journalists in Ottawa, John A. Stevenson. King had obtained a copy of the manuscript and at once complained to the author's employers, the London *Times*. The journalist revealed later that he needed his job more than publication of the book, and accepted King's demand that the biography be burned. The alternative was that King would have had him declared persona non grata, forcing the *Times* to replace him. Still, Stevenson had the last word. In the copy of his manuscript passed to Bill Stephenson, there was this prophetic passage: "History will pronounce the record of [King's] achievements in the field of statesmanship singularly barren and see the opportunities which he has missed towering in magnitude above his meagre accomplishments."

PROFESSOR MAY WALKS
THE PRIMROSE PATH

By the time of his flight, Alan Nunn May knew only that the University of London needed him urgently enough to command a priority seat on the RAF's transport service. Stephenson dared not speed him on his way by direct intervention. The more he kept out of the picture, the better.

"The PRIMROSE has top priority to fly RAF Command from Montreal next September 16," said a coded message that arrived on his BSC desk two days before the departure. Things seemed to be going according to plan . . . but they weren't.

Two RCMP officers were to be put aboard the same converted bomber on which May would travel. Bombers were at the time the substitute for regular commercial planes. They ran more or less on a schedule, and carried passengers whose seats were reserved through military channels. It was a ticklish business for passengers on secret missions: bookings had to be made through some neutral third party; if the passenger traveled under another name, there was the danger of this becoming apparent to the passport officers. The two RCMP men were listed under false names and they were traveling in civilian clothes. One was a friend of the commander of secret movements at the Montreal base. There was a grave risk that the sociable commander might greet his friend in front of May, and give the game away. Someone had to lure the commander, known as Popeye, from his duties. But who? The number of people who knew about the Corby Case was still limited to an absolute minimum, so the plan had to involve someone already briefed—and someone with sufficient authority that the commander could hardly refuse. Mackenzie King? An invitation to tea? But neither man knew the other. Popeye would guess something important was going on. No senior security officer could extend the invitation. That would provide the commander's sensitive nose with a whiff of scandal. And he loved gossip.

It was the kind of idiotic, seemingly trivial problem that crops up at the last moment. Stephenson had a vision of Popeye bouncing through the VIP lounge, yelling, "Why aren't you in uniform?" to his RCMP friend. Professor May would guess that something unusual was afoot. Yet it would be unthinkable to confide in Popeye. He was notoriously indiscreet. On one occasion he had briefed Alexander Korda, the moviemaker of legend, on how to inflate a Mae West life preserver, in case his bomber had to ditch in the Atlantic. "It will keep you afloat for hours," he said.

Korda brooded a moment. "But," he answered finally, "I do not wish to float around the Atlantic for hours."

It had seemed a funny retort to the commander, who told the story several times before someone pointed out that Korda's intelligence work was supposed to be secret, and broadcasting the fact that he flew as a VIP on bombers hardly helped to protect this status.

Somebody suggested slipping Popeye the proverbial Mickey Finn during the crucial hours that May would be on the base. But the commander was a good fellow at heart, and the suggestion was quickly dropped when Malcolm MacDonald volunteered his services.

"I'm the British high commissioner, and it's about time I had this senior RAF officer over for a drink," he said, a sturdily patriotic statement made in the teeth of his own recollection of the man as a witless bore. "Sherry and biscuits, I think," he added hastily, shrinking from the prospect of a long evening.

As it turned out, the sherry ran into the hour for whisky, which led to dinner and a prolonged exchange of anecdotes through port, then brandies. This painful delay was entirely because the plane, with Professor May and his RCMP shadows already aboard, had run into a series of mechanical problems on the ground. Popeye was overwhelmed by the attention lavished upon him by the representative of His Majesty the king, and was slightly taken aback when MacDonald dashed to the telephone late that night, listened, said only, "Thank you!" and scampered back to the library to jerk the somewhat sozzled guest out of his chair and propel him to the door.

"So nice of you to come!" murmured MacDonald, breathing heavily. "Know you've got a long drive ahead; frightfully sorry I kept you chin-wagging so long. 'Bye, my dear chap. Goodbye!"

After the commander, goggling, had gone, MacDonald rushed back to the phone. The caller had reported, "PRIMROSE is planted," meaning May was at last airborne and technically in British hands. MacDonald's concern was the commander, whom he perceived as more dangerous than anyone had anticipated. He had told MacDonald he "thought something funny was going on" to do with "Commies and spies" and mentioned "two suspicious characters in government service" traveling on phony orders. In a frenzy to warn London that it might get some odd and possibly panicky signals from Popeye that must at all costs be ignored, the British high commissioner fired off signals to MI5.

It was too late. Popeye had sped back to base, checked into the causes of the delayed departure, and brooded about MacDonald and left-wing conspiracies. Wasn't MacDonald's father "a Commie prime minister"?* Then he sent an alert to the RAF police at Prestwick, Scotland, where the Ferry Command plane was scheduled to land. The two RCMP officers, known to the commander only as "phony civilians," were to be held for questioning. Popeye was only displaying a caution normal in wartime. Transatlantic flights had been handled as highly confidential. Few got to see passenger lists because there had been cases where long-range German aircraft intercepted VIP flights, as if forewarned. The wartime precautions were such that a British carrier-borne fighter had once destroyed an allied plan by mistake: there had been no warning that the converted bomber even existed, let alone that it would fly over a convoy trigger-happy about long-range German bombers.**

Professor May's plane had to refuel in Labrador, however, and further delays were caused by headwinds and bad weather. This gave MI5 time to post a man with priority authorization at Prestwick. Otherwise, the ludicrous spectacle would have unfolded of two RCMP officers being detained as possible subversives while a real spy went free.

May was at last under the eye of MI5 counterintelligence. It seemed a guarantee that all was going well. He was watched while he moved into lodgings near King's College on the Strand. He was watched while

---

*Ramsay MacDonald had been a Labor prime minister of Britain.

**Some allied aircraft were easily confused with German Condors, which often shadowed British and American convoys to radio details to the waiting U-boat packs. British navy fighters were catapulted from freighters with very little time to destroy the Condors. A fellow pilot of the author, intercepting in thick cloud and *expecting* to see the enemy whose presence had been reported by ships' observers, shot down a planeload of allied VIPs. At the subsequent court-martial, the pilot's camera-gun film was screened, together with similar film of an attack on a confirmed enemy bomber. The presiding admiral could not distinguish between the two aircraft and the nineteen-year-old pilot was exonerated. When highly trained policemen, like pilots, expect to see the enemy, they generally do—with devastating results for innocents who stray across their path.

he picked up the threads of life in a country still suffering from the war. He learned to deal again with food rationing and coupons for "utility suits." He revisited old haunts, now reduced to rubble by bombs and rockets. And nothing else happened. Alan Nunn May behaved exactly as might be expected of a respectable, somewhat eccentric professor returning to London after wartime adventures in the new world of atomic bombs.

The watch on Professor May went on. The date of his first scheduled contact with the Soviet network in Britain approached. There was no reason why the scientist and his RIS handlers should fail to meet. They would be arrested as soon as they had clearly compromised themselves. The decision to move against them was known to a very select few at SIS headquarters. Today, it would clear up many mysteries if a list of those in the know had been preserved. Thanks to "weeding," that information has been removed from relevant files, classified or otherwise.

"When the arrests are made, there will be some leakage," Cadogan in the Foreign Office innocently warned his friends. The message must have amused one or two of his colleagues, since the leakage had already occurred. "This may have political repercussions in our relations with Russia," Cadogan added, doubtless evoking a smile or two in Moscow, where the message was intercepted as soon as sent. "His Majesty's government are prepared to accept this consequence and they would like to know if the Canadian and U.S. governments agree."

Mackenzie King performed another clumsy somersault. He had planned to make a direct appeal to Stalin, through V. M. Molotov, the people's commissar for Soviet foreign affairs. King had just learned through Gouzenko that it was Molotov's office that received some of the intelligence stolen in Ottawa. Whatever King thought he could do with Molotov was now threatened by the new British initiative. Cadogan must be smarting (thought King) from Molotov's intransigence at the Council of Ministers in London; still, it was no excuse for telling the U.S. and Canada that London would break open the case on its own, if need be. King mentally hovered upside down while he considered all this. If the British did make arrests, and if there was publicity, how would it look if King meanwhile had done nothing? Then he came right side up again. He would have everything ready, just in case.

Special orders-in-council would be drawn up, by which suspects could be arrested and interrogated without regard for their civil rights. Squads of police experts were meanwhile flown into Ottawa to study the Gouzenko papers, widening the circle of those partly in the know. "By almost superhuman efforts the RCMP was to be made ready by the evening of October 7th, the first date May had with the unknown Soviet handler," recorded the BSC history. "Time was running short. Everyone worked feverishly for the emergency that might arise."

In the United States, Hoover and the FBI made their moves, treading warily, aware the Corby Case could play a large role in the FBI's future but also conscious of the disastrous consequences of a false step. The State Department was not enthusiastic about the strong British line. President Truman's distaste for secret police methods still prevailed. ("The Director of Centralized Snooping," Truman had once said, "ought to be equipped with a paper cloak and a wooden dagger.") Hoover depended heavily on Stephenson, BSC, and the foreign alliance to build up the case with which, eventually, he hoped to change Truman's outlook. He had to be content with allowing Stephenson to call the shots, and this meant especially the avoidance of premature action.

Then suddenly, on the very eve of his journey to the White House with the Corby Case file under his arm, King pirouetted off in yet another direction. His "leading advisers" had cautioned him "to move very slowly and cautiously," he told the British. "We are not ready in Canada to take proceedings."

It seemed at the time that King was neurotically indecisive. Only much later was it speculated that he might have been a puppet dancing on invisible strings. In Washington, Hoover had already concluded that pro-Soviet advisers were responsible for soft-headed U.S. policies, and he was convinced the situation was worse in Canada. He had grave doubts, for instance, about the Canadian ambassador in Washington, Lester B. Pearson, the future Nobel Prize winner and UN secretary-general. Stephenson preferred to wait, even though each day's delay was now a clear bonus for the enemy. A few more days, and Professor May would make his compromising move. Then King would be forced to act.

In his message to London, King quoted the same advisers as saying it would be "very difficult to get a conviction on the material, considering its source."

The last phrase is revealing. It implied that the source was not reliable.

Yet the source was Gouzenko. There was no possible excuse for down-grading Gouzenko, unless pro-Soviet officials were now trying to discredit the man.

Everything seemed to hang on May. His testimony could not be dismissed with a contemptuous "considering its source." The man's eminence in the new field of nuclear physics, his reputation among scientists the world over, turned him into an imposing traitor. Nobody would have the gall to protest that police operations had been undemocratically coordinated in three countries, once he was caught.

But PRIMROSE seemed to be rooted in the soil of routine. He continued his legitimate walks through the narrow alleys and drab courtyards around King's College. He had come home to a gray land, gray skies, gray faces. Everything in those days in Britain seemed to be covered in the gray ash of a war from which the country would never really recover. "Blitz-weeds" flourished in bomb craters, symbols of the neglect with which most returning soldiers were greeted. There was no British equivalent of the American GI Bill; no repair work was performed on disrupted lives. The veteran had to fend for himself. Often, he could never make up for the six precious years of youth he had lost. There were no frontiers for him to conquer: the old empire was shrinking, and such a traditional settlers' territory as Canada took steps that made immigration from England difficult. The English veteran reacted to the situation with bitter jokes. "The trouble with Yanks in England," he said, "is they're overpaid, oversexed, and over here." Perhaps it was envy. Perhaps it was fatigue. Perhaps it was the seldom-voiced acknowledgment that North America was now the center of power and wealth, seeming to threaten traditions and a culture and an empire built up through centuries of fierce struggle.

Professor May had crossed not only the Atlantic but a gulf in time and mood. People in Britain had forgotten American generosity of spirit; and material generosity they tended to resent. It was five and a half years since the *New York Times*, with the start of the Battle of Britain, had editorialized: "Is the tongue of Chaucer, of Shakespeare, of Milton . . . to be hereafter in the British Isles the dialect of an enslaved race? . . . We have to look back a good many centuries to find the beginnings of English liberty. We see it as a rough and obstinate growth, heaving the rich soil under the oaks of lordly estates . . . never perfected, never giving up. . . . It is twelve o'clock in London. Not twelve o'clock for empire—there is no empire anymore. . . . Twelve o'clock for the common people of England, out of whom England's greatest souls have always come. Twelve o'clock for all that they are and have been, for all those things which make life worth living for free men."

The good feelings had turned sour. A new American president, Harry Truman, heard from his secretary of state, Dean Acheson, a view that later became public (provoking a protest from London): "Britain lost an empire and has not found a role." Determined to remain a great world power, without ever redefining a great power's role in a nuclear age, Britain was adrift. There were two governments in Britain: His Majesty's political government in Westminster, and the permanent government of bureaucrats, whose crucial organ of perception was the Secret Intelligence Service. The second seemed to take an oddly languid attitude to Soviet spies, despite the recent creation of a super-secret Section IX operating exclusively against Soviet intelligence. The gray figure of Professor May merged into that gray landscape, and he was, through benign neglect or calculated treachery, permitted never to put a foot wrong.

FIFTEEN

HARRY TRUMAN
TAKES HOLD

Harry Truman, thirty-third president of the United States, was up before dawn on Sunday, September 30. He showered and shaved, dressed with a finicky care that belied his casual demeanor, and by seven o'clock was crossing Lafayette Park for his 120-paces-a-minute constitutional.

Half a mile away, in the new State Department building on Virginia Avenue, the American most favored by the Soviets as secretary-general of the UN conference in San Francisco skimmed through a brief sent over by the Canadian embassy. He was Alger Hiss, director of Truman's Office of Special Political Affairs.

The brief came from Lester B. Pearson, the Canadian ambassador to the United States, today playing host to his prime minister. It summarized what King would be telling Truman later that morning: "What we have learned about espionage in the United States [and] Soviet intelligence requests for information about U.S. military matters . . . the case of a courier to the U.S. who turns out to be an inspector in the Red Army, sizing up chances for further espionage in the U.S."

Truman was not totally unprepared for this disclosure of Soviet aims against the United States. What surprised him that morning was the tentative manner of Mackenzie King, leader of the vast neighbor to the north, a country Truman only vaguely understood as a last rump of the British empire. He himself seldom worried about the electorate's opinion of his decisions. He found King's disquiet about public opinion "strange" until it dawned on him that the subject at hand was treason on the grand scale. "This will fairly tear the roof off the American nation," Prime Minister King warned. "It shows a fifth column operating in all our countries."

King had arrived with a brown paper parcel under his arm. He had neither slept nor breakfasted well, and he found Truman's optimistic air "inappropriate." As if to prick the presidential balloon, he unwrapped the parcel, removed a large envelope, and said almost casually, "Among these statements is something about an assistant secretary in the State Department being a Soviet plant. . . . This is what Corby says."

Unknown to the Canadian leader, the statement had already reached the president. The name of Alger Hiss had come to mind. Hiss had been at Yalta, as special assistant to Edward Stettinius. How much had been betrayed to Stalin at Yalta was still a matter of conjecture.

Truman said after a pause, "We thought Corby was talking about an assistant to an assistant."

"All I know is what's in the statement," King said evenly. "Perhaps the story's got no foundation."

The secret meeting lasted two hours. At one point King said, "You'll have to do something about the Soviets in New York. Vice-Consul Yakovlev is running a spy network there. If you or we denounce them, we have to pack them off to Moscow. That means breaking off diplomatic relations—with consequences to the UN too awful to contemplate."

"Get all evidence before action," murmured Truman.

King was leafing through more papers. He looked up. "You agree we should all act together?"

"No use going off half-cocked. The British won't want us to do anything without checking with them, and we'd appreciate similar considerations."

King looked grateful. Truman was known for his hatred of procrastination. This sounded more like a prudent delay. He took out one of the progress reports on PRIMROSE. "Now, sir, this Professor May. . . ."

King began to read the secret summary. Later, it would be said that this was the precise moment when President Truman lost all innocence about Russia's good intentions. The United States had spent two billion dollars in the extraordinary four-year search for the bomb. The best scientists had been matched with the greatest industrial resources to produce "the keystone for a very fragile arch" in military plans to defeat Japan. The Soviets had benefited from that defeat; indeed, they had with a great show of bravado declared war on Japan at that last moment in order to share the spoils. The Soviets could never have duplicated the U.S. effort on the bomb, though they understood the theoretical physics. Instead, by stealth and double-dealing, Moscow Center had acquired a cornucopia of charts and formulas, and volumes of data on everything from the gaseous-diffusion process for separating U-235 and U-238 to methods for detonating the two kinds of bombs. The Soviets had thus skipped costly and time-consuming research. Truman found this appalling. He said courteously, "Mr. King, would it be possible to tell me where this PRIMROSE is now?"

"He reached London ten days ago."

"When will he be arrested?"

"The day I arrive in London myself," replied King, folding the papers in his lap. "That's the day PRIMROSE should meet his Russian controller, and that's when I'll brief Prime Minister Attlee."

"You'll brief Mr. Attlee, sir?"

"Well, Mr. President, he'll want to know your views, of course. Scotland Yard are on the job, but the political implications. . . ." King let the words hang.

"Then with your permission, sir, I'll make a suggestion," said Truman. "Go see Halifax before you leave Washington."

Mackenzie King cocked his head, surprised.

"Lord Halifax," murmured Truman, "is a good ally but unpredictable as an enemy."

"That's very good advice, Mr. President."

"Good," said Truman briskly. "I'll tell him you'll be over after lunch."

Truman ushered the prime minister on his way and returned to sit at his desk. He had replaced his model gun with a toy plow once the bombs were dropped on Hiroshima and Nagasaki. Like Churchill, he hoped the atomic bombs were a blessing in disguise. They made war unthinkable.

Truman nurtured his reputation as a businesslike man. No subterfuge. No playing off one faction against another. Yet he had suggested that King see Lord Halifax, the British ambassador in Washington, for what could only be called reasons of intrigue. Halifax was remembered as the British foreign minister in Neville Chamberlain's "peace-in-our-time" period of appeasing dictators. In Washington he was an elegant figure-head, but he could be obstructive in London if he thought things were being arranged behind his back.

In fact, Truman reflected, arrangements could very well be going on behind his own back. The early reports on the Corby Case had been relayed through Hoover, who might try to use the case to advance his own ambitions. Truman believed anyone operating both the FBI and the new agency would get "too big for his britches." He had instructed Hoover to "just hold your horses," but the man kept right on trying.

Truman turned the toy plow over in his hand. He'd been delighted to get rid of the army gun. After all, plowshares weren't being beaten out of swords. Not yet. Still, a secret war, by being secret, could be contained. Maybe the Soviets could be scared with proof of their treachery. The trouble was, J. Edgar Hoover was the only man to handle investigations, and these would have to be coordinated through BSC. Any continuation of the wartime alliance with British intelligence went against Truman's instincts. The British were *not* running American policy. Lord Halifax understood how Americans felt about the concealed, imperial hand. You could say that much for him. He saw Stephenson and BSC as a necessity in moments of crisis, best buried in more tranquil times.

No, it would never do to offend Halifax with secret deals through secret channels. If he did move against the Soviets, Truman wanted his foreign allies to be in agreement. He was, for once, undecided. Hoover needed time for his investigations, but too much delay would help the Russians get agents to safety and destroy some of the evidence.

It would be later claimed that Truman was not as concerned as King. "Although the Russians were clearly working on the bomb," Truman felt there was "no precious secret the United States could withhold." The American monopoly of the atomic secret would, in the nature of things, vanish over the next five to ten years.* But such interpretations were made by critics who believed the spy scares were used to set off the Cold War between the Americans and the Russians, and by those spreading the gospel according to Moscow that Americans should share all weaponry secrets.

In fact, the president had learned very quickly that "force is the only thing the Russians understand" and that Russia "plans world conquest." He still considered it important to keep the Russians talking. The devil of it was, Stalin behaved as if he was doing his allies a favor by talking at all—as if the president of the United States were a weakling at the head of a nation tortured by strikes, rising prices, black markets, and severe housing shortages. There was a kind of arrogance in the way the Soviet intelligence chiefs had gone about searching out the secrets of a country they said was falling apart.

Dean Acheson in the State Department had followed part of the King-Truman talks and would say later, with the loftiness of a professional policymaker, that Truman was naive—"not a serious indictment [because] he was still learning the awesome responsibilities of the President of the United States." Yet the speed of learning was not acceptable to those determined to spread an impression that the United States, not the Soviet Union, was the troublemaker. These ill-wishers preferred to project a picture of Truman as a man pushed by warmongers. The reality was that he regarded the atomic bomb as "too dangerous to let loose in a lawless world," expressing the view after the Big Three conference at Potsdam and shortly before the meeting with King. "That is why," Truman added, "we who have the secret of production do not intend to reveal the secret until means have been found to control the bomb [and] to protect the world from total destruction."

*J. L. Gaddis, *The United States and the Origins of the Cold War, 1941–47* (New York: Columbia U. Press, 1972, pp. 252–53).

He wanted to think carefully about joint action with Britain and Canada against Soviet spies. If the facts were as ominous as the Corby Case indicated, the publicity given to them as a result of such action could damage the UN dream. American public opinion might become so greatly aroused that all hope of somehow muddling along with the Soviets would be lost in the atmosphere of general outrage. The list of Moscow's intelligence requirements, revealed through Gouzenko, showed the scope of the Soviet attack:

(a) The technological processes and methods employed for the U.S. production of explosives and chemical materials.

(b) Information as to the transfer of American troops from Europe to the United States and the Pacific; and also the army headquarters of the 9th Army, the 3rd, 5th, 7th, 13th Army Corps, the 18th Armored Division, the 2nd, 4th, 8th, 28th, 30th, 44th, 45th, 104th Infantry Divisions, the 10th Tank Division and the location of the Brazilian Infantry Division. Whether or not there had been organized a staff for the American troops in Germany and, if so, its location and the name of officer-in-command. The location of the 1st Parachute Troops and the plans for their future use.

(c) Models obtained from the Canadian government agency for secret weapons, the National Research Council, of developed radar sets, photographs, technical data, periodic reports characterizing the radar work carried on by the council, and future developments planned by the council.

(d) Formulas of explosives and samples from the secret explosives establishments.

(e) Specifications of the electro-projector of the "V" bomb.

(f) Research work relating to explosive materials and artillery.

(g) American aircraft radar locator, navigation periscope (specifications required).

(h) List of army divisions returned from Europe and details of divisions divided, re-shaped or undergoing re-shaping.

(i) Numbers of postwar troops and system of organization.

(j) Information from [Canadian] Department of Munitions relating to chemical warfare . . . plants producing same . . . weapons in general.

(k) Electronic shells in use with U.S. navy.

(l) Depth "bombs" and double-charge shells. . . .

The BSC account of these RIS requirements concluded: "It may be seen Moscow's objectives are extremely broad and transcend what Soviet apologists describe as the logical consequence of Western atom-bomb secrecy."

One giveaway was Russian interest in the morale-raising value of American help for beleaguered Britain. The RIS had asked its Ottawa network for details of a countermeasure to Hitler's first "vengeance weapon," the V-1 flying bomb. A replica V-1 had been testflown over the U.S. site of the first atomic explosion, enabling American scientists to perfect a proximity fuse, codenamed VT, to be screwed into the nosecone of anti-aircraft shells. The crash project was completed in time to reduce the destruction in southern England. Some 8,000 V-1s had been launched against London, killing 6,000 civilians and seriously injuring another 18,000 before the new VT-equipped shells went into action. They detonated on coming within range, and achieved immediate results—90 flying bombs out of the next clutch of 94 were destroyed. "Englishmen still alive should be grateful to Johns Hopkins," wrote a British nuclear scientist. The applied-physics laboratory at Johns Hopkins had produced the V-1 antidote. What Moscow Center wanted to know was just how grateful the British might be, and how much this might affect future collaboration.

The first presidential message on atomic matters was to be delivered to Congress three days later. Truman drew a sheet of paper across his desk. The draft speech would need some adjustment. "I propose to initiate discussions," he wrote, "first with our associates in this discovery, Great Britain and Canada, and then with other nations, in an effort to effect agreement for cooperation in atomic power. . . . These discussions will *not* be concerned with disclosures relating to the manufacturing processes leading to the bomb itself."

It was a statement that would challenge the Association of Oak Ridge Scientists, said to represent 96 percent of the scientists involved in the U.S. atomic-bomb project. During the past week, the association had issued a warning that the bomb must *not* become the cornerstone of foreign policy for the Atlantic alliance, and that "no enduring monopoly of the atomic bomb by the Americans and British is possible."

After hearing about Professor May, Truman was beginning to question the political wisdom of the scientists.

To Mackenzie King, it was beginning to seem as though business regarding the bomb and spies, at least where the British were concerned, always took place at garden parties. Lord Halifax was presiding at one in the embassy grounds that afternoon and could spare the prime minister only a few moments in the library. Seated on a sofa directly in line with the late Indian-summer sunshine slanting through the French windows, King wondered if Halifax had put him there on purpose: the noble lord himself sat on a separate chair with his back to the light. "It was," King said later, "the sort of thing people of the Mussolini type do. They watch your face and keep their own in the dark."

Squinting and shading his eyes, King quickly reviewed the Corby Case. He was aware, while he talked, of a third man in the room. The name of this silent observer was Donald Maclean. King shifted about on the sofa but found it impossible to escape the blinding sun.

"I have, of course, heard some of these particulars from MacDonald in Ottawa," said Halifax.

"I considered it my duty to give our American friends the same information I am giving Britain." King recrossed his legs.

"Yes, yes, of course," replied Halifax. "I'm quite sure the British prime minister and President Truman can work things out together when Mr. Attlee comes here shortly—"

"I shall be sailing early tomorrow for England," said King with some asperity. "I plan to tell Mr. Attlee that we Canadians expect to be fully consulted. Indeed, we are in the most serious position of all. The whole dreadful business originated in Canada, and if anyone suffers from the consequences, it will be ourselves."

"Quite so," murmured Halifax. *

Had King thought to inquire, he would have discovered that the third man, Donald Maclean, was using his position at the British embassy to

---

*These and other quoted comments are taken from published recollections, and the diaries of William Mackenzie King. The conversations are reconstructed from the memoirs of participants and from personal interviews (see author's preface).

become the foremost Foreign Office expert on matters relating to the American bomb and further atomic research. There is no record of King's raising the matter with the Canadian ambassador in Washington, Lester B. Pearson, who certainly knew Maclean's job. Pearson was taken fully into King's confidence with regard to the Corby Case, and he very soon afterwards redoubled his efforts to pressure Stephenson into dissolving BSC, claiming that it was politically embarrassing to have a Canadian running that type of operation on United States soil. Pearson had already rejected an offer to have the FBI help build a postwar Canadian security force, observing that "Canadians are quite capable of managing their own security."

Meanwhile, King sailed regally across the Atlantic on board the liner *Queen Mary* with Norman Robertson. The two men discussed international control over atomic energy, and argued back and forth about the desirability of simply giving the Soviet Union all the secrets of the bomb, just as Stalin's friends said they should.

On the evening PRIMROSE was scheduled to meet his Soviet contact, the liner docked at Southampton. Already on board, having gone out in the pilot boat, was a messenger with the highest security clearance. This anonymous figure would later be identified as Roger Hollis, the man alleged to have questioned Gouzenko; after serving as MI5 chief, he was to die before he could answer the gravest, unsubstantiated charges. Hollis had come to give Mackenzie King a message from Dean Acheson, who was acting as go-between for the president. Truman requested that PRIMROSE should *not* be arrested unless caught in some treasonable activity.

The request had been forwarded through Lord Halifax. It seemed a circuitous route for a presidential message. Mackenzie King had set up a small committee to handle this sort of thing, with direct and secure links through BSC in New York and Camp X. King smelled an intrigue but put it down to Truman's own need to tread warily in Washington. After a thoughtful hesitation, he said he agreed with Mr. Truman. The spy should not be arrested "unless circumstances warrant."

That same night, October 7, only MI5 watchers turned up outside the British Museum. Neither PRIMROSE nor the unknown comrades appeared.

CLEMENT ATTLEE
GOES IT ALONE

The news that PRIMROSE had taken fright was brought to Chequers, official country residence of British prime ministers, by a dispatch rider well acquainted with the tiny hamlets and narrow lanes of Buckinghamshire. A few hours earlier, he had driven over from nearby Bletchley Park with a decoded report out of Moscow that the Russians were insisting there was "no atom bomb secret"; "the Soviet Union would have atomic energy very soon and many other things."

Another message from Bletchley Park had been received via high-speed Morse links with BSC in New York, through Camp X: "The *New York Times*'s science correspondent, W. H. Lawrence, reports, 'Top-flight atomic scientists warned Congress continuing monopoly of the atomic bomb impossible.' "

Tramping among the sheep in the grounds of Chequers, Clement Attlee considered these newest developments while he waited for his dinner guest. He had taken office just two and a half months before, when Churchill was defeated by the Socialist vote. Attlee's greatest political moment had coincided with the first explosion of an atomic bomb. It would haunt him for the rest of his days. At Potsdam he had urged the Big Three to declare: "This invention makes it essential to end all wars. . . . The only hope of staving off disaster is joint British, American and Soviet action."

Tonight, Attlee was facing a terrible choice. Either renounce the bomb or take the lonely road to building one without U.S. help.

His own constituency, Limehouse, had taken the brunt of German bombing. The Cockneys of that grimy London slum knew from experience that once a bomb was invented, no matter how frightful, it would get used—the German land mine, for instance, and the giant time bomb, the incendiary clusters, the booby-trapped torpedoes that killed the rescue squads, the parachuted one-tonners sliding silkily out of the night on invisible cords, the doodlebugs and unheralded rocket V-2s. The only way to keep the enemy from using a new bomb was to hit back with a bigger and better one. Attlee feared that, despite the part Britain had played in producing the biggest bomb, Americans would shut her out of future atomic development. The reason seemed clear: he was a Socialist, which to the Americans meant he was the bogeyman, practically a Communist in the allied camp. In fact, he was a Fabian Socialist, drawing more on the Bible than on Karl Marx. The Kremlin, in its assessment, saw him as a greater threat than dyed-in-the-wool rightists. He was the dissident whose example might encourage others to challenge Russian doctrine that socialism should be built first in the Soviet Union and therefore that Moscow must command the loyalty of comrades everywhere.

Mackenzie King brought Attlee back to the house and to present concerns. The two men did not like each other very much. King was still inflated with self-importance despite a dreary drive from Southampton. He was shaken at first by Attlee's news about PRIMROSE and the mysterious failure of the spy and the Soviets to keep their rendezvous. Then he saw the brighter side. More delay. He told Attlee about Truman's desire to keep the case secret until all investigations had been completed. Now, he said, he had just received a special message from the president recommending *no* arrest of Professor May.

Attlee frowned. This was the first he'd heard about Truman's message, though it must have passed through his Foreign Office, and probably through SIS. Still, he was more worried about Soviet behavior. He read out to King the background to the Moscow telegram. Soviet Foreign Minister Molotov proposed to say publicly that the technical secrets of the atom bomb could not be confined to an elite circle. "The discovery," Molotov would say, "should not encourage a propensity to exploit it, nor encourage complacency about peace."

This was a challenge from Stalin, remarked Attlee. Either share the secret or face a race in atomic development that would make all previous arms races dwindle to insignificance. "I'm afraid," he said, "events are forcing me in a direction I would prefer, as a Socialist and a pacifist— I would prefer not to go."

He had, in fact, decided that his "atomic bomb committee," known in bureaucratic jargon as Gen (for General) 75, should begin work in absolute secrecy on Britain's own bomb.

◆ ◆ ◆

The next morning, the two ministers drove together through "leafy Bucks."
Clem Attlee had a particular purpose. He had seen British airmen progress
from the careful bombing of strictly military targets to wholesale destruction of cities. Americans, with the same traditions of liberty and chivalry
toward the weak and helpless, had been forced along the same road to
massacring civilians from the air. Attlee had also watched with alarm the
growth of secret methods of warfare. In his mind, Fourth Arm skills were
those of terrorists who threatened the civilizing rule of law, and had no
place in these new days of peace. The Fourth Arm of the West, like the
RAF's Bomber Command, had been directed against the Nazis from the
secret places of Buckinghamshire. The countryside symbolized for Attlee
the innocence that allowed the growth of all these new weapons. In
dealing with Gouzenko's alarming disclosures, Attlee wanted to be sure
there would be no panicked rush down the road to self-destruction, and
he hoped with this journey through winding lanes in the heart of England
to show King the nature of the dilemma.

They drove first to the scene of what had been, in wartime, the heart
of history's greatest concentration of air power, the underground nerve
center of RAF Bomber Command. From Number One Site at High
Wycombe had poured out the teletyped orders to bomber groups based
around southern England, launching as many as ten thousand young
airmen on a single night against a single city until the urban areas of
Germany had been systematically destroyed, block by block. The two
leaders drove past Springfield House, where "Bomber" Harris had lived
within easy reach of Chequers, his staff bicycling through the woods to
the shelters where targets were selected. Air Chief Marshal Sir Arthur
Harris was also known as "Butcher" to those repelled by his squandering
of air crews and civilians. Attlee recalled that once, while in Washington,
Harris had been stopped by a traffic cop for fast driving. "You might
have killed someone, sir," the cop scolded. To which Harris replied,
"Young man, I kill thousands every night." Yet Harris had started out
in life humbly enough, as a boy bugler. He had served in all corners of
the empire, working his way diligently to the seat of power.

"All power corrupts," said Attlee. "Nobody is beyond that kind of
corruption. Give a man the atom bomb and someday he'll find a reason

to use it." The drive angled northward, and Attlee modified the familiar phrase: "Secret power corrupts absolutely."

They were entering the wartime center of the secret world of the Fourth Arm, about which even Attlee had only dim notions. He knew Bletchley Park was a Gothic-Victorian mansion in the center of a web of hidden bases linked to the secret armies, the spies and saboteurs and partisans of Nazi-held Europe. The bases were concealed in some of the loveliest of England's rural retreats, from Great and Little Brickhill to Fenny Stratford, where professors of codebreaking once drank their beer in the Cock on the Old Roman Road. Across the way, at the Bull, women intercept operators slaked their thirst. Long ago, tall tales told at these two pubs had become known as "cock-and-bull stories," a fitting precedent for the deceptions dreamed up here against the Nazis. In these simple surroundings—the English meadows, the tall elms heavy with ravens, the crumbling Norman churches—miracles of improvisation had produced victory in secret warfare. Here, halfway between their spiritual homes in Oxford and Cambridge universities, the dons and scientists who called themselves "boffins" had created COLOSSUS, a photoelectric punched tape that would eventually encode or decipher thousands of groups a second. The few survivors were on thin rations now, and the Corby Case was meat to them.

This was ULTRA country. In this complex, the means had been found to help allied commanders anticipate enemy moves. Attlee had associated it with fierce patriotism, total discretion, unquestioning loyalty to the cause of liberating the oppressed of Europe. It was, in his mind, comparable to the atom bomb that brought the Japanese warmongers to their knees. It represented integrity, brilliance of intellect, and unity of purpose. The scholars who had worked on the atom bomb were from the same rich traditions of scholarship as the dons who broke the codes. God forbid that such genius had suffered a twist of conscience.

Today the countryside bore a bedraggled air. There were few cars on the road, for gas rationing was still severe. Few village chimneys showed signs of use, for domestic coal was unobtainable and wood was needed for small industry. Smoke from the tall stacks of Bletchley brickworks introduced a gritty aroma, irritating to the lungs. Low clouds scudded overhead, trapping the smoke and casting a pall.

Near Leighton Buzzard, Attlee offered a lift to a young naval lieutenant walking bareheaded in the rain. The lieutenant explained that he was a fighter-pilot who'd been sent home on extended leave. There wasn't much flying to be done, he said, what with the need to conserve fuel on everyone's mind. He wasn't officially demobilized, so he didn't have a civilian suit, but he'd started work because they'd already cut his flying pay. That was why he wasn't properly in uniform—just battle dress, no cap, and he didn't have a raincoat. "There'll be a revolution here if things don't improve," he said as they drew alongside Ivinghoe station.

Before the lieutenant left, King suggested with a glimmer of pixyish humor: "Instead of becoming a revolutionary, come to Canada. Look me up if you've got the time."

The young flier grinned and shook their hands. He knew who they were, all right. He'd faced worse prospects than a couple of prime ministers in the last few years. Then his face became grave. Standing by Attlee's window, he said, "I meant no disrespect, sir."

Attlee thought he referred to the scruffy bits of his uniform and waved the apology aside with a joke about brass buttons and gold braid.

"No, sir," said the lieutenant. "I meant about the revolution."

"By peaceful means, we'll achieve it," Attlee promised. "It has to mean no cake so that everyone gets some bread."

It was a bleak philosophy. Many young veterans were considering King's proffered solution of emigrating. But such was the mood of the times that Brits who migrated, like girls who married Yanks, were regarded with as much enthusiasm as rats leaving a sinking ship. It was one of Attlee's most powerful weapons, this postwar patriotism. And just in case the moral persuasions failed, he had made it extremely difficult for a migrating Brit to take his money with him, even if he had any.

Attlee's niggardly scrimping and scraping of resources was due to the huge cost of building an independent nuclear deterrent. The man "with a good deal to be modest about," in Churchill's phrase, was taking fullest advantage of Britain's draconian Official Secrets Act to gamble on a bomb of Britain's own. He explained to King that the Soviet attitude left little choice. Neither did the American reaction to Soviet intransigence. The momentum of RAF bombing strategy made possible a step up to the next logical level, the RAF's own atomic weaponry. But Attlee wanted his Canadian visitor to know how painful the decision was: Britain's "hopes for the economic betterment of the people are nonexistent," the econ-

omist John Maynard Keynes had informed his Socialist admirers. And
the likeminded historian, A. J. P. Taylor, considered that Britain had
already beggared herself in the war, while the United States grew rich
from it.

It became clear what Attlee's purpose was. He needed the British
scientists who had undertaken work on the bomb in Canada, and who
were now involved in Canadian development of the peaceful uses of
atomic energy. He needed, too, Canada's backing in the creation of an
independent deterrent. But Mackenzie King was determined about one
thing: Canada would never become an atomic power in the military
sense.

Attlee sent Lord Addison to see King in London at his Dorchester
suite. "Russia will very soon acquire the secret of the bomb," he told
King. "Their espionage capabilities are nothing short of astonishing.
Wherever they occupied territory in Germany, the Red Army's intelligence officers knew exactly where to look to find the German scientists
they needed. And the equipment. These scientists and this very valuable
equipment we *know* is now at work inside Mother Russia. There's no
question they've built up very effective spy networks in all three allied
countries."

Addison was a London mandarin, looking after dominion relations.
The role of a dominion under the British Crown was not much relished
by Canada, and his visit had elements of condescension. He was more
interested in telling King what was going on, and it took some time for
the Canadian leader to get it through Addison's head that his lordship
was not as fully briefed on PRIMROSE as he thought. Addison had not
been informed, for instance, that the Russians were so well organized
that a courier had taken back to Moscow a sample of uranium supplied
by PRIMROSE in Canada.

Attlee seemed to have problems with his own ministers and officials, who
played down Gouzenko's importance. This alarmed Norman Robertson,
who was puzzled that senior British Foreign Office men treated PRIMROSE
as a simple criminal matter. At dinner with Ernest Bevin, he was just as
astonished as King had been by the British foreign minister's unawareness
of what had happened. How could Bevin live in such ignorance? Was
it a case of deliberate concealment? In an attempt to find out, Robertson

went to see the man described in the King diaries as "the chief of the Secret Service." Stewart Menzies had been head of SIS since the start of the war. His dingy office was close to Section IX, the new anti-Soviet department on the fourth floor of Broadway Buildings, a warren of wooden-partitioned offices and frosted-glass windows, symbolically sited between Buckingham Palace and Parliament Square.

This meeting also baffled the two Canadians, because the legendary Secret Service seemed to be running counter to Clement Attlee too. King wrote later that the chief of the Secret Service in London had come to the conclusion it was better to postpone action on Soviet espionage until after the meeting of Attlee, King, and Truman, back in Washington. Earlier action, and the resultant publicity, "might arouse public opinion in a very serious way . . . might spoil the chance of getting a settlement on the atomic bomb." Even SIS General Menzies, it appeared, did not know much about the case.

MOSCOW CALLS THE SHOTS

SEVENTEEN

THE KREMLIN COVERS
ITS TRACKS

Unseen hands were meddling in the case. Stephenson could only sit in his New York office and fume. His wartime authority had originated with Churchill. Now, the war was over, and Churchill was out of power. Talks between the Canadian mission and the SIS director-general in London had restored the routine security relationship, which was good. Stephenson had no personal ambitions there, and wanted only to get back to his normal civilian pursuits. He didn't mind being nudged into the cold. But the alarms ringing in his head signaled that a counterintelligence operation was going wrong.

PRIMROSE had failed to turn up at any one of the three meetings scheduled by Moscow Center for the scientist-spy. The BSC historian's note for October 7, 1945, captures the sense of impending catastrophe: "The few men in London, Washington, and Ottawa who knew what might happen waited anxiously while M15 drew their unseen net of watchers around the dark streets near the British museum. But PRIMROSE did not stir from his lodgings that night." Nor did he stir on any subsequent night specified by Soviet intelligence.

Someone had alerted Professor May. A Soviet "resident" might have done that, working under diplomatic cover. But it would require a Soviet-controlled agent deep inside the West's security system to put brakes on the investigation. Stephenson was reluctant to voice suspicion. In war, men trusted one another absolutely. Stephenson placed loyalty very high on his list of priorities. He must believe the SIS chief, Stewart Menzies, knew what he was doing. The questionable position of BSC left Stephenson in limbo. The BSC director could act only on the basis of the services he still ran, his own formidable talent for persuasion, and bold use of the personal influence he might still command because of first-hand knowledge.

The briefings given Clement Attlee were clearly denigrating the importance of the case. Despite obvious Soviet awareness that PRIMROSE was under surveillance, Attlee shocked Mackenzie King at dinner in London by asking if he "might begin an inquiry."

Begin an inquiry? It was now seven weeks since Gouzenko's break for freedom! Stephenson heard about the exchange with feelings of dismay. Here was Mackenzie King agreeing that "it isn't well to delay much longer," and mentioning with evident embarrassment that some papers were missing from the Canadian passport office "which we are a little suspicious about."

Stephenson saw that the steam had been taken out of the Canadian prime minister again. On October 21, King was shifting responsibility onto the minister of justice, St. Laurent. "I will communicate with the minister," King told Attlee, "to see if some way could not be arranged whereby we can immediately question the different persons involved in what we have discovered."

Stephenson consulted Hoover. The FBI had been given the job, almost by default, of pursuing investigations within the United States. On the day of King's departure for England, veterans of U.S. intelligence had become "ex-OSS" and found themselves wandering along strange corridors: 1,362 officers in the new State Department building, 9,028 in the War Department. "My dear General Donovan," Truman wrote to the OSS chief, "peacetime intelligence services of the government are being erected on the foundation of the facilities and resources mobilized through the OSS during the war."

"So thank you very much, Bill Donovan, and here's your bowler hat!" to quote Stephenson. The BSC director saw this as a most dangerous time. The Corby Case reflected the uncertain policies of the Atlantic alliance on future atomic warfare. Within all three countries, rival factions jockeying for power left Moscow Center free to rescue its blown agents, to bury the "sleepers" deeper, to replace the compromised networks, and to mount a vigorous propaganda campaign opposing Western work on a new line of bombs. This Soviet strategy was almost certainly pushing the hardliners among the Atlantic allies in the opposite direction, because they now tended to view legitimate concerns about future nuclear weapons as Communist-inspired.

Hoover was running into difficulties with rival intelligence chiefs similar to those Stephenson had with SIS in London, but he enjoyed the huge advantage of having disciplined the bureau, with political acuity, for as long as anyone could remember. Furthermore, his biggest rival, Donovan, had been knocked out of the ring.

While King and Attlee mumbled away in London about on-again off-again operations to round up spy suspects, Hoover now had hard evidence that Moscow Center had spent the past weeks in "damage control." This was standard RIS procedure. In covert activities, it meant limiting the harm done to existing networks and switching to backup espionage systems. In diplomacy, it meant fashioning a positive strategy to divide the allies about what action to take against Moscow. "Window" would be scattered—a term taken from the strips of tinfoil released around an allied bomber force to blind and confuse enemy radar. RIS "window" consisted of false clues that helped strain the limited resources of Western security. In all of this, the allies were handicapped and the RIS was enormously helped by the West's own democratic way of dealing with a crisis. Hoover, for instance, had no powers under the law to stop the spy first known as "V," whose activities during the period of delay demonstrated beyond doubt that the Soviets were getting inside information on the Corby Case and were offering their endangered agents protection—*on U.S. soil!*

The Soviets had realistically sacrificed spies like PRIMROSE. Alan Nunn May, no matter how useful he might have been as a nuclear scientist in Russia, was "hot." No Soviet handler would be risked trying to save him. This was evident to Stephenson. Meanwhile, he had been working with Hoover and Gouzenko on the identity of the other spy, "V," still operating in the United States.

During the past summer, the Russian director of military intelligence (GRU) had radioed Colonel Zabotin in Ottawa about the urgent necessity to "paper agent V." Someone known as the Executor in the Canadian immigration office was to forge application forms to back up a doctored passport taken from a Canadian volunteer who had fought in the Spanish civil war. The Executor's price for this service was $3,000, a small fortune in 1945.

This much was deduced from a study of a dossier labeled FRED taken from the Soviet embassy by Gouzenko. The dossier recorded FRED's contacts with the Doctor and other unidentified agents in Canada.

The FBI, through the unofficial agreement between Hoover and Stephenson, examined all dossiers relating to possible U.S. operations. With Gouzenko's help, they matched up V to a man living in Los Angeles named Ignacy Witczak. But this was not the real Witczak, a Polish Jew who had migrated to Canada in 1930 and had later been killed in Spain.

The imposter had claimed to be Witczak on entering the United States, September 13, 1938, on the S.S. *Veendamk* out of Boulogne. This Witczak, with a young wife, settled in California as a "student" and, each month for the next seven years, received regular payments into his Los Angeles bank account from an unnamed source.

In mid-1945, the need must have arisen to cover the Soviet agent with fresh documents, still using the old Canadian passport with the false identification and photograph in it. From the GRU traffic, it was clear that the Canadian passport office was the source of "documentation" for large numbers of Soviet agents in the Western Hemisphere. The case of Witczak was taken up by the FBI ten days after Gouzenko's defection— swift action, compared with the sudden delays that mysteriously bedeviled British inquiries. By mid-September something had alarmed Witczak, who traveled to New York and began writing letters to his wife, Bunia, using an "open code"; the FBI, steaming open the letters, had no difficulty deciphering them.

Two days before King's journey to brief Truman on the Soviet spy rings, Witczak met a known Soviet intelligence agent in New York and was told to go to Washington. His letter to Bunia said: "In the morning my uncle called me, saying he wanted to see me at two—so up to two there were worries. . . . He just wants me to go to Washington for a visit."

The day after the Canadian prime minister left President Truman, Witczak wrote: "Things look more complicated for me and therefore it is quite possible a change of climate is necessary for my health, but I don't know for sure. . . . Have you seen Dr. H? . . . Maybe you have already spoken to him."

Who was Dr. H? The FBI read Bunia's reply with interest: Dr. H had made some suggestions for the joint improvement of their health. Bunia was placed under surveillance.

Witczak was becoming unsettled by what his Soviet contacts had been telling him. He now referred to himself as "Harry," and wrote: "When one Harry arrived in D.C. at the station he was met by two doctor specialists, and for three hours they did not take their eyes from Harry. . . . Now, if everything is OK, why such a fuss? It is quite possible that doctors in the U.S. were *informed from Canada* about Harry's sickness. [Italics added.] When Harry went to D.C. he thought the whole sickness was exaggerated. . . . Suddenly when Harry felt bad in D.C. it became clear there is something and since then Harry [has] had to be careful. . . . Harry was told in case of a bad attack he should immediately go to the New York hospital and stay there."

The "New York hospital" was the Soviet consulate general. And Anatoli Yakovlev, the vice-consul, was "the doctor."*

Thus in the first week of October, before PRIMROSE's first scheduled Soviet contact at the British Museum, Moscow Center had issued warnings concerning Gouzenko's break! This was now startlingly clear, and telegraphed the existence of undetected Russian double agents. Stephenson informed the Canadian and British authorities by way of BSC channels: "There can no longer be any doubt that Soviet intelligence has been alerted." The lack of action in London would take on significance later.

On the first night PRIMROSE failed to keep his appointment with Soviet intelligence, Witczak wrote to his wife that "the doctors said they want decision to be postponed until next Sunday evening for case history from home hospital."

This suggested that his Soviet controllers were waiting to hear from Moscow what had happened in London. The Russians were still not sure if PRIMROSE might be arrested, whether or not he kept the rendezvous. If he was not arrested, they would be strengthened in a belief that the West was afraid to act because of the larger issue at stake—the desire not to annoy Stalin.

"There was another aspect," commented Stephenson later. "The Russians were well aware of our respect for the law. The end of the war meant an end to emergency regulations. That in turn meant a return to the most scrupulous regard for the rule of law. Spies are always difficult to arrest in peacetime because evidence is very difficult to come by. The Russians knew this. They were testing the extent to which we'd gone back to peacetime normality. It would guide them in the future, allowing them to practice espionage in an increasingly flagrant manner."

So far, Witczak had done nothing flagrantly illegal. He had forged documents, but the FBI wished to leave those alone for now. Instead, FBI agents made their presence more obvious in an effort to scare him into a false move. A BSC report gives an almost Keystone Cops picture:

---

*From BSC report, previously classified as secret, recounting FBI cooperation in the Gouzenko case.

The only comic relief in the Gouzenko case was provided by Witczak's antics trying to shake off the FBI. . . . In New York he registered in various hotels under false names. . . . He slept in the waiting rooms of railway stations or in a Turkish bath. He neither washed nor shaved nor changed his clothes. He became an extremely odd-looking creature and the amused glances of passersby (which no doubt he mistook for FBI surveillance) only served to aggravate his "sickness," which he now referred to in his letters as "liver trouble" or "toothache." . . . Once, this ill-kempt figure suddenly broke into a wild dash down the street, turning a corner sharply to shake off the "shadows" whom he suspected every passerby to be. He rounded the corner with such speed he ran directly into an FBI agent whose apparent concern and kindly face led "Witczak" to invite him to coffee in a drugstore. There, the strange couple spent the rest of the day talking. . . .

It is normal practice for an agent being followed to pass through a revolving door and move quickly to one side to observe who follows. "Witczak" elaborated this procedure . . . entering a revolving door, for reasons best known to himself, he refused to leave, travelling round and round until forcibly ejected by the hotel clerk. In another hotel, an FBI man was amused to see "Witczak" thrown out by the hotel detective, who found him climbing down the fire escape. The only excuse "Witczak" could offer was that he didn't know the way out. . . .

Had an over-all decision been reached and the FBI empowered to arrest "Witczak," they would have had little difficulty persuading him, in his nervous condition, to talk freely.

In California, the FBI had established that Dr. H was the NKVD resident attached to the local Soviet consular office. Witczak's wife met him on street corners for advice. Again, there was nothing the FBI could do but watch and wait. From Ottawa, they received confirmation that passport applications for both the man and his wife had been falsified, providing the legal basis for criminal prosecution of the Executor. It was this information that Prime Minister Mackenzie King meekly introduced to Attlee as something "we are a little suspicious about."

Stephenson was convinced that Moscow Center's flying start in the struggle over Gouzenko must owe something to RIS disinformation. All three leaders—Truman, Attlee, and King—were getting advice from knowing or unwitting "useful idiots," and it was this that must account for the soft-pedaling, the changes of mind, the timidity, and the costly delays. The techniques of disinformation and "useful idiots," as old as the Russian Revolution, could always be opposed by truth. Stephenson leaned more and more to his private belief that in the end he would have to force action by breaking the case wide open. Gouzenko had provided incredible leads, and Stephenson agreed with Hoover that it might yet be possible to get action by presenting President Truman with some of the evidence.

Igor Gouzenko had confirmed, through stolen Soviet documents, that a woman named Elizabeth Bentley had acted as liaison between Soviet informers in U.S. government departments in Washington and the Soviet "hospital" in New York. A middle-aged Vassar graduate, Miss Bentley seemed all wrong for the role of traitor. Yet she, like other seemingly fine, upstanding citizens, had felt an ideological need to report to the Russians on the innermost councils of the Western allies, including the biggest military-operations secret in the history of warfare: the D-day invasion of Europe.

Soon Elizabeth Bentley began to provide the FBI with details of her five years' service as a Soviet courier, her compulsion to confess triggered by personal tragedy and remorse. She had carried U.S. government documents from Washington to her Soviet controllers in New York. Her suppliers included thirty or more public servants: among them, Lauchlin Currie, special assistant to President Roosevelt from 1939 to 1945; Harry Dexter White, former assistant secretary of the U.S. Treasury and executive director of the International Monetary Fund (already identified by BSC earlier as one of the most dangerous of Soviet agents); and Alger Hiss.

In the belief that it would become impossible for Soviet intrigue to muddy the final picture, Stephenson and Hoover kept to themselves, for the time being, the weight of evidence now building up. Their calculations were these: Democracy had more strengths than weaknesses, and it was time to make use of the strong points. Certainly the American press could not be muzzled by government invocations of secrecy laws. Publicity would force the obscene mess into the open if, for political reasons, the leaders tried to cover up. President Truman had never cared to pander to public opinion for purely political reasons, but he was sensitive to criticism. Neither his administration nor King's government would wish to risk a public outcry over the concealment of Soviet agents within the public services.

King, however, was a political survivor whose urge to keep power translated into sanctimonious arguments about the need to get along with the Russians. King identified himself with the ruling Liberal party. To him, the Liberals represented the only good in Canada. Therefore, he could also rationalize that the good of the world was served best by accommodating the Soviet Union. This would make it difficult for the other two allies to take action decisive enough to impress Stalin. And Stalin, in Stephenson's experience, was contemptuous of weaklings and grew more ambitious as he climbed over their bodies.

All three ABC leaders were to meet soon in Washington. The sooner the better, thought Stephenson. He was confident they would reach a bold and sensible conclusion, once freed from undermining influences at work in London. Truman was not easily pushed around, and took a simple view of those who lied and saw him as a foolish little haberdasher with no qualifications for performing on the world stage. The president epitomized the stubborn character of ordinary Americans. He was already incensed by his personal discovery of Soviet bad faith. Molotov had glimpsed this stubborn quality during a visit to assess this successor to President Roosevelt. Truman accused the Russians of failing to stick to the Yalta agreement. Molotov replied that the Soviet Union had been faithful to its word. Not in Poland, retorted Truman. Stalin's promise of free elections had been hogwash; so long as Red puppets squatted in Eastern Europe, Poland would not get into the UN. Molotov was enraged: "I've never been talked to in my life like this!" Stick around, Harry Truman snapped back. He would not talk that way "if you carry out your agreements!"

The Soviet Union continued unabashed to mobilize its friends in a campaign to pressure the Americans into providing details of how to make atomic bombs. "The only workable way to prevent an arms race and nuclear self-destruction is to reject atomic secrecy," went Moscow's argument. Many eminent nuclear scientists took up the cry—among them Niels Bohr, a political innocent who had been smuggled out of Nazi-controlled Denmark partly to keep him from unwittingly helping Hitler's scientists to build an atomic bomb. And now Moscow would benefit.

DISCORD AMONG
THE ALLIES

Four days after PRIMROSE for the third and last time failed to contact his Soviet controllers in London, Truman delivered his first foreign-policy speech in New York. He was about to meet British and Canadian leaders to discuss the atomic future, he said. "The process of manufacturing the atomic bomb," he emphasized again, "will not figure in the talks."

The alliance was crumbling. But before that happened, Mackenzie King planned to have his own little talk about the atomic bomb with the Soviets. His intention was to put forward the proposal that if the Soviets would stop spying on the West, perhaps the West would turn over its atomic secrets. King was still inclined to return Gouzenko if this would make for better relations with Moscow. How far King was prepared to go, we may never know. The relevant diary notes are gone. What is known, however, is that the Soviets turned a cozy and secret meeting into such a display of cockiness that they diverted King from a path that surely led into the same treacherous quagmire in which the scientist-spies had foundered.

Now Stalin shifted the pressure onto Mackenzie King. In conditions of such discretion that it would have an eerie aftermath, a meeting took place between the Canadian prime minister and the Soviet ambassador, Feodor Gousev, known to the British as boss of NKVD operations. British counterintelligence had gone through the motions of trying to catch Professor May passing secrets to his Soviet contacts, but nothing was done to see that Prime Minister King did not discuss the case with Stalin's most powerful secret-intelligence chief living abroad.

In Kensington Palace Gardens, a private thoroughfare bordering the urbane brick of the palace inhabited by George VI's royal relations, the Soviets ate, drank, slept, and worked in a mansion built in the grand Victorian days of empire. Ancient elms and oaks arched above the approach, once part of the royal vegetable gardens. Piles of dead leaves blocked the driveway. When Mackenzie King arrived for lunch, he noted with customary finickiness that the embassy windows were dirty, the curtains grubby, everything barred against intruders.

Inside, though, all was sweetness and light. Feodor Gousev bearhugged his distinguished visitor, in odd contrast to the cold shoulder he had given King publicly only thirteen days earlier at a diplomatic reception. "We're old friends," growled the ambassador. "You and I can talk openly and undisturbed."* There was another NKVD man present—officially a commercial counselor.

The Soviet embassy was secure from British counterintelligence. Safe within, Gousev said he understood Attlee was soon to meet with Truman about the bomb. Since Canada had played a role in creating the bomb, surely her prime minister should be present, too? King replied this was exactly so. He would be off in a couple of days' time to Washington. Gousev affected pleased surprise. Doubtless Mr. King understood there should be a fourth person at this meeting, to represent Russia? Gousev quoted the American Federation of Atomic Scientists: "If the West does not share the bomb secrets, there will be a nuclear arms race." This was a convenient quotation that should have alerted King, already aware of the federation's role as a Soviet mouthpiece.

The commercial counselor asked if King had seen the previous night's *Evening Standard* cartoon of Truman carrying in his arms a baby bomb labeled SECRET. Bemused, King replied that he remembered something of the sort.

"But nothing is secret," said the counselor, and burst out laughing.

The humor was heavy at lunch, and grew heavier with the lubrication of liquor. Gousev drew attention to how well the Russians catered to their stomachs.

---

*The Soviet embassy was not bugged in those days. British security had better things to do. Since Hitler's death, resources had been strained by the sheer hard work of clearing up wartime mysteries, interrogating knowledgeable survivors of the Third Reich, and reviewing military and political operations. Since all of this was treated as highly secret, nobody outside the magic circle quite knew what SIS and its reinforcements were really doing. But it would become clear, as the result of later spy scandals, that some actions concerned the suppression of embarrassing information. Anthony Blunt, the art historian and wartime MI5 man, was despatched to the American zone of occupied Germany to retrieve letters written by a former king, the Duke of Windsor, to Nazi leaders before the war. It was feared the unscrupulous Americans might find the letters and publish them in New York. After his dangerous excursion into what he must have regarded (for more than one reason) as "enemy territory," Blunt became a royal favorite, enjoying protection from subsequent spy-hunters with a knighthood and the post of surveyor of the royal household's pictures. Blunt finally confessed to being a double agent.

"Revolution is good for nothing," he said, "if it isn't good for eating and drinking." In England, he remarked, even the aristocracy knew nothing about good food. The fox-hunting squires were, he said, repeating the Oscar Wilde joke, "the unspeakable in full pursuit of the uneatable."

King noted all this in his diary, with a prudent comment that he had been careful to merely "taste the liquor." He was picking up the signals Gousev had been instructed by Moscow to send out. In typical Russian fashion, the message was buried in hints and obscure references. Sure enough, there came a veiled threat, clearly intended to be passed along to Truman at the approaching summit: If the United States refused Russia access to the atom-bomb factories, the Soviet Union would ignore the UN and start to build its own bombs. Implying that Soviet espionage was needless when information was freely available, Gousev aired his knowledge of the big nuclear-energy projects in western Canada and at Chalk River, of the West's principal source of bomb materials from a Canadian mine, and of *military* atomic research at Petawawa, the army base in southern Ontario.

Petawawa, said King heatedly, worked on substances released by atomic energy and was incidental to work on peaceful uses of the new science.

Gousev digested this information with an approving smile. Wouldn't Canada be wise, he asked, *officially* to renounce the bomb altogether?

King was noncommittal. Small danger signals fluttered across his mind. He remained affable, for he was still convinced that more could be achieved by quiet diplomacy to allay *genuine* Russian anxieties about the West's military intentions. But he was on guard against Gousev's clumsy manipulation. It revealed an arrogance that said, in effect, "We are ideologically pure and the rest of you are contemptible and therefore fools."

King concealed his annoyance and the conversation continued in the heavily furnished "withdrawing room" in an oppressive atmosphere of heavy floor-to-ceiling drapes, thick red carpets, and Soviet art: a full-length portrait of Stalin, a bronze bust of Stalin, and a painting of Stalin's head in heroic profile.

King was far from the fool the Russians thought him to be. He reflected later that they frequently took the West at its own valuation. Leaders of the democracies had so many outspoken enemies that inhabitants of a dictatorship might suppose the leadership to be "both daft and doomed." He was sure now that Gousev knew about PRIMROSE and the hunt for the Soviet networks in Britain. He felt a sudden sense of urgency. Under Gousev's goading, he turned from timid politician to angered patriot—and his anger was all the more formidable for being rare. The Russians had outwitted themselves. King wrote later: "The Russians may come back on any disclosure we make [regarding the Corby Case] by presenting the view that the bomb was really conceived in Canada and worked out there by scientists from the U.S. . . . This will be the excuse they make for having found it necessary to have espionage.*

Was Prime Minister King as guilty of treacherous conduct as those later dubbed "the atom spies?" Not really. King knew something that remained secret for the subsequent thirty-eight years: that there had been an official NKVD mission in London whose agents were assisted by both British Special Operations and the American OSS. Gouzenko's action had started a process that led to the total breakdown in this onesided, highly secret arrangement in which the Soviets were kept informed on Western intelligence operations. A Soviet "counsellor" to governments-in-exile in London was in fact using what influence he could to bring into postwar Europe a new crop of pro-Communist governments. It had been quite normal between 1943 and 1945 for government leaders to sit down with Russian intelligence chiefs in London, disguised as diplomats. The whole story of a situation that now seems incredible was suppressed until friends of Mackenzie King broke official silence to defend him against accusations that his NKVD lunch was, to say the least, indiscreet. But even they felt constrained by the secrecy laws to keep the facts from the public. Only now is it clear that Moscow had received, by the time of King's meeting, hundreds of top-secret OSS research studies; and that the British had supplied guerilla warfare expertise to the chief of the NKVD's subversive operations, Colonel A. P. Ossipov!

◆　◆　◆

*Among the NKVD directors under Gousev in October 1945 were the old master of Soviet espionage, Sergei Kudryavtsev, and another gnarled veteran, Vladimir Naboychenko. These were GRU representatives whose names would later gain some awkward prominence. They were part of the team handling pro-Soviet Britons, from as far back as the 1920s, to whom the ringmasters of the so-called Red Orchestra could turn in emergency. But the Red Orchestra's operations under Moscow Center's control were not widely known in 1945, and the Soviet embassy in London was not aware that its roots were being painfully disinterred by American investigators, from captured Gestapo files and other sources. It was the "other sources" that would propel Anthony Blunt of M15 into sudden action, seemingly on behalf of the royal household, in fact to provide Moscow Center with material embarrassing to the British monarchy.

In the week following the NKVD lunch, Molotov made his awaited speech in Moscow. It was clearly based on the same body of analysis revealed by the NKVD to King: Atom-bomb secrets could not be monopolized by any one country or group of countries.

The next day, November 7, Churchill rose in Parliament and retorted, "The United States does not wish to disclose the practical production methods which they have developed at enormous expense and on a gigantic scale." Churchill, of course, was speaking on the basis of Stephenson's decision to bypass the usual channels and let the deposed leader into the whole story of the Corby Case.

"This is not an affair of scientists and diplomats sending over formulas [if the United States were to cooperate with Russia]. To be effective," said Churchill, "any such disclosures would have to take the form of a considerable number of Soviet specialists, engineers, and scientists visiting the United States arsenals. . . . They would have to dwell there so that they could have it all explained to them, and the officials would then return to their own country with all the information and with any further improvements which might have occurred to them."

Churchill picked his words carefully. He was paving the way for a stronger statement, but he was aware of the political niceties. He must first let the British government's elected leader, Attlee, confer with King and Truman on what to do about Russia and the bomb. That approaching conference would be colored by what King had learned from his strange and confidential lunch with the interchangeable diplomats and secret police in the Soviet embassy. Churchill was once again an ordinary member of Parliament, forced to the sidelines—a hard place to sit so soon after the wartime years of glory. But he could still exercise his parliamentary influence, which was, to Stephenson's mind, the least corruptible form of power, and one that the Canadian had used when another dictator, Hitler, was trying to cheat the democracies without going to war. It was almost a decade since Churchill, out of power, had tried to warn the democracies against the earlier threat of nazism.

The secret meeting between King and Gousev of the RIS made it easier for Stephenson to convince the Canadian prime minister that police action against Soviet agents in all ABC countries should be coordinated to begin as soon as possible after the summit. With November 26 agreed upon as the starting date for these counterintelligence operations, Stephenson flew ahead to Washington and took the Pennsylvania Avenue entrance to FBI headquarters. "Go right in, Mr. Williams," said Sam Noisette, the director's driver, bodyguard, and general factotum. Around the FBI, Stephenson had graduated from Whoosis to Williams.

In Hoover's office, the greeting was, "Hey, Bill, look at this!"

Hoover slid over a stack of documents. Stephenson put his hand on the files. First, though, he had something to tell Hoover. Police action would begin in Britain and Canada after the Truman-Attlee-King talks.

Hoover looked pleased. There had been attempts to keep him from rounding up spy suspects, amid arguments such action might jeopardize ongoing intelligence operations. Hoover suspected the Soviets were the ones who really wanted more delay. They had already benefited from it immeasurably. "We know for sure now," he said, "that Soviet networks extend right through this country. We've got the same weevils in the same woodwork."

The FBI papers under Stephenson's hand detailed the leakage of "thousands and thousands" of secret U.S. government documents to the Soviets. More spy rings had come to light as a result of Gouzenko's talks with the FBI. One agent, Jacob Golos, had been director of RIS operations in the United States. It was his recent death that had jarred his mistress, Elizabeth Bentley, into volunteering information.

"We're just getting to the heart of things," said Hoover. "We need time. Yakovlev has been alerting his people to the Corby Case, and we're getting leads as a result."

It was Friday, November 9, and the high-level bomb talks were to begin the following week. Mackenzie King had worked out a proposal: D-day would be the twenty-sixth. Then police would detain, search, and interrogate suspects under emergency powers; and commissions of inquiry would be launched.

On November 15, 1945, three months after mankind had come into the atomic age, the Truman-Attlee-King statement was finally issued from the White House. This long-awaited declaration on atomic policy said nothing at all about atomic espionage. Nor was there a public rejection of what the Soviets had been campaigning for—an invitation to participate and to send observers to the U.S. atomic centers. Instead, the invitation was conspicuous by its absence from the summation: "There should be full and effective cooperation in the field of atomic energy between the United States, the United Kingdom and Canada." *But not on the bomb,* was the unspoken addendum.

The difficulties in the way of coordinated ABC intelligence action on atomic espionage arose in part from clashes of personality. There was open hostility between Attlee's chief atomic adviser, John Anderson, and the U.S. overlord for the Manhattan Project, General Leslie Groves. It was more than three years since Groves, then a forty-six-year-old colonel, had been told: "Do the job right and you'll win the war." The job, the first atomic bomb, stretched Groves's skills as an engineer. He imposed his authority over the scientists, "the longhairs," and established this ascendancy to the point where politicians accepted the Groves version of things atomic. In this world according to Groves, the engineers made all things possible by their realism. The scientists were apt to fly off in all directions. You would never find spies infiltrating the ranks of the engineers. Groves's own origins were within the U.S. Army Corps of Engineers, a self-contained bureaucracy with a proud reputation for building the best bridges, the firmest roads, the least troublesome sewage systems. It was Groves who had supervised the building of the first Pentagon.

Groves disliked Attlee's scientist adviser on sight. John Anderson, the man who had the most knowledge of Britain's bomb plans, "behaved high-handedly." Nicknamed Pompous John, he was the caricature of an old-fashioned imperialist—big, booming, florid-faced, the strong man of the colonial office. Groves ridiculed him in private as a stuffed-shirt and the bully who "quelled rebellion" in the Ireland of the 1920s and "put down insurrection" as governor of Bengal in the India of the 1930s. Anderson was the bitter enemy of socialism, but his unrivaled familiarity with British atomic research made him indispensable to Attlee. He was now *Sir* John, chairman of the Atomic Energy Committee, and delivered his judgments with the authority of Jehovah. Grumpily watching him perform at one of the Washington sessions, Attlee muttered, "We're all Jehovah's witnesses here."

Anderson lectured the Americans on the need to keep atomic secrets from Stalin. But the Americans were in no mood to be lectured. The result was an almost fatal misunderstanding. Many were unaware of the British and Canadian contributions to the bomb. General Groves was not about to enlighten them. At the end of the talks, he insisted on a revised resolution that severely limited atomic cooperation. A strong lobby in the Senate later resulted in a bill introduced by Senator Brien McMahon prohibiting the disclosure of information to *any* foreign power.* Trust between allies had corroded. The Corby Case raised questions within the inner circle of the bomb's guardians: Were other British scientists stealing information? Did spies exist in all Canadian government agencies? The discovery of Soviet espionage had accomplished a kind of victory for the Soviets.

But Soviet espionage had also hurt itself by hardening the minds of those who might have listened to the pressure groups arguing that the real issue was "whether in the postwar world Russia was to be treated as a friend or enemy."** Secretary of State James Byrnes said in private discussions that he was utterly opposed to giving Russians access to U.S. atomic centers. It was all very well for the scientists to waffle on about science knowing no boundaries, but, "Tell that to Stalin. We can't even get into Hungary or Poland, let alone expect Stalin to let us inspect Russian factories making the bomb."

It was a tough response to those scientists who had protested against the following White House statement: "Ninety percent of the brainpower that went into the production of the atomic bomb," reported the *New York Times* on November 18, "joined in a resolution that said in effect the scientists were unimpressed by the communiqué and were frankly scared."

"Frankly scared" was a fair description of Clem Attlee. He had gone to Washington hoping Truman would lift presidential restrictions on the commercial exploitation of atomic energy. Instead, the United States insisted on confining cooperation to scientific data.

---

* Senator McMahon was prevented from hearing about ABC cooperation. "James Chadwick, the leader of the British scientific team in the U.S., was advised by someone in the British embassy against discussing this with McMahon," notes the Corby Case file. McMahon would later say that if he had known of British and Canadian work on the bomb, he would have modified the bill to allow for continuation of the wartime collaboration. The first important gift from Britain, he acknowledged, had been "the first memorandum in any country to foretell with scientific precision the practical way to the bomb." In 1946, he was prevented from learning this by Donald Maclean, the "self-taught expert" in the British embassy in Washington.

** William A. Reuben, *The Atom Spy Hoax* (New York: Action Books, 1954), p. 11.

"Britain has a grasp of that already," said Attlee. He wanted details of how fissile material was produced, "which is information due to us and will save us vast and needless expenditures." He was refused.

The British were thus confirmed in their resolve to go it alone, no matter what the cost to their crippled economy. John Cockcroft, who had made the estimate of what PRIMROSE betrayed to the Russians, was warned he must return to England soon. He was to start work on Britain's own bomb. When he asked what had happened to PRIMROSE, he was advised to curb his curiosity.

During the next fifteen years, Britain would devote precious human and material resources to designing and making the bomb without further exchanges of information. "We actually got ahead of the Americans," crowed Attlee later. He never said what it had really cost his country, which had lost its empire, its stature as a great power, and the trust of Americans, whose earlier help had saved it from Nazi conquest. It was to the breakdown of trust, and the fomenting of anti-American or anti-British feeling, that Moscow Center was devoting its energies.

WAIT — BUT FOR WHAT?

Christmas approached. Gouzenko and his family were still in hiding. The long Canadian winter had lost its charm. Camp X was not Ottawa, where thick snow and ice brought out the gaily clothed skiers and skaters. Igor was visited at long intervals by interrogators, including Peter Dwyer and a team assembled out of the SIS agents who came under Stephenson's wartime direction within the Americas. Anna expected to give birth any day, and amused herself with writing notes about her life "before Igor," a book she would eventually publish. Both had the talent to justify their ambitions as writers, but the outlook at this moment was not encouraging.

They could not hide from themselves the reality that they were living in a no-man's-land. The Soviet motherland still claimed that Igor was a criminal; and they knew that under Stalin's laws they could be sentenced to death *in absentia* for what they had done. The secret base was bleak at the best of times. Their security escorts were kind and took them out on brief excursions into a countryside equally forbidding, dotted with small communities where strangers were viewed with dangerous curiosity.

Igor Gouzenko was keenly aware that he must not seem neurotic or melodramatic. Yet he wanted to talk about so much more than the nuts and bolts of Soviet spycraft as detailed in the documents he had stolen. He was convinced that the most important part of his experience concerned the infiltration of Western security agencies by Russian-controlled agents. He was astonished by the innocence of Western politicians who could not see that those who professed anti-Communist sentiments might be the most dangerous double agents.

He was told that public silence about his disclosures was a matter of policy; that security men were moving cautiously, taking care not to alarm those agents and suspects already identified with his help. Familiar with the ways of the secret police in Russia, he could not shake off the fear of betrayal. He had thought he knew the democratic ways of the West. He listened to the radio and he read periodicals, and these all reinforced his faith in a free society. But he found himself reading and hearing arguments for trusting the Soviet Union in atomic affairs, and he wondered why the public was still unaware of Soviet espionage.

Attlee was now saying "full-scale atomic warfare will result in the deaths of millions and the setting back of civilization to an extent unimaginable." Meanwhile nothing was done to warn the world about Moscow's hostile intentions. Soviet possession of the bomb was the only way Attlee's spine-chiller could come about. Why not say so? Why not tell the world what Moscow had done to get the bomb?

"It became clear to me that the Communist party in democratic countries had changed long ago from a political party into an agency net of the Soviet government," Gouzenko wrote. He was preparing a formal statement during this curious period of suspense. "Instead of gratitude for wartime help, the Soviet government developed espionage operations." He wanted to issue a public warning about the specific use of idealists by Moscow, the recruitment of "agents of influence" in democratic societies, and what he himself knew from Moscow Center about double agents. He was told to save this for later discussion. He began to write a more philosophical account of events: "I saw, while I worked for Soviet intelligence in Ottawa, how people in the West sacrificed their sons to deliver help to Russia, and how the Soviet government delivered in return a stab in the back." Gouzenko's warnings failed to hold the attention of his interrogators. Like the dragnets he expected would be thrown out to capture the spies, such generalities would have to wait. But wait for what? Gouzenko wondered.

New measures were taken to ensure Anna's safety. Pavlov and the NKVD, fully aware she was approaching her term, would be watching the hospitals over a wide area. Unless her identity was concealed, an informer could easily give the NKVD a clue to where the Gouzenkos were kept, inviting an attempt on Anna's own life. Anna would be admitted to a nearby hospital as the wife of a Polish immigrant; a Mountie would pose as her husband, an illiterate farmer who could not be expected to fill out the complicated forms.

Gouzenko could feel the security tightening around his family with great efficiency, while he remained in the dark about the steps being taken to deal with the RIS menace outside his gilded cage. In frustration, he put more thoughts on paper. He was outlining his future novel, *The Fall of a Titan*. He wrote that a great writer was intolerable in the Soviet Union if he took an independent line because he then became an alternative government. Such a writer had to be broken. He sketched the story on the drawing board in the form of a large mansion. As an artist and a trained architect, he could visualize this way how his characters met and traveled from room to room on their journeys through this Russian saga about a great writer's family and their struggles with bureaucrats whose purposes were dark.

About his main character, he made some preliminary notes: "He had thought he was writing of himself—so great was his desire to do something big, unforgettable, to help people find the truth of life, to accustom their eyes to the bright sun of justice. . . . Could it be that his heart was covered with ashes? No, what he was going through would pass, as a cold passes."

•   •   •

It seemed incredible that, knowing all they did, the three allied governments could not prevent the NKVD from continuing to exercise terror.
All three leaders—Truman, King, and Attlee—should have had before
them the BSC study warning that "from a security point of view, the
Soviet networks cannot be left at large indefinitely. . . . The people must
be told of Russia's apparent intentions. . . . Moscow's instructions to the
networks can be taken as meaning Russia is preparing for a war against
the Western powers."

But these reports from Stephenson and BSC were now subject to
distortion and diversion as they wound their way through the restored
labyrinths of the peacetime security agencies. Moscow Center knew all
about the investigations, supposedly conducted in total secrecy, although
this would not become evident for decades. RIS agents simply played for
time. Some of the big birds had flown. Colonel Nikolai Zabotin, Gouzenko's chief, had slipped away by a maneuver that would be recognized
in time as a feature of Soviet spy cases. Using diplomatic passports, he
and his NKVD escorts crossed into the United States, where the colonel
boarded the Soviet freighter *Alexandrov* at night in New York. The freighter,
bound for Murmansk, sailed without clearing customs or immigration.
Zabotin was reported by a later defector to have jumped to his death in
the North Sea. A Communist party paper said he "died of heart failure"
four days after reaching Moscow. It was a grim end to the journey made
by air with Gouzenko across the Arctic more than two and a half years
before. In Ottawa, Malcolm MacDonald lamented his death: "He was a
good soldier," the British high commissioner said with curious compas-
sion, "and a true Russian patriot."

The same fate would overtake the GRU chief at Moscow Center whose
shocking miscalculations, the NKVD was eager to point out to Stalin,
had lost a major battle in the secret war. Gouzenko had known him as
Major-General Bolshakov, head of the 1st Intelligence Directorate. He
had turned up in Washington as a Soviet military attaché. Suddenly there
were no records to testify to his having once existed. It was far from certain
that the officer using his name in Washington was the same man. He
became a total, worldwide nonperson, only his name remembered even
in the West. His mistake had been to permit Gouzenko to fight his recall
to Moscow, and then to fail to check Gouzenko's loyalty.

Zabotin's GRU assistants in Ottawa, Motinov and Rogov, had to be
hustled home for fear of what they might reveal if they followed Gou-

zenko's example and defected. How they got out remained secret. Colonel Sokolov, the Soviet "commercial counselor" who got his instructions from a GRU control in the "New York hospital," would vanish on a diplomatic trip to Washington. Before he got there, he boarded another Soviet vessel in Philadelphia. Paveli Angelov, the Soviet handler of PRIM-ROSE in Canada, would also disappear after his Ambassador Zarubin was recalled "for routine consultations."

There was a certain implied contempt in the way the Soviets slowly and carefully rolled up the blown networks. In many cases, their American, British and Canadian agents had been warned within a week of Gouzenko's defection: they burned incriminating documents at their leisure. They had been advised that very little legal action could be taken against them by law-enforcement officers unless they confessed.

The contempt was justified, in Stephenson's judgment. Moscow Center had been fully briefed on Western counterintelligence action. The postwar secret agencies were being made to look like fools. Among his own BSC "wartime amateurs" were dons and professional writers, now working their way through BSC records. They were preparing a discreet account of covert action against nazism and the Japanese warlords. He put their summary between leather covers, stamped it TOP SECRET, and prefaced it with the statement: "An account prepared at my instruction by BSC officers who have drawn on organizational files." On December 31, 1945, Stephenson authorized the project to provide "a record, should future need arise for secret activities of the kind described." He continued, "Against possible atomic attack, the only chance of survival is to be forwarned [and] this necessitates a worldwide Intelligence Service. . . . The concept of coordinated operations, which BSC originally exemplified, was the basis on which the Americans built, with astonishing speed, their own highly successful wartime Intelligence Service."

The BSC summary was an end run to salvage something from the ruins left by rival intelligence chiefs and bureaucracies. It approached secret warfare as a topic more complex than atomic energy, and far less understood by the public. "If we had been restricted to collecting intelligence by conventional means," wrote Stephenson, "our wartime BSC operations would have been altogether inadequate. . . . The success of secret activities was primarily dependent upon the coordination of a number of functions falling within the jurisdiction of separate government departments. . . . Only as a result of such coordination was BSC to develop the vital elasticity to meet urgent demands."

With these words, Stephenson planned his own dissolution as Intrepid, and the dignified end to his BSC organization. He would explain later: "We grew out of the greatest emergency ever to face our civilization. A new war had started, but it was secret and the West refused to acknowledge it. My job had been fighting the Nazis, and it was over." Fighting the KGB would become another challenge to private enterprise, which was what Intrepid had always represented. In the early months of 1946, he put his BSC at the West's disposal, though he knew its days were numbered unless the new danger spurred imaginative action.

Top Secret documented some of the FBI's wartime successes and handsomely acknowledged FBI help in keeping abreast of German improvements in espionage technology. Hoover was not presented in quite the flattering light in which he saw himself—in *Reader's Digest* he had claimed the spectacular breaking of Nazi German microdot methods— but his difficulties were sympathetically described. "Before Pearl Harbor, BSC was an undercover agency, winked at by the State Department," the *Top Secret* summary confessed. "The FBI protected it from official curiosity and guaranteed its good behavior." It had been BSC's dependence on the FBI that led Stephenson to lean over backwards to build up Hoover's image.

The official but confidential history gave this version of the 1940 origins of FBI-BSC collaboration:

WS saw J. Edgar Hoover, director of the FBI, and explained the purpose of his mission. Hoover said frankly that, while he himself was not opposed to working with SIS, he was under strict injunction from the State Department to refrain from collaboration with the British in any way which could be interpreted as an infringement of United States neutrality, and he made it clear that he would not be prepared to contravene this policy without direct presidential sanction. Further, he stipulated that even if the president could be persuaded to agree to the principle of collaboration between the FBI and SIS, such collaboration should be effected initially by a personal liaison between WS and himself and that no other U.S. Government Department, including the Department of State, should be informed of it. . . . Mr.

Roosevelt, upon hearing the arguments in favor of the proposed liaison, endorsed them enthusiastically. "There should be the closest possible marriage," the president said, "between the FBI and British intelligence." . . . Thus an agreement was reached, some six months after the start of the European war, for Anglo-American cooperation in the intelligence field. . . . The fact that it had to be kept secret even from the State Department provides striking illustration of the strength of American neutrality at the time. . . . In London [after the February 1940 mission to the United States] WS reported these findings to CSS,* and he advocated that a British secret organization in the United States, though founded on the basis of liaison with Hoover, should not confine itself to purely SIS functions but should undertake to do all that was not being done by overt means to assure sufficient aid to Britain and eventually to bring America into the war.**

The great secret was now officially acknowledged, even if only in part and printed in a severely limited edition: one copy went to each of the three leaders of the alliance. The contents became known to SIS, with peculiar consequences. At once, Hoover felt a renewed effort in London to make SIS the British agency with which any U.S. counterintelligence or secret-intelligence agencies must deal. Hoover had reasons of his own for feeling distrustful of this shifting emphasis. He was careful not to talk about it with anybody except Stephenson, who was like an old sparring partner, an opponent he could respect. Even to Stephenson, though, he merely mentioned his dislike of British career diplomats in Washington, "pushing bits of paper around and playing silly buggers."

* CSS: Head of Secret Intelligence Service.

** From "Origin, Development and Functions," historical file, British Security Coordination (BSC) 1940 section: Vol. I of *Top Secret*, Copy No. (i)

THE BOGEYMAN'LL GET YOU...

THE DETERRENT
OF PUBLICITY

To comprehend the enormity of what began happening . . . imagine a large household whose children insist that they are pursued by a bogeyman. Others in the family repeatedly assure them that there is no such thing as a bogeyman. . . . Then one evening when the family is gathered together one child notices that a closet door is ajar. He flings it open—and out steps a real bogeyman, ten feet tall and all teeth. Igor Gouzenko in Canada had been such a child.*

Five whole months after Gouzenko had risked everything to defect, he remained under wraps, his disclosures kept secret from the public. Moscow had almost succeeded in reducing its secret war on Western security to the dimensions of a myth. Stephenson turned to the chief weapon in his armory: "the deterrent of publicity." He had always believed that concealment resulted only in confusion of motives, misunderstandings, and dangerous competition among departments. Concealment was an automatic response to the new political problems created by the atom bomb. The truth was being hidden, for instance, about the long-range effects of the Hiroshima bomb's radiation. A new generation's qualms, it was thought, needed to be quelled. But the new generation had an instinctive sense of the real size of the menace: "What do you want to be when you grow up?" went the current classroom joke. The answer was one word: "Alive."

At least half a dozen separate investigative agencies in three countries were now handling different aspects of the Corby Case. Some rough form of coordination had been achieved because BSC was still controlling communications. The Soviets had gotten away with much of their counteraction. The FBI's files on Soviet spy rings in the United States, if made known, could meet the same resistance encountered in Canada.

---

* William Manchester, *The Glory and the Dream* (Boston: Little Brown, 1974).

There, the ruling Liberals were again wondering if it wouldn't be best to forget the whole scandal.

Stephenson decided to begin by embarrassing the Soviets in Canada.

Colonel Zabotin's replacement had arrived in Ottawa at the end of 1945. According to Grigori Popov, the new spymaster, Canada's silence had been interpreted by Moscow Center as weakness, irresolution, and stupidity, and he said as much in resuming contact with a pro-Soviet informer still at large. He was perfectly certain the Canadians lacked both legal means and the intestinal fortitude to prevent him from building new networks and reconstituting the old ones that had escaped any damage from Gouzenko's disclosures. The contact, a Marxist theorist known as JAKE, had been uncovered by RCMP I-Branch investigators. Confronted with questions about his betrayals, JAKE realized he had been used by the Soviets and agreed to help the Mounties in exchange for immunity from prosecution.

On the night of February 2, Popov contacted JAKE in a downtown Toronto bar. Three hours later, staggering in an apparent drunken stupor through the red-light district of Jarvis Street, Popov was picked up by the local police and thrown into the drunk tank while inquiries were made. What intrigued the police was Popov's handgun and his identification as a Red Army military attaché.

By the following day, Mackenzie King himself had been informed of renewed Soviet intelligence operations. A medical receipt, signed by one of the old GRANT network agents, had been found in Popov's wallet. "It is part of the inevitable," the prime minister wrote in his diary, resigned now to facing a public outcry.

The timing of the arrest, facilitated by rendering Popov "drunk" with a special BSC-developed pill slipped into his first and only drink,* was arranged with exquisite care. It came one day after King had been secretly visited by Truman's chief of staff, Admiral William D. Leahy, who was also the president's confidential agent in dealing with intelligence problems. Admiral Leahy's sudden arrival on the prime minister's doorstep was to ensure that Gouzenko was neither "lost" nor forgotten. The admiral was about to take over stopgap coordination of U.S. intelligence. Rivalry

---

* The "knockout drug" had been used during the war on enemy agents after experiments in New York. See A Man Called Intrepid.

between the new spy agencies was getting out of hand, and the admiral distrusted some of the advice Truman and other leaders were getting from their respective diplomatic experts. The RIS intercepts had revealed some worrisome references to a Soviet agent known as HOMER and to another identified as Number 13, both in the State Department. The department's adventures into the field of covert operations also bothered Leahy, but his mission on this trip was to say to King, on a strictly confidential basis, that both their countries should investigate the possible infiltration of the public services by Soviet agents and that Gouzenko should be given every opportunity to openly state his views. Moscow must be allowed no more delays that would limit Gouzenko's effectiveness.

In an attempt to impress on King the gravity of the betrayal of atomic secrets, Leahy talked of something that had so far received no public attention. The Hiroshima bomb differed from other bombs because it was not the explosion that did the most killing; it was the heat and radiation. The admiral confided what was then still secret: victims mostly died from radiation sickness—and would continue to die from it at Hiroshima, where the bomb's effects still lingered.

Admiral Leahy's personal appeal for action on Gouzenko might still have been rejected if Stephenson had not put into effect the third phase of his assault on secrecy. On February 4, Drew Pearson, one of America's most influential and widely read columnists, announced:

Prime Minister Mackenzie King has informed President Truman of a very serious situation affecting our relations with Russia, *which I don't like to report.* A Soviet agent surrendered some time ago to Canadian authorities and confessed a gigantic Russian espionage network inside the United States and Canada. . . . This Russian told Canadian authorities about a series of agents planted inside the American and Canadian governments who are working with the Soviets.

This information had been carefully leaked to Pearson by Stephenson's BSC team in Washington. The relationship, which began early in World War II, was described in the BSC operational summary, in a section labeled "Intelligence & Propaganda": "WS gave instructions that Pearson should be cultivated as a potential source of important intelligence and the necessary contact was made. A BSC officer in Washington spent many months gaining Pearson's confidence and by 1943 the acquaintance began to produce solid results in the form of reports on, *inter alia*, political changes, the president's intentions and the views of high naval and military officers."

A lighthearted proso-profile by the BSC officer also survives. The flavor is captured in this extract:

> Pearson is a tall, tight-lipped individual who looks uncomfortably like a horse . . . snorting as he speaks. He has little sense of humor. He is a Quaker who still occasionally addresses members of his family as "Thou" or "Thee." The garden pool of his Washington house is stocked with goldfish bearing [the names of the president's brain trusters such as] Harry Hopkins. . . . His cows in Maryland are similarly named Henry Morgenthau, Eleanor Roosevelt. . . . Cordell Hull was slaughtered in the spring of 1945 and eaten by Drew Pearson and his family with relish. . . . Washington was Pearson's beat. Cabinet members, senators, and congressmen were his servants.

By the end of the war, Pearson was a nationally known broadcaster and his column appeared daily in the *Washington Post* and 616 other U.S. newspapers. He was the perfect channel for Stephenson's "deterrent of publicity."

King now had little choice. "It is the way that a certain kind of politics is played by a certain type of man," he noted in a barely concealed, spiteful reference to Stephenson. But Stephenson had not enjoyed the operation. It had seemed urgent to leak the story, and to engineer Admiral Leahy's journey and Popov's arrest, in order to offset pro-Soviet influences edging Gouzenko toward extinction. Gouzenko knew things that should be exposed to a wider audience through a special commission of investigation. U.S. and Canadian leaders had been put under all kinds of pressure to avoid such an inquiry, not the least being the claim that spy hunts infringed on the rights of citizens.

"Unless the deterrent of full publicity were used," the Corby Case file warned, "other citizens of the Atlantic alliance might be led to betray their countries in the same way that the agents of the GRANT net had done."

This warning was possibly the most important to come out of the case, but it was smothered by the very organization that it threatened—the Soviet secret services, whose operations would depend upon betrayal on a rapidly expanding scale during the decades to come.

Pearson's first broadcast was a warning shot. He promised more disclosures in subsequent Sunday broadcasts. The sudden flurry of activity before his next Sunday broadcast was significant. Action by government agencies, before the third broadcast, amounted to near panic.

In Canada, the prime minister assembled his Cabinet the following day to report the Gouzenko case for the first time. He said little about the source, but disclosed that the government had documentary evidence. King then read out the order-in-council appointing Supreme Court justices Robert Taschereau and R. L. Kellock as commissioners to take testimony. These royal commissioners began, the very next day, to review transcripts of Gouzenko's debriefing. On February 13, after Drew Pearson made a broadcast predicting a spectacular spy trial, Gouzenko finally got what he had wanted for so long. He stood before the commissioners, the president of the Canadian Bar Association, a Justice Department official, and a Montreal lawyer to tell his story.

He was no longer talking to security men in a wilderness of secrecy. He was exercising his right as an individual to speak out before the public in a democratic society. By the following morning, the commissioners had heard enough to justify advising the government that many of those named in the RIS telegrams should be taken into custody.

Thirteen alleged spies were picked up by Canadian counterintelligence officers early on February 15. *

For the first time since Ambassador Zarubin had gone hunting through the night for Gouzenko in Ottawa, an official summons was sent to the Soviet embassy: Would the ambassador's stand-in please report to the Canadian prime minister's office?

* Asked in Parliament later if Pearson's broadcasts were responsible for the timing, King demurred: "The United States told us it was better to proceed without delay." The BSC record tells a different story. "It was decided to anticipate Pearson's next broadcast," states the official Corby Case narrative written at the time. "The date for arrests was therefore set for the dawn of February 15."

Action in other fields was timed precisely to coincide with King's belated move. In London, a decision had been taken to haul in PRIMROSE "for a chat" with the most dangerous of professional interrogators, William "Jim" Skardon, and the first confrontation took place on this day. That afternoon, the thirteen arrests were confirmed. By evening, the Gouzenkos had been transferred to another protected area, from where Igor could give his first oral testimony to public commissioners. The efficiency of the police services did not counterbalance Mackenzie King's alarm, which was entirely due to the fact that the Russians had never replaced their ambassador. Such Soviet diplomatic inaction amounted to a form of moral blackmail of King, who was forever in a stew about provoking Stalin's displeasure. He would have been surprised to learn that Moscow Center already had a description of Skardon's formidable interrogatory powers, now being applied to PRIMROSE.

The director of NKVD operations in Canada at this time was still Vitali Pavlov, and it was this man who responded to Mackenzie King's summons, although he brought along the nominal Soviet chargé d'affaires, N. Belokhvostikov. The effrontery of Pavlov's appearance was interpreted by Stephenson as proof that the Soviets expected no further serious repercussions. It also confirmed reports that the NKVD had won the battle with GRU military intelligence, and now dominated the Soviet intelligence scene. Pavlov, far from pretending embarrassment or contrition, took the offensive (through Belokhvostikov) by protesting the arrest of military attaché Grigori Popov.

The Soviet protest was couched in offensive, hectoring language: Popov had been treated like a common criminal; the Canadian police had shown indifference to the proprieties of diplomatic immunity; and the police were "fascists," akin to the Nazis' gestapo; therefore, Popov would be withdrawn from Canada to demonstrate Moscow's extreme displeasure.

Since Popov had been caught red-handed, at work on a new spy system, his withdrawal simply anticipated his deportation. The bizarre and unpredictable attitudes that politicians and so-called public servants could adopt, however, were at once demonstrated by Mackenzie King and Norman Robertson. First, Robertson *apologized* for the alleged breach of diplomatic immunity. Then King recited the basic outline of the Corby Case and said, "We regret having to speak of these matters at all. We are all close friends and nothing should destroy this relationship."

Pavlov remained wooden-faced and contemptuous. The chargé shook hands all round with great enthusiasm.

"You will notice," King said ingratiatingly, for the second or third time, "we are taking action only against members of our own public service." It was a comment that puzzled everyone.

After several days' silence, there was a response from Moscow. Solomon Lozovski, deputy commissar for Soviet foreign affairs, called in the Moscow representative of the Canadian government and accused Ottawa and the press of setting out to make bad blood between the West and Russia. "Soviet organizations," blustered Lozovski, had become aware that some members of the Soviet military mission had received from Canadian acquaintances certain secret information. This did not, however, interest the "Soviet organizations" because "of the more advanced technical accomplishments of the Soviet Union." Anyway, all the U.S. information could be found in technical works and Professor Smyth's recent *Atomic Energy for Military Purposes*. It was ridiculous to say this insignificant body of scientific data posed any threat to security.

Still, when the Soviet government "became aware of the above-mentioned acts of certain members of the staff," military attaché Grigori Popov had been recalled, not because of any sense of Soviet guilt, but in order to show goodwill. The Soviet Union had turned embarrassment into a display of self-righteous magnanimity. Confronted with a tough resistance, Moscow was backing down. The lesson, even for King, was obvious. The Russians admired strength and had contempt for weakness.

Gouzenko was at last giving evidence to a public commission. The commissioners could impose a security blackout on some of the material, but it would be difficult to conceal most of what he had to say about Soviet spying in general.

"I can see where a great hue and cry will be raised," King had written in his diary. "I will be held up to the world as the very opposite of a democrat." After Drew Pearson cast him in the mold of a knight defending democracy, the prime minister's tune changed: "There has never been anything in the world more complete than what we will reveal of the Russian method to control the continent," King purred. "We are only at the beginning of the real disclosures. . . . There will be certain major sensations."

Igor Gouzenko's actions were associated in the public mind with the birth of the bomb. Unseen was the rise of the powerful forces leading to the KGB. In 1941, the political thought-police had been separated from the NKVD to become the NKGB. Gouzenko's escape resulted in the dismissal and probable execution of his boss, the GRU chief. The NKVD argued that further GRU incompetence could be prevented only by granting wider powers to the security administration (which since 1941 ran SMERSH). The result was the emergence of a much more powerful MVD-MGB state security apparatus combining the old NKVD powers with greater authority in Soviet covert action abroad. The foundations were laid for the KGB. Under whatever title, one long-term Russian aim was to wipe out Gouzenko's effectiveness.

But Gouzenko had hardened Washington opinion in favor of an American agency that should eventually prove more than a match for the RIS. A week after Pearson's broadcast, Admiral Leahy became "the president's eyes and ears" on a new Central Intelligence Group. The birth of a full-blown CIA was still delayed, but its conception was confirmed.

THE
MENACE OF
INTERDEPARTMENTAL
STRIFE

Winston Churchill now stepped back on stage. Those Americans who mobilized in 1940 to challenge the Nazis had invited Churchill to the United States. On March 5, after reading Stephenson's proposal for the formation of "a secret organization of sufficient stature in the U.S. to carry on where BSC left off,"* he arrived by train with President Truman in Fulton, Missouri. Two days earlier, the Canadian royal commission had issued its first Corby Case report. The previous day, Detective-Inspector William Whitehead of Scotland Yard had with grave politeness arrested PRIMROSE, Professor Alan Nunn May, on charges under the British Official Secrets Act.

Churchill delivered his speech on the campus of the modest little Westminster College at Fulton, in a gesture of respect for the president and his humble beginnings: "It would be wrong and imprudent to entrust [to the UN] the secret knowledge or experience of the atomic bomb while it is still in its infancy. . . . [It would be] criminal madness to cast it adrift in this still agitated and ununited world. . . . From Stettin in the Baltic to Trieste in the Adriatic, an iron curtain has descended across the continent. . . . There is nothing [the Russians] admire so much as strength. There is nothing for which they have less respect than weakness."

Churchill was, as so often before, ahead of his time. The Iron Curtain part of the speech, his criticism of Soviet foreign policy, evoked the same

---

* Stephenson had written, "In the light of continuing Soviet aggressive intentions, it is vital to Britain's interest (a) that the closest possible working liaison with American intelligence should be maintained and (b) that American public opinion should be properly informed. These were the two chief responsibilities which BSC assumed in 1940 and . . . had they been taken several years earlier the Second World War might have been averted or at any rate curtailed."

general reaction as his 1938 thunder against Hitler. He was a "warmonger" again, a canard popularized now by Soviet agents.

Stalin openly responded by denouncing the speech as "a call to war against the Soviet Union." In turn, Truman offered Stalin the same opportunity to come to Fulton "for exactly the same kind of reception, the same opportunity to speak his mind."

Truman was finally committed to the creation of a force that might confront the Soviets' secret war. He had spoken, in his first State of the Union message on January 21, about a foreign-intelligence service becoming part of the regular U.S. government establishment and had thereby given unprecedented public recognition to the status of intelligence. Even Roosevelt had never done this. "Truman," commented *Time* magazine, "put the U.S. in the business of international espionage. . . . The U.S. is joining in the game of spying . . . ending, for a while at least, a bitter homegrown feud."

For the first time in history, an American president had publicly put his country into the spy business—but he was still far from regulating it. The feuding became worse than ever. Freebooters swarmed over Europe in search of spectacular coups that might provide a competitive edge in winning presidential approval. Out of this, ironically, came the mobilization of Germany's rocket experts for the future U.S. space program and the collection of other German scientists before the Soviets could catch them for their own research-and-development programs.

Stalin's agents in America, with the help of "useful idiots," seized upon Churchill's speech and on a running report by newspapers of FBI arrests arising from the Corby Case. All, it was said, had been timed to poison the first meeting of the UN Security Council in the United States. "The leading powers of the world have come forward for the defense of democracy and peace. But the real prosecutors of this case," said a West Coast labor lawyer defending a Soviet naval officer accused of spying,* "aim to destroy this unity and their ultimate objective is war. . . . A spy scare was needed."

Truman was accused of using the "spy scare" to distract attention from

---

* Lieutenant Nikolai Redin, charged with seeking atomic data, was found innocent for lack of evidence, not unexpectedly.

very real problems at home. In his State of the Union message, he had asked for another year of Office of Price Administration controls. But businessmen argued that free enterprise was doomed by this "government within government" poking around for evidence that price controls were being circumvented; if any "Gestapo" existed in the United States, it was the OPA, a tyrannical mockery of freedom. Nonetheless, the OPA fought inflation so well that prices had risen only 30 percent over their 1939 prewar levels. Still, black markets flourished, and within a few months Truman was forced to begin lifting all controls.

The president was also heading into a confrontation with striking miners and railroad workers. He had drafted a speech to the nation in which he proposed to say that young Americans had "faced bullets, bombs, and disease" to win victory, while the coal and railroad unions in effect "fired bullets into the soldiers' backs." The draft concluded: "Let's put transportation and production back to work, hang a few traitors. . . ."

Luckily, he was dissuaded from giving that speech. Nevertheless he drew a parallel, publicly, between treachery at Pearl Harbor and the new domestic crisis caused by men who put their selfish interests above the nation's welfare. He challenged the union leaders to a showdown, and eventually won. There was a perceptible shift of public opinion in his favor. An aide commented that "when he walked, you could hear his balls clank." Truman was becoming known as his own boss at last.

The U.S. president's first stumbling steps in the direction of a centralized intelligence agency to meet the RIS challenge were not enough to satisfy General Bill Donovan, now back in Manhattan, practicing law.* He was angered to see wartime experience tossed aside to pacify a handful of generals and admirals, plus "a striped-pants State Department dandy or two." He ridiculed as a "committee of secretaries" what Truman had established as his first directorate of central intelligence, subservient to a National Intelligence Authority. He wrote in *Life* magazine that the wartime United States "had the makings of a real intelligence service, but chose to disband it and dissipate its assets."

* He was living with the knowledge, never revealed until thirty-seven years later, that a political decision had resulted in the OSS's being forced to surrender to Moscow Center the captured Soviet military and diplomatic codebooks that should have accelerated the decoding and analysis of Russian intelligence traffic during and just after the war against Hitler.

This dissipation included the ongoing analysis of captured Gestapo files and deductions made from them about the operations of Soviet intelligence networks. The efficient use of this knowledge, gleaned from intercepted RIS intelligence traffic with Moscow Center, was hampered by the hit-or-miss way intelligence was pooled. Donovan had watched this with growing concern; he knew that if Stephenson and BSC had not contrived to keep functioning in this muddled time, there would never have been a Corby Case. Twenty-three different agencies were now pouring different kinds of intelligence into Washington—"an absolute bedlam," complained Allen Dulles, whose wartime OSS successes were still unknown. Now a private citizen, he drew attention to British intelligence triumphs resulting from London's coordination—an overview conducted by a separate and independent agency. Without a similar structure, the United States would be doomed to repeat the failures of Nazi German, Italian, and Japanese intelligence services.

The Corby Case illustrated the force of the argument. But U.S. defense services were entirely diverted by the spread of the Wanna-Go-Home riots from London and Paris and Frankfurt to Tokyo, Guam, Shanghai, and Calcutta. Morale was lower than ever, according to Hanson W. Baldwin, military editor of the *New York Times*. In that spring of 1946, U.S. prestige abroad was at a low ebb and U.S. military discipline seemed nonexistent. General W. D. Styer, commander of U.S. armed forces in the Western Pacific, was booed by 20,000 GIs in Manila when he tried to reassure them that demobilization was being carried out as swiftly as possible. The truth was that schedules had been cut from 800,000 to 300,000 men a month returning home from the Pacific, amid rumors that troops were to be used in anti-Communist operations in China and Southeast Asia. In Frankfurt, 4,000 GI agitators taunted their commanding officers and called on others to support their Manila buddies. The rioters were not combat veterans, most of whom had in fact gone home. As the *Times* claimed, "the breakdown of Army discipline" was being directed by political rabble-rousers who had heard no shots fired in anger.

Stalin seemed to do as he pleased in Eastern Europe. In Japan, warned the American military chiefs based there, a revolt would be timed to coincide with displays of widespread dissatisfaction among American troops. General Dwight D. Eisenhower said he needed 350,000 troops in Germany, 375,000 in the Pacific, and another million elsewhere, but there were only 400,000 volunteer American soldiers in all—and army strength was down 80 percent. A withdrawal of *all* troops from Korea was contemplated before summer. In China, Mao's Communists ("agrarian reformers" to their American apologists) concluded that the United States would not fight again on the Asian mainland; and Stalin reinforced the Communists of North Korea, who began to view the capture of the south as a certainty.

Stalin had powerful apologists in the United States. A wealthy Washington lawyer, Joseph E. Davies,* had been ambassador in Moscow and now defended the motives of those Western scientists who had worked so diligently to help the Soviets. During Davies's ambassadorship, in 1937–38, the Russian Division in the State Department had been abolished and its unique files on the Soviet Union were destroyed. A veteran Kremlinologist, George F. Kennan, would later write in his memoirs of his surprise that McCarthyites never got hold of the incident, "for here, if ever, was a point at which there was indeed the smell of Soviet influence.**

Kennan's refreshing realism was in sharp contrast with the unadulterated admiration shown for the Kremlin by some previous American visitors in Moscow. Submitting a report in 1946 on Soviet intelligence aims, he noted that the NKVD had been assigned a budget *for administrative purposes alone* of "two-thirds of the total spent by the entire remainder of the Soviet government apparatus." If anything signaled a declaration of secret war against freedom, this did. It failed, however, to discourage the battle royal shaping up over the proposal of Lieutenant-General Hoyt S. Vandenberg for a genuine central intelligence agency.

General Vandenberg had become director of the Central Intelligence Group, succeeding the brief rule of Rear Admiral Sidney W. Souers. It

---

*Ambassador Davies was married to Marjorie Merriweather Post, heiress to a fortune based on Grape Nuts, Post Toasties, and Jell-O. Their post in Moscow became a base for shopping sprees in which the Soviet government gladly cooperated, selling off priceless antiques for the dollars then badly needed after the spectacular failures of Stalin's Five Year Plan.

**George F. Kennan, as counselor in the U.S. embassy in Moscow, had studied Stalin's hard-line 1946 speech and was preparing an even more refreshing blast of realism in the form of an article, signed X, in the influential American quarterly *Foreign Affairs*. He analyzed the Soviet leadership's commitment to world revolution in terms of a kind of religion with its own dogma and sense of mission. This pseudoreligion could be limited to the nations already captured by the faith, Kennan argued, but only by a policy of containment. Kennan's views were adopted by President Truman in the following year and became known as the Truman Doctrine of containing communism.

was not so much that Souers *ruled* as that he *sat* in the middle of the agencies competing for favor. The CIG was denied any "internal security function" out of the widespread fear of a gestapo "blossoming under the rear admiral's rear end." General Vandenberg was skeptical about such excessive concerns and by the end of June had decided upon the need for order and a single, independent agency. He drafted "A Bill for the Establishment of a Central Intelligence Agency," self-sufficient in every aspect of intelligence activities, untouched by political expediency. It was Bill Donovan's proposal resurrected. It was Stephenson's plea made visible. But it would take until July 26, 1947, almost two years after Gouzenko's defection, to establish the Central Intelligence Agency, whose director would be "appointed from civilian life by the president with the advice and consent of the Senate." The 1947 law, said Tom Troy's official CIA history in an uncharacteristic burst of effusiveness, "was a return to the Donovan plan [of 1944]; to the Donovan plan with its provocative proposal for a new, strong, central agency; to the Donovan plan with its ideas for an agency headed by a civilian, serving the president. . . . Yes, to the Donovan plan with its restrictions on the CIA's domestic activities."

What it might have added was that the concept originated with Stephenson and the BSC appeal to prolong wartime alliances against tyranny—and that only the Russians had understood what *that* meant.

Gouzenko was enjoying a sense of false security. He believed that his knowledge of other spy networks, symbolized by the second ELLI codename, had been conveyed to Stephenson, whose real identity he did not know. Nor could he know that the organization behind the man was finished.

Gouzenko had touched upon the second ELLI in his testimony to the royal commission, whose sanitized report was expected to become public in mid-1946, four months or more after the hearings behind closed doors. He had volunteered little information because he believed the full details should be restricted to one trustworthy man of Stephenson's caliber. And this is exactly what he thought had been done.

But such information no longer passed through Stephenson's hands. His organization had lingered on, in part because it had again proved indispensable with HYDRA and other wonders of ultra-fast secret communications. Stephenson had always argued that the machinery for moving information swiftly and secretly was the key to superior intelligence, which in turn was the key to the successful defense of democracy. The secret war of 1939–45 had vindicated him. It would be decades before the public learned about ULTRA, MAGIC, PURPLE and other ABC code-breaking triumphs. Even after these secrets were partially unveiled, the whole subject of "illicit wireless intelligence" (the BSC phrase) remained taboo. Stephenson, since his invention of the wirephoto and involvement in electronics, had always stayed on top of the art. He had nursed into existence, during the war and in the months of Gouzenko's first ordeal, a complex system of protected communications. The new toys excited the envy of his rivals.

There are no precise records to give guidance to the sequence of events. Somewhere in that period before mid-1946, however, the anonymous figure known to Gouzenko only as "a gentleman from England" confiscated everything Gouzenko had said about the second ELLI and other possible infiltrators into Western security. Even if Gouzenko had known about this, he would have had little hope of being taken seriously, as the official skepticism of later years would demonstrate. His only real hope would have been Stephenson. And Stephenson, in his own wry phrase, had been "deactivated."

HYDRA, at Camp X, was an outgrowth of the special BSC role in linking U.S. and Canadian monitors with ULTRA at Bletchley Park, which was not merely the home of ULTRA. How Bletchley was in turn linked with the wartime anti-Nazi networks in Europe is still, at this time of writing, secret.

What is no longer secret is that the Gouzenko case prompted the planning of a hundred high-speed monitoring stations in Canada to cover Soviet posts, illicit or diplomatic, and to cover Soviet activities in the Arctic, the results being shared with American and British cryptographers. HYDRA sped the work on machines evolving rapidly to handle the increasing volume of traffic: ROCKEX-II and others, some based on TYPEX, TELEKRYPTON, and even some old German *Kleinschmidts*.

This was then also highly secret, and the rival agencies competed to take full responsibility. The BSC organizational files contained a section entitled "The Menace of Inter-Departmental Strife." It was prophetic in its descriptions of civil war within the bureaucracies.

This strife helped those who wished, for more sinister reasons, to force Stephenson and BSC into voluntary liquidation. The Fourth Arm, devoted to fomenting unrest among oppressed peoples, was the unorthodox means by which a Soviet empire could be broken up. The wartime system for knitting together anti-Nazi resistance in Europe through radio networks was, of course, the very foundation of any scheme for keeping hope alive among those in secret rebellion against tyranny. Meanwhile, Stalin was preparing his own style of guerrilla warfare against the West, and the RIS had developed its own sophisticated apparatus for linking agents with Moscow.

The regular armed forces of the Atlantic allies were naturally opposed to any Fourth Arm competing with them for money, manpower, and supplies; and they were philosophically unsympathetic to irregular-warfare schemes. Thus they joined the attack on BSC in the United States. Its headquarters had been provided by Nelson Rockefeller, grandson of John D. The young Nelson had been "the voice and ears of the United States in Latin America," self-assigned to the task of fighting Nazi influence with the first American psychological warfare agency. His work had benefited from Stephenson's operations in that region, and it was unthinkable that he would expel his tenant after the war to satisfy pro-Soviet influences. But valid objections were brought against a British organization now so deeply involved in communications intelligence.

The State Department was conscripting Nelson Rockefeller for the highly secret Office of Policy Coordination (OPC), the first covert spy agency set up in the United States after the dissolution of OSS and before the birth of the CIA.* The OPC's immediate concern was to fight the Soviets in Europe, using covert action as its chief weapon. The creation of the State Department's own intelligence service was in reaction to the operations of the British Foreign Office intelligence service, which was in effect the SIS, treated as *Most Secret* by the British. The Americans believed that the permanent British government in Whitehall used the SIS as its crucial organ of perception. This had always made the State Department uneasy, and that unease rubbed off on Stephenson's organization; the department was resolved to speed its termination.

The U.S. Joint Chiefs of Staff were the department's unwitting allies. General Donovan, when his wartime OSS was at the peak of its success, had set forth arguments for the Fourth Arm that intrigued President

---

*The existence of State's OPC was never admitted until a U.S. Justice Department investigation led to questions in the late 1970s. During Eisenhower's administration the presidential advisers on OPC affairs were C. D. Jackson, former publisher of Time-Life, Vice-President Richard Nixon, and Nelson Rockefeller.

Roosevelt but caused the service chiefs to grit their teeth. When Donovan recommended a presidential award for Stephenson soon after D-day in 1944, the U.S. Joint Chiefs of Staff were in a mood to block any of Donovan's moves. The U.S. Military Intelligence Division said it was unaware of any activity meriting the award. The U.S. War Department suggested Stephenson had certainly been helpful enough to deserve the Medal of Freedom. Nevertheless, Donovan was resolved to get Stephenson the far more prestigious Medal for Merit, even if it had never gone to a foreigner before.

Always sensitive to changing winds, J. Edgar Hoover wrote a formal letter to Stephenson on official FBI stationery. Sent to the BSC director's official address—Room 3553, 650 Fifth Avenue, New York 20—the message expressed "a feeling of sadness at the termination of the pleasant relationships which existed between us during the war years." Hoover broke their mutually agreed silence, uncharacteristically, by adding that the direct liaison between them "contributed immeasurably to our efforts in protecting the internal security of this country and what I regard now as successful intelligence coverage achieved by your organization and ours on behalf of the whole allied cause." The FBI director concluded by hoping "Anglo-American collaboration in intelligence work will continue." But he knew that Stephenson was falling victim to the domestic strife in Washington.

President Truman finally awarded the Medal for Merit "to Sir William S. Stephenson for extraordinary fidelity and exceptionally meritorious conduct" on July 18, 1946.

Even so, General Donovan had been obliged to scale down his original justification for the award. "Without Stephenson's help," wrote Donovan in his revised recommendation, "it would have been impossible to establish the instrumentalities" in time for U.S. wartime secret-intelligence operations. A later CIA history broke out of its bureaucratic reserve to comment: "One wonders whether Donovan felt some indelicacy in detailing [this] assistance."

Well, that of course was the point. Donovan wrapped things up in the appropriate bureaucratic gobbledygook so that the postwar crop of chiefs in Washington might avoid the "indelicacy" of sharing with wartime allies the credit for the new weapons of secret intelligence and the bomb. It was also necessary to avoid alarming further the conventional military minds disturbed by the secret Fourth Arm concept.

A FRENZY OF INACTION

In mid-1946 a 733-page document was released by the Canadian royal commission investigating the Corby Case. A quarter-million words related RIS operations against the West. But the report did not tell all: the preface admitted that sections had been suppressed "for security reasons," a phrase meaning that political factors continued to influence the handling of Gouzenko. Government officials were afraid of losing face if extensive subversion should be uncovered in their administrations. And confession was often the only way—in a democracy—to prove a case of espionage.

The report implied that a citizen's ideological beliefs would affect national interests. Those who had sworn an oath to serve their country had been induced to pass information to the Soviet Union because of their attachment to Marxism. Little more was said about the curious innocence of academics and those who pretended to intellectual superiority.

On May 1, an English criminal court had demonstrated that those trying to build a defense against the Soviets were sabotaged by intellectual innocents. Professor Alan Nunn May was tried and sentenced in double-quick time at London's Old Bailey, to the loud dismay of some members of the academic world. PRIMROSE had finally confessed, but meekly insisted he had passed secrets to the Soviets "only because it was a contribution I thought I could make to the safety of mankind." He was sentenced to ten years in prison.

William "Jim" Skardon, the interrogator described by Rebecca West as "a quiet man to whom people confess,"* had called at May's lodgings near the University of London on February 14, within hours of Gouzenko's completing his oral testimony to the Canadian royal commission. Skardon wondered if the professor might help Scotland Yard with its inquiries. Skardon in fact worked for MI5, but since counterintelligence had no powers of arrest, the mystique of the Yard was invoked to imply

*The New Meaning of Treason (New York: Penguin, 1967).

some sort of police authority. May invited him into his cramped quarters with the observation that he really couldn't imagine what he could do to help in a police matter.

"Well, it's really more a matter of national security," Skardon said softly.

Dr. May showed an appropriate surprise. The name PRIMROSE fairly described his shrinking style and conservative dress. The primrose had become a symbol of conservative politics in England. Alan Nunn May, however, was a Communist to the bone. He offered to brew up some tea.

"That would be very nice, sir," replied Skardon. His manner nicely blended the English bobby's respect for the citizen's privacy and the barest touch of menace. Skardon had developed his style during wartime interrogation of Nazis and captured German commanders. U-boat captains, in particular, were disarmed by the man's concern to offer no discourtesy. A London newspaperman who worked in wartime with Skardon to squeeze intelligence out of high-ranking prisoners of war was awed by his unruffled patience. "He built up a curious relationship between himself and the person under interrogation," the newsman said later. "When he'd finish with a 'subject,' the poor chap would actually seem grateful and volunteer all kinds of stuff." Skardon's methods were polished with practice on wartime enemy prisoners who were protected, of course, by the international rules of war, and knew they need only answer with their name, rank, and service number. They found him so affable and understanding that, though he never raised his voice, he managed to extract the information he needed. Part of this technique required a decent expense account for entertainment (U-boat officers were given a night out in London with British "naval officers" who took the line that "sailors are all brothers, even in war"). It also included some even less sporting devices like hidden microphones during bouts of drunken, but bogus, camaraderie.

When Professor May shrugged his narrow shoulders and made a polite disclaimer to Skardon's hearty opener, "You seem to have helped the Yanks build their bomb," Skardon added playfully, "Mustn't hide our light under a bushel, now, must we, sir?"

Skardon went on, "We're a trifle bothered, Professor May, by reports you might have known some rather dubious characters in the United States—"

"But I was working in Canada."

Skardon looked blank. "I'm afraid there's been a mistake, then, sir. We understood you spent time in Los Alamos."

May shook his head.

"Or Chicago?"

Again the scientist shook his head. He was taken in by the humble manner of Skardon, who seemed, after all, only a bloodhound from the Yard's Special Branch. May, an intellectually arrogant man, thought he could have a little harmless fun with him. Also, undeniably, Skardon aroused his curiosity by letting drop tantalizing bits of information. How much, Professor May must have wondered, did this rumpled, tired-looking investigator really know?

Skardon had him hooked now, and asked if he might return the following day. Perhaps, if the professor could spare the time, he wouldn't mind looking over some material?

The temptation was too much. Dr. May actually enjoyed the subsequent chat. Indeed, as Skardon expected, his reaction was visibly one of relief. The scientist had known he was under observation, and it was oddly reassuring to come face to face with one's shadow.

After four visits, Skardon had started to trip up the scientist. Over yet another cup of tea, he said, "It's a funny thing, sir, but the U.S. authorities have a record of your crossing the border on these dates." He still spoke in the same slow, heavy manner, still played the part of a streetwise but otherwise simpleminded cop. He plodded remorselessly on. "Didn't you say—let me see. . . ." More flummery, thumbing his way through a policeman's notebook. "Yes, here we are, sir. You said here you had no knowledge of Colonel Zabotin?"

May had denied any knowledge of his Soviet contacts in Canada. Now Skardon tugged out of his jacket pocket some crumpled telegrams. "I'm afraid we've got statements to the contrary, sir."

It was on February 20 that Alan Nunn May cracked. On that same day, the Soviet deputy foreign minister issued his protest against Canadian government accusations of espionage. At the time, nobody seemed to make the connection.

Skardon had delivered his customary little lecture to Professor May on the advisability of cooperating with the authorities. If a spy confessed fully and frankly, life could be made tolerable. In some cases, where no confession was volunteered, the spy would be promised immunity from later prosecution. In May's case, the cooperation was strictly limited. He would not disclose his fellow conspirators' names, and he pretended to forget the details of the contacts he was to have made in London. He was advised to continue with his lectures at King's College as if nothing had happened, but he was asked to hand over his passport. Without it, PRIMROSE would be unable to skip off to the Continent—and down one of the rabbit holes provided by the RIS for its escaping agents.

The light punishment May received at his trial was contrasted with the swift hanging a few months earlier of another traitor, Nazi propagandist William ("Lord Haw-Haw") Joyce. Writing in the *New Yorker*, Rebecca West commented: "The guilt of Joyce was a light matter compared with the guilt of May." Yet everyone in court seemed aghast that May would go to jail at all; even the prosecutor, Sir Hartley Shawcross, who "wished to make it abundantly clear there is no suggestion that the Russians are enemies or potential enemies."

Lord Haw-Haw was hanged because the authorities had determined that he should hang. Professor May would have suffered the same fate if the authorities had judged that the public mood demanded it, for he had committed treason in time of war too. But the scientist was an intellectual among intellectuals. William Joyce, on the contrary, was a poor fool who had affected an aristocratic English accent (hence "Lord Haw-Haw") to mock English leaders when nobody else dared defy Hitler. It had been difficult *not* to hear Joyce if you lived in England and tuned in to his nightly broadcasts prefaced with the eerie cry, "Jairmany calling! Jairmany calling!" He gloried in the daily U-boat claims of English ships torpedoed when, wrote Rebecca West, "to open the newspapers was to see the faces of drowned sailors." Still, he had betrayed no secrets. He had established an American birthright, though he had become a naturalized German. Unfortunately for Joyce, however, it had been laid down in 1608 that any man who came to England "owed to the king obedience, that is, so long as he is under the king's protection. . . . If he commit a treason, he shall be judged and executed as a traitor." Joyce had enjoyed the protection of English law for thirty years before his move to Nazi Germany, and it was an anachronistic technicality that led him to the executioner.

The Crown, in its prosecution of Professor May, never invoked ancient treason laws. Even the judge, winding up the short day's proceedings, merely regretted that "a man in your position could have had the crass conceit, let alone the wickedness, to arrogate to himself the decision to share atomic secrets with Russia."

Hearing about the public trial, Gouzenko naturally assumed that much more was happening beneath the surface. He started to make a new life for himself and his family, freed of the restrictions of "protective custody." He began to build a new life under another name in a rural setting that brought out his unfulfilled dream of becoming a sort of Tolstoyan farmer, a cultured man who might write and paint canvases on the land he tilled.

Professor May was behind bars. To Gouzenko, that meant the security services were plodding steadily along the trail of other traitors. The second ELLI, and what he represented, receded in his memory.

Meanwhile, Alan Nunn May's scientific colleagues were pleading for clemency. The Soviet-influenced British Association of Scientific Workers demanded a reduction of "the extremely harsh sentence." The news of May's sentence caused a shudder among British scientists at Los Alamos. "Poor Alan!" was the general comment.

The only poker face belonged to a certain physicist who considered himself brighter than May and who was a fellow graduate of the British Tube Alloys nuclear project. He said, as an afterthought, "I don't think Alan could have told the Russians very much." It was a curious display of pettishness, for he speaker was himself a Soviet spy named Klaus Fuchs. He still had four years to run before the formidable Skardon finally caught up with him. If the rogues and vagabonds in sensitive Western posts had not been able to protect the surviving spies, and if wartime intelligence coordination had been in effect, this scientist-spy would have been among many whose careers ended earlier. But by 1950, his betrayals of American atomic secrets were breathtakingly extensive. This particular "spy of the century" (there were so many, the very title became controversial) was caught in England, where the laws dictated that his espionage was provable only through confession, since no tangible evidence existed. He had been active since 1942, providing all details of the U.S. bomb "substantially as the U.S. perfected it."

And though Gouzenko had led investigators to the spy's controller, Anatoli Yakovlev, the doctor in the "New York hospital," Yakovlev continued to flourish in his New York diplomatic post for another ten months. Indeed, the spymaster left at the end of 1946 in a flurry of fashionable Manhattan farewell parties.

What was betrayed through Soviet espionage conducted under Moscow Center's GRANT headquarters in Ottawa? How much continued to be betrayed, as the Russians switched to other networks, contemptuous of the way democratic procedures hampered the lawmen? For how long had the Soviets used Canada to spy on the Western Hemisphere, knowing easygoing Canadian ways? In 1946, such questions were not properly asked. Attention was focused on limited atomic espionage, the full extent of which remained unexplored. Further inquiries were cut short by Moscow, working through agents in influential positions in the West, exploiting dogfights between seniors in Western intelligence. Despite Gouzenko's efforts, there was no assessment of infiltration by Soviet agents into the centers of Western policymaking.

Among the diversions launched by the RIS was an attempt to create a Canadian external-affairs intelligence service that would have been ultimately controlled by Moscow through the proposed new agency's chief architect, a top-level RIS agent who was still undiscovered. Stalin had learned the lesson expressed by the chief of British SOE, Colin Gubbins: "One nation penetrating the security and intelligence of another can pull the strings." Gubbins referred to manipulation by the British of Nazi German intelligence operations, but the principle remained the same.

So the "betrayal" exposed by the Gouzenko investigation was confined to the theft of wartime atomic secrets. The custodian of those secrets was the United States, although Britain and Canada had been in at the ground floor of the bomb's development. The Russians, fishing in troubled waters, had no difficulty stirring mutual suspicions. The RIS would be able to keep at the center of the controversy such questions as: Is it worth guarding secrets in the modern world? Should atomic scientists or other technologists be punished for sharing secrets out of idealism? Was execution an unjust punishment for alleged atom spies like Ethel and Julius Rosenberg?

Of course the related questions were *not* asked: Why does the U.S.S.R.

guard *all* information with secrecy laws backed by the death penalty? Why don't Soviet scientists talk freely about their work? Is execution and exile an unjust punishment for Russians who give away "state secrets" such as the figures for annual production of petroleum products?

And Gouzenko's second, mysterious ELLI vanished from view. But neither this ELLI, nor his companions, were inactive.

THE McCARTHY ERA AND THE COLD WAR

TWENTY-THREE

ELITISTS AND
WITCH-HUNTS

I used my Marxist philosophy to establish in my mind two separate compartments: one compartment in which I allowed myself to make friendships . . . to help people and to be in all personal ways the kind of man I wanted to be. . . . I knew that the other compartment would step in if I approached the danger point. . . . I had succeeded in the other compartment in establishing myself completely independent of the surrounding forces of society. Looking back, it seems better to call it a controlled schizophrenia.

This was Klaus Fuchs's own explanation of how he operated as an atom spy. For many years, an approved version of his story went something like this:

The FBI studied notebooks taken by Gouzenko from the Soviet embassy in Ottawa. Among the names was that of Klaus Fuchs. This rang alarm bells. FBI agents digging through captured German Gestapo files had discovered an entry referring to a Klaus Fuchs, identified as a Communist by the Gestapo Field Office at Kiel. The description fitted Klaus Fuchs, respected chief of the British atomic energy establishment at Harwell, theoretical physics division. Fuchs was a man of genius. Director Hoover of the FBI notified MI5. British intelligence had turned up information through its debriefings of Alan Nunn May and other agents of Soviet intelligence. Fuchs had fled Germany to escape the Nazis. He had worked on atomic research in England and then joined the Los Alamos project in 1943. He had maintained contact with a Soviet agent, Harry Gold, a Philadelphia chemist. Fuchs finally confessed in 1950. He named Gold, who in turn named his contact as David Greenglass, who had worked at Los Alamos. Greenglass pointed to Julius and Ethel Rosenberg.

In fact, Fuchs had also been spotted through the partial interception of RIS traffic between outstations and Moscow Center. Similar decoded traffic in 1949 spotlighted Julius Rosenberg as a source of Soviet intelligence on the bomb. The intercepts could not be disclosed. ABC counterintelligence experts went through the difficult detective work of building up independent cases. These cases relied, as Hoover very well knew, on confessions of the sort Jim Skardon was skilled in extracting. "A conspiracy trial is the most difficult to prove," a later presidential aide explained. "You're usually left with circumstantial evidence."*

By making use of background knowledge gleaned from the monitored traffic, Skardon had finally persuaded Fuchs to confess during the week of Monday, January 30, 1950. Sitting in the War Office, in a room reserved for MI5, he gently coaxed Fuchs into describing his eighteen years as a traitor, and his betrayal to Russia of details of the U.S. gaseous-diffusion process, the plutonium bomb, and the postwar British development of an independent atom bomb.

In the summer of 1949, five months before Fuchs confessed, Russia had tested her first atom bomb. The Soviet Union's graduation to the status of a nuclear power came at a critical moment in world affairs. "Are you sure? Are you *sure*?" President Truman demanded when told that a B-29 flying laboratory, returning from a photographic mission in Asia, had found traces of radioactive material from what could only be an atomic explosion in the Soviet Union. Truman had believed the Soviet Union could not develop a nuclear bomb for another ten years yet. Soon the details trickled in of a Soviet bomb detonated in the Kazakhstan desert. "This means we have no time left," said Truman.

Stephenson had revealed earlier, on February 18, 1949, that the first Russian bomb was scheduled to be exploded in September. "He was long out of service, on special mission," wrote the former liaison officer with the OSS, Washington lawyer Ernie Cuneo.* "In September, Truman

---

*Quoted in the "oral biography of J. Edgar Hoover," *The Director*, by Ovid Demaris (Harper's Magazine Press, 1975).

*Ernest Cuneo had been appointed by General Donovan to serve as liaison between the OSS, British intelligence, the FBI, the State Department, and the White House, where he was a familiar member of President Roosevelt's "brain trust." The former Brooklyn football player had been legal adviser to New York's Mayor LaGuardia. His knowledge of the law and experience in American political life made him, Stephenson said later, "one of my most priceless assets."

made the announcement. . . . I asked Stephenson where he got this staggering information and how good the source was. 'We have a little window,' said Stephenson, 'and the source is Triple A, Triple 1.' "

Russian espionage itself was seen as a clear threat to U.S. security. Four years after Colonel Zabotin's GRANT operations had been exposed, the extent of Soviet success was finally faced. The Hiroshima bomb's most intimate mechanism involved two hemispheres brought into contact until the mass reached a critical point and detonated. The details—the size of the two halves, the speed of collision, the amount of U-235, the range of the neutrons to be projected by the chain reaction, the method of focusing the detonation waves to trigger the bomb—all this and more had been delivered to Moscow with such efficiency that the Russians might just as well have been full partners with the bomb's manufacturers.

If ever there was a real need to ruthlessly reexamine the aftermath of the Corby Case and the neglect accorded Gouzenko, it was now. Four days before the arrest of Fuchs, Albert Einstein warned the world that "radioactive poisoning of the atmosphere and, hence, annihilation of any life on earth has been brought within the range of possibilities. . . . General annihilation beckons."

Einstein was thinking of the H-bomb. The news of Fuchs's treachery had shocked President Truman's advisers on atomic energy into recommending the "super bomb." The decision to go ahead was announced on the last day of January 1950, the day after Fuchs began his long confession in London. Fuchs had been at the center of Anglo-American scientific discussion and "knew everything," according to Hoover, reporting to Admiral Lewis Strauss, one of Truman's "supermen" on bomb matters. Privately, Hoover was asking why it had taken so long to detect Fuchs when the clues were all contained in the Corby Case. But politics being a game Hoover was obliged to play to survive, he was to find himself devoting a disproportionate amount of time to the questions provoked in Congress by the wild charges of Tail-Gunner Joe McCarthy.

Fuchs did not have nearly the impact upon the public mind that Senator Joseph R. McCarthy did when he delivered his speech that February to the Ohio Women's Club in Wheeling, West Virginia. His tale of traitors, and of "bright young men born with silver spoons in their mouths" betraying their country, sparked a witch-hunt that was offensive to many but touched a nerve. Anti-Communist zealots popped up everywhere. The junior senator from Wisconsin read from "classified" documents, refused to submit this "evidence" to public inspection on the grounds of national security, and set a style for televised inquisitions that blighted innocent lives.

The congressional interrogations were nourished by conclusions from the Canadian royal commission investigation into the Corby Case. Some of the suppressed sections had reached Washington. No honest observer could ignore even the sanitized public Gouzenko report. An investigative writer, Joseph C. Goulden, who had always shown the healthiest incredulity about official versions of any event and who detested all that McCarthy stood for, nonetheless wrote of the Gouzenko report that it showed:

> . . . domestic Communists [could] no longer be dismissed as harmless "parlor radicals." Secret Communist party members "played an important part in placing other secret Communists in various positions in the public service which could be strategic not only for espionage but for propaganda and other purposes." Many of the bureaucrats implicated in the espionage network were "persons with an unusually high degree of education, and many were well regarded [by colleagues] . . . as persons of marked ability and intelligence." All acted from ideological motivation. . . . The Soviet Union stood exposed as a nation willing to spy on its friends.*

In Washington, as the Gouzenko report took effect, there was a widespread feeling that Senator McCarthy might be a lout but there had to be something in what he said. Sections of the report kept secret from the public, but known to the FBI, were leading to the conclusion that Soviet spy rings in the United States had functioned with insolent confidence over many years. These sections had been suppressed in accordance with

*Joseph C. Goulden, *The Best Years: 1945–50* (New York: Atheneum, 1976).

an agreement between the ABC countries to limit the publication of security investigations to each government's own area of responsibility. It was a face-saving device: President Truman was not the only leader who feared that stories of spies prospering under his administration would hurt him at the polls. The news about Fuchs, and the probability that more traitors would be unearthed in the investigations following his confession, helped Truman decide on a thermonuclear crash program. He was responding to the outcry typified in the Senate by Homer Capehart: "How much more are we going to take? Fuchs . . . and Hiss and hydrogen bombs threatening outside, and New Dealism eating away the vitals of our nation!"

Without the atom spies who gave the Soviets their competitive spur, the new age of atomic weapons might never have moved into the ultimate horror of the H-bomb, capable of so much more devastation than the first atom bomb. After the first Soviet atomic explosion had been announced in September 1949, the Atomic Energy Commission met in Washington to consider the "super bomb." Sentiment was against it. After Fuchs's arrest, though, the pendulum swung the other way. The first American fusion bomb was exploded in the Pacific in November 1952, but it was only a static bomb. Nine months later, the Soviet Union gained nuclear superiority with the successful testing of a *deliverable* H-bomb. The theory of thermonuclear weapons (so-called because fusion takes place only at very high temperatures in a process by which the sun gives light) had been known to the Anglo-Americans for a long time—and, as Fuchs told the FBI when Hoover's agents flew to London to interrogate him, the theoretical mechanics to trigger the heavy-hydrogen charge had been conveyed to Moscow Center by Fuchs himself.

Prime Minister Attlee told the British Parliament: "Here you have a refugee from Nazi tyranny, hospitably entertained, who was secretly working against the safety of this country." But a complacent British public did not send Fuchs to Traitors' Gate to remove his head. Opinion came down in favor of letting Fuchs discharge his guilt by sewing mailbags.

Once again the intellectual arrogance of the "new privileged class"*

---

*Rebecca West used the phrase when she covered the PRIMROSE trial of Dr. May, and recoiled in disgust from the scholarly apologists who constituted "a new privileged class" claiming that scientists were exempt from traditional concepts of loyalty.

seemed to be making excuses for the sensitive conscience of science. The spy who had once boasted, "I *am* the British research establishment," who had opened the way for Russian nuclear superiority over the West for the brief period when Moscow alone had a deliverable hydrogen bomb, was sentenced to a term of fourteen years in prison. Deprived of his British nationality, which he clearly viewed as no great punishment, Klaus Fuchs would be released after nine years and allowed to fly to Communist East Germany to become deputy director of the East German Central Institute for Nuclear Physics, a subsidiary of Soviet nuclear weapons research.

Meanwhile Professor Alan Nunn May would serve only six years of his ten-year sentence, then head for a nuclear-physics job in one of Africa's new, Soviet-influenced republics. Eventually, he returned to England and the decent obscurity of village life near Cambridge, where so much polite scholastic treachery began.

The Fuchs papers increased U.S. suspicion of the British. The excesses of McCarthyism swung liberal opinion against counterintelligence. The damage was more effective than any Soviet disinformation campaign. McCarthyism distracted the West from legitimate anxieties about Soviet activities, forced the FBI to waste time on high-profile leftists in Hollywood, and made an honest man like Gouzenko sound worse than any McCarthy-like opportunist.

Gouzenko was now gently tugging at the sleeves of other counterintelligence officers. They seemed unreceptive. Had the unthinkable occurred? Had he spoken to a Russian mole when he confided all he knew and suspected about the second ELLI to "the gentleman from England"? By the time this question began to trouble him, Gouzenko was already feeling the consequences of a careful, surreptitious campaign to discredit him. McCarthyism helped that campaign, because the witch-hunts disgusted many within the counterintelligence agencies too.

Defectors from the RIS after 1950 would confirm that the Soviet Union quickly learned that McCarthy, by his extremes, proved its best friend. Witch-hunts and spy-fever were a cheap way to create dissent and distrust. "I have here in my hand a list," proclaimed McCarthy in Wheeling, claiming to have the names of Communist agents in the State Depart-

ment. The words "I have here in my hand a list" would be repeated
again and again with increasing contempt.

The witch-hunts had to compete for newspaper headlines after the Communist attack on Korea. At the beginning of 1950, the Central Intelligence Agency predicted that Communist North Korea would attack the
South in June of that year. It was a prediction of astonishing accuracy.
It demonstrated that the new agency had built firmly and rapidly on the
old. The fact that this clear warning was ignored is typical of the times,
but another element was present: treachery. From the standpoint of military security, Korea was regarded as having little strategic interest. Truman's doctrine of containment, however, implied a commitment to confront
Communist aggression anywhere. It was easier, said America's critics,
for the blowhards in Washington to confront communism at home by
way of a witch-hunt. This was a cheap shot, but it was the popular British
view even after war broke out in Korea and the two countries again became
allies in the field. Political distrust made possible the leakage of secret
intelligence to the Russians in ways that would have seemed inconceivable
to the American, British, and Canadian patriots who fought and sometimes died in Korea.

Right on schedule, the North Korean People's Army crossed the 38th
parallel, led by crack Communist troops who had fought with the Soviets
against the Nazis. Moscow attempted at first to win Western sympathy
for these "anti-fascist forces," by recalling its relatively brief alliance with
the West against Hitler. This time the ploy failed. The United States
found itself standing in for the United Nations as defender of South
Korea, through Stalin's own miscalculation. He had earlier broken an
agreement at Potsdam by which the Korean peninsula's future was to be
determined by supervised elections: when it came to the test, the Russians
refused to let UN commissioners cross the 38th parallel to scrutinize the
Communist North's interpretation of "democratic elections." The United
States had thereupon taken on the task of representing the UN, and soon
found itself involved in war. By the irony of fate, the Atlantic allies
tumbled one after another into the conflict, fighting under the banner
of the United Nations which, they had once insisted, the Soviet Union
must help create—at almost any cost in appeasing Stalin. Otherwise,

they had once argued, there might be a conflict between the UN and the Soviets. . . . Clearly, the appeasement reflected in handling the Corby Case had not coaxed Stalin into a better frame of mind, any more than it had Hitler.

North Korea's attack was Soviet-inspired, Soviet-equipped, and Soviet-timed. Stalin had been told the Americans considered the peninsula to lie beyond their new Pacific defense lines. It would be many years before investigators concluded that this information had been part of a series of major leaks from Washington to Moscow. It demonstrated the dangerous possibilities in secret intelligence, for in this case the analysis was wrong. The United States, and indeed the free countries of the UN, were prepared to fight for South Korea. Stalin's miscalculations were partly a result of predictions, made before the outbreak of war by "agents of influence," that Korea lay beyond Washington's active concern.

The "police action" cost 100,000 American casualties in three years of fighting, the penalty paid by the United States for taking the initial brunt of the attack and then providing the leadership to turn back the invaders. But "victory" in this case was nothing more than a cease-fire. Soviet influence had been pushed back to where it was before. It was the later study of BRIDE/VANOSA traffic, and the abrupt disappearance in 1951 of two Soviet moles in Washington, that began to define the boundaries of betrayal. The full extent of the perfidy was kept from the American public until 1983, when it became clear how American troops had been ambushed and killed as a consequence of high-level betrayals. Stalin may have blundered in misconstruing the West's willpower. His agents, though, produced a notable military victory.

Apart from specific military intelligence, Soviet agents in Washington provided material for political propaganda. Information had been delivered to Stalin, after the Communist Chinese crossed into Korea to help fight the UN at the end of 1950, that General Douglas MacArthur had recommended dropping thirty to fifty atomic bombs on Chinese air bases north of the Yalu River. The Yalu marked the boundary between Chinese Manchuria, once coveted by the Soviets, and North Korea. Stalin had reason to fear an expansion of Chinese power and he was not averse to getting the Chinese out of Manchuria. But he knew the atom-bombing of their bases was unlikely, because he was soon furnished with a full report of talks between President Truman and Britain's Prime Minister Attlee. Truman told Attlee the bombing proposal was "a bunch of rhubarb." A serious proposal was put up, however, for laying a belt of radioactive cobalt along the Yalu to stop further Chinese incursions. This was leaked to Mao's Communists through Soviet agents in Peking. Out of this grew the tall tales of U.S. "germ warfare" that won sympathy for the Chinese in Asia and the West. The truth was regularly supplied from Washington to Moscow Center: Truman had no plans for using atom bombs. The supposedly secret cobalt-along-the-Yalu scheme had been rejected, but it was distorted by Communist propaganda to support the "germ warfare" line.

Also in question at this time was how many sympathizers served Stalin in the State Department. The investigations became a circus, with McCarthy cracking the ringmaster's whip as he drove intellectuals into protesting his methods.* Legitimate anti-McCarthyist rage was turned into Soviet propaganda. Those who had opposed an American H-bomb were joined by those who deplored McCarthy. The ease of making Soviet "useful idiots" out of articulate citizens was described later by a Soviet agent whose name had floated unnoticed through the Gouzenko hearings of 1946.

Hede Massing had "married into the Communist party" in 1920. Her husband was highly placed in the Comintern, the international arm of Soviet foreign policy for espionage and propaganda. A champion recruiter of agents, she finally broke with the party and in 1981 described how easy it had been to orchestrate indignation among academics and scientific workers, turning anger away from active Soviet collaborators, and directing it against targets like Gouzenko. Hers was the voice of long experience, and her words deserved a public consideration that would have been denied them in the McCarthy era:

---

*America's McCarthy era produced a phenomenal number of sackings: 9,500 federal civil servants suspected of Communist affiliations were dismissed. Another 15,000 resigned while under investigation. All names were publicized. By comparison, only 25 British civil servants were dismissed for security reasons between 1948 and 1981; another 25 resigned; 88 were transferred to nonsensitive work. And of that number, 33 were reinstated. Nobody was named. Does this prove greater laxity in Britain? Or greater American propensity for intrigue? Another conclusion might be that many Americans were unfairly hounded out of office by the McCarthy publicity.

"An idealistic approach works best with the privileged of America. It would be almost impossible to recruit the working class . . . but easy to win recruits among the intellectual and middle class. Communism appeals to the elite. What can it offer? Great ideas. The freedom of all time. Marxism. A different economic system. Thoughts. New medical experiments. The world . . . the world."*

TWENTY-FOUR

THE FLOWERING
OF SOVIET
ESPIONAGE

The political climate became better for spies than for defectors.

Gouzenko's was a burnt-out case in the mythology of Western security in the 1950s, and conveniently regarded as Stephenson's last big one. "Gouzenko is a nonentity whose only cause is himself, a minor cipher clerk with big ambitions," a reviewer of his first novel wrote in a Communist-financed Indian newspaper. The Bombay critic might be forgiven for thinking Gouzenko was a minor clerk, but the campaign to scorn him was deliberate.

Gouzenko was talking more freely now to investigative committees in

---

*From Hede Massing's interview shortly before her death in 1981, with Martyn Burke in a Canadian Broadcasting Corporation TV documentary on KGB operations, produced by Norfolk Communications.

the United States, though he used an assumed name, fearful of Russian vengeance and still intimidated by the secrecy laws of his adopted land. These laws were British-based, and much stricter then than now. It would be thirty more years before the British government would formally acknowledge the existence in peacetime of the Secret Intelligence Service, MI6, or the Security Service, MI5. The penalties for breaking secrecy were severe, and it was difficult for Gouzenko to voice his fears without referring to such agencies.

Stephenson could be told of those fears without danger of retaliation, but otherwise Gouzenko was stuck with the fact that legally he could confide only to officers of those very agencies he thought had been infiltrated by Soviet-run spies. Stephenson's own situation was comparable to that existing before World War II when, as a private businessman, he ran his own informal intelligence agency to keep Winston Churchill informed about Hitler's preparations for war. He now lived in an old plantation house in Jamaica, having helped to create a postwar investment organization, World Commerce, with Bill Donovan. It was intended to finance pilot industries in underdeveloped countries that, after decolonization, faced the problems of economic as well as political independence.

Stephenson believed Gouzenko's assertions: that the Russian Intelligence Services controlled agents in a position to choke off self-investigation among the Western security agencies; that the RIS exploited failures of coordination between those agencies; that the RIS trained terrorists for the assassination of the Kremlin's targets abroad.

All these allegations would be proved valid in the long run. But at the time, Gouzenko was denigrated as unreliable, even paranoid.

Stephenson cast around for proof that Gouzenko was right. He had looked into two RIS operations by 1950 that confirmed Gouzenko's claim that the RIS used Canadian passports as tickets to major operations. One case involved the doctoring of such a passport to help one of Stalin's killers destroy Trotsky. The other concerned a Soviet satellite's confiscation of some three thousand Canadian passports, taken from Canadian citizens tricked into returning to their native, Communist-run countries.

The wholesale theft of Canadian passports for Moscow's fake-document factories was dealt with quickly. When Tito's Communists took over Yugoslavia after the war, Canadians of Yugoslav origin were persuaded to return. Thousands responded. Many wound up in jail when, disenchanted, they tried to leave again. They couldn't leave because their passports had been taken away. Stephenson publicized the high-handed action. He was also on speaking terms with Tito, partly because of his prewar business interests in Yugoslavia. Tito fired his secret-police chief and released those who wished to return to Canada. The confiscated passports, however, were already on their way to Moscow. The Canadian government had shown no concern for its own citizens, caught in the trap; but the publicity did force some action. A description of the lost passports was eventually circulated—too late, however, to prevent some of them being altered to cover certain RIS agents. Tito himself, before the war, had traveled on a Moscow-doctored passport under the name of a Canadian engineer, Spiridon Mekas.

The assassination of Trotsky by another fake "Canadian" presented more complex problems. Stephenson, in Jamaica, had been invited by a disillusioned MI5 chief to join a private agency fighting international crime. Sick of departmental strife, the MI5 chief was seeking a challenge in the competitive world outside. He told Stephenson that the Gouzenko files were missing in London—an example of how vital dossiers disappeared for reasons never clear. He thought the loss of Gouzenko's files ominous. Did it foreshadow an attempt on Gouzenko's life? He described the mystery of Trotsky's skillfully planned execution near Mexico City, where Stephenson still had contact with a former SIS officer placed under his wartime BSC direction.

Here was a way to expose Soviet intelligence methods and help Gouzenko win credibility from the public. It was also vital to convince the protecting authority that Gouzenko's own life was in greater danger because of Stalin's certainty that he could silence any enemy, anywhere, and would act accordingly if Gouzenko continued to threaten RIS operations.

The Western intelligence agencies were gullible, to put it mildly, in 1950. Stephenson was prepared to believe the MI5 chief, who suspected that their vulnerability was not entirely accidental. How else explain the fact that Trotsky's killer was still alive and living in some luxury at the expense of the state of Mexico, where he had carried out his Kremlin-assigned task of assassinating Stalin's old rival? Nothing had been done to end the public ignorance that enabled the assassin to assume an official Canadian identity.

Gouzenko had testified that Soviet agents within the West's public services could erase the tracks of fellow agents, using techniques and equipment supplied through Moscow Center. Four years after Gouzenko's warnings, there was no evidence that these had been acted upon.

Leon Trotsky, co-founder with Lenin of the Soviet regime, organizer and leader of the Soviet Red Army, had been assassinated on August 20, 1940. The killer carried a Canadian passport identifying him as Frank Jacson. He was taken alive. He had been only one of several assassins who had pursued Trotsky around the world for eleven years after Stalin rejected him. "Jacson" ran Trotsky to earth finally in his heavily fortified Mexico home.

"Jacson" was taken alive because of Trotsky's last words to his bodyguards, ordering them not to kill the assassin. Trotsky had been struck down with an ice pick. Trotsky knew Stalin's methods and he wanted them exposed. His last cry was intended to preserve the killer as evidence that could talk.

But the killer talked in confusingly different languages, telling different and equally convincing, though contradictory, stories. Trotsky, who had earlier announced that his own son had been executed in Paris by Stalin's assassins, had hoped this killer would break down under interrogation. But "Jacson" had been trained and prepared to perfection. In his clothes were misleading letters and official papers. He could pass for a Frenchman, a Belgian, a Spaniard, a Canadian. . . . For ten years, held in a Mexico City jail, he resisted the expert analysts. Then, through a brilliant counterintelligence operation that was covered by the pretense of an accidental discovery of old criminal records in Spain, he was identified as Jaime Ramon Mercader del Rio Hernandez, son of Caridad Mercader, who had dedicated the illegitimate child to Stalin's service. Born in Barcelona in 1914, he was "reborn" within the RIS as a terrorist.

In 1950, again using the old-boy network, Stephenson publicized the truth. The killer's forged papers were based on information taken from a Canadian killed in the Spanish Civil War. The killer had trailed Trotsky, traveling on Canadian papers through Canada to shake off his past, moving to New York to pick up the woman earmarked to gain him entry into Trotsky's fortified home. A full account was published in a Royal

Canadian Mounted Police journal. It started questions circulating in the political assemblies of the West, reminding many that Gouzenko had exposed the presence in Canadian public service of the Executor, the man Moscow used to keep records in line with altered RIS documents.

Stephenson's purpose was to bring to light several issues obscured by the secrecy laws. In the case of the confiscated Canadian passports, he forced a reluctant Canadian government to take a strong position with Communist Yugoslavia when Ottawa had hitherto refused to make any fuss at all; and he dramatized the barefaced exploitation of slipshod Western security measures against the use of falsified passports by Soviet agents. In the case of Trotsky's killer, he demonstrated the criminal stupidity of those in Manhattan who had feted the Soviet consul, Anatoli Yakovlev, even after Gouzenko had exposed him as a spymaster. For now it was known that Yakovlev was the one who had supplied the killer with the money and means to kill Trotsky.

Trotsky's killer continued to live in style, however, receiving his mistress in his Mexico jail one night a week and lecturing to fellow prisoners on communism with Soviet propaganda films that were replaced monthly. Another ten years passed, and he was released to fly to Cuba and then to Czechoslovakia, where he became an instructor in terrorism.

Soviet espionage, far from being impeded, flourished. One of its bad side effects was described by the veteran American newsman Don Whitehead: It "created doubts that never should have been injected in the stream of American political life."*

One whole year later, in late 1951, another nuclear physicist who had betrayed secrets was able to escape to Russia. He was Bruno Pontecorvo, who had taken full advantage of the American distaste for distrust and suspicion.

Pontecorvo's escape substantiated Gouzenko's claim that it was indeed possible for vital security information to be "lost'" between one intelligence agency and another. This was important to prove, because one of the discrediting stories that had been slipped into the Ottawa files on Gouzenko was that no single security officer could hope to conceal any

---

*Whitehead, twice a Pulitzer Prize winner, had in 1956 written *The FBI Story*, covering Soviet spy cases.

of the Russian's testimony; that the second ELLI, said to hide near the top of British intelligence, could not keep to himself the debriefing reports, nor "lose" evidence that might incriminate himself. The reason Pontecorvo could betray secrets of the H-bomb's manufacture was that each of three Western security organizations had been hoodwinked into thinking the other had cleared the spy for super-secret work. He became privy to the most sensitive knowledge, shared by only a select few, that an essential component in the H-bomb was lithium deuteride.

Bruno Pontecorvo had escaped from Italy in 1940, another refugee from the Nazis. He had gone straight to a senior post in the U.S. as a physicist. His reputation had preceded him as one of the authors in 1935 of the remarkably prescient paper "Artificial Radioactivity Produced by Neutron Bombardment," published when he was only twenty-two. He had joined the wartime ABC nuclear research teams, knew about advanced work at the Manhattan Project, and after the war became part of the British atomic-weapons group. After the Fuchs confession was confided to President Truman, the FBI raided Pontecorvo's American home. What they found was startling proof of Communist and anti-American sentiments. A warning was sent to London through the liaison office for MI6 in Washington. Pontecorvo was tipped off by Soviet agents before the British authorities could act. With complete aplomb, he went to his security office and confessed with disarming candor that he had a brother in Italy who was a Communist. He promised that the brother had nothing to do with science. His frankness made a good impression and gave him time to prepare his escape.

The FBI now learned Pontecorvo had never gone through a security screening. Each agency in Britain, Canada, and the United States had been led to suppose the others had already made the customary checks. When Pontecorvo moved to the Canadian atomic plant at Chalk River, the RCMP thought he had been cleared by the FBI. The British thought the RCMP had cleared him. During his trips to U.S. atomic projects, the U.S. authorities thought he had British and Canadian clearances. Pontecorvo escaped, to contribute his genius and his unique knowledge of the U.S. hydrogen bomb to Soviet weapons research.

Pontecorvo had unwittingly demonstrated that Gouzenko was also right about the ease with which Soviet agents slipped through the loosely woven security screens of the West. By now, CIA counterintelligence had developed into a strong and independent force with a sympathetic view of Gouzenko's plight. The suspicion was hardening in Washington that all these security failures could result not only from carelessness and innocence about Soviet ruthlessness, but also from double agents. The McCarthy years, however, had stiffened resistance to the claims that Russian agents could climb high in Western councils.

Still Gouzenko insisted, within the limits set by his uneasy situation, that he had been aware, during the Moscow period of his wartime service, of such agents. Then along came another case illustrating that he knew what he was talking about.

A Soviet agent had joined OSS during the war, and moved on to become an adviser to John Kenneth Galbraith and George Ball, a future U.S. undersecretary of state for economic affairs. The agent's sister appeared to be a British housewife but had in fact been chief of the British section of the Soviet Red Orchestra, and the Soviet control for Dr. Klaus Fuchs.

The "housewife," known as Mrs. John Brewer, lived quietly in an Oxfordshire thatched cottage. Her brother, identified only as "Juergen" in a special counterintelligence file derived from BRIDE/VANOSA intercepts, had written studies on Nazi Germany for Galbraith and Ball. He had concentrated on matters of vital concern to Stalin, who was the first to get his reports: on plans for postwar economic recovery, on the fate of a Soviet-backed plan to reduce all Germany to one vast field for the plow, on the effects of strategic bombing. Soon after MI5, prodded by Washington, began looking for "Juergen," he vanished. "Mrs. Brewer" received the MI5 men with an invitation to come inside and share a pot of tea. Over the teacups, they said they were sorry to delve into her political beliefs, but wasn't it true that she had been a Communist until disillusioned by the Russians' treacherous attack on tiny Finland? Why, yes! said Mrs. Brewer, clutching at the straw. Would she mind answering some questions, then? Yes, said Mrs. Brewer, she would mind. She objected to being interrogated when she had done nothing wrong. Her visitors shared the general distaste in Britain for McCarthyism. They put away their notebooks, finished their tea, and left. It was not long before Mrs. Brewer also left, for East Germany, and resumed her real identity as Colonel Ruth Kuczynski of Russian military intelligence.

Events now made it hard to scoff at Gouzenko. Yet there continued to be an unexplained intelligence gap between the super-secret part of his testimony and Western countermeasures.

At fifteen minutes before midnight, on Friday, May 25, 1951, Donald Maclean and Guy Burgess caught a boat train to France. They were not seen again until five years later, when an enterprising Australian newsman, Richard Hughes of the London *Sunday Times* and *The Economist*, flushed them out in Moscow.

Both British diplomats had come under a shadow even while they were in Washington. How much damage they had done, while nicer feelings prevailed to delay action, could only be surmised. The FBI reported later that Maclean "had full knowledge of . . . cooperation between the U.S., Canada and England in atomic energy." Burgess had access to the BRIDE/VANOSA decrypts and was able to add to what Russia had already gathered about American tapping of Soviet secrets by coded telecom. Both men supplied Stalin with intelligence on U.S. military plans in Korea, resulting in the deaths not only of Americans but also of their own fellow countrymen. Moscow Center was kept abreast of American intentions, from the brushfire wars of Asia to the launching of anti-Soviet Fourth Arm activities in Europe. All these betrayals made nonsense of the housecleaning that supposedly followed the Corby Case.

At the time of Gouzenko's defection in 1945, Maclean was the tall, slim, darkly handsome "golden boy of the British Foreign Office," known as the expert on political aspects of atomic research. He had devoted himself to the subject since his arrival the year before and had enjoyed rapid promotion. Neighbors who watched him tend the English tea roses in the front yard of the Macleans' modest Washington home regarded him as almost the caricature of a young, pinstriped diplomat; one of his ambassadors judged he was "a sweetie"; the British Foreign Office saw him as its watchdog in the American atomic establishment. He had a sharp perception of Anglo-American research and could recognize when the Americans were secretly entering new fields "to steal a march on their allies." He sat on the Combined Policy Committee established during the Quebec conference of 1943 to coordinate allied efforts to produce the first atom bomb—and he must have reflected that there was a certain irony to the arrival of the Canadian prime minister in Washington that fateful day late in 1945 when Mackenzie King confided the great secret of Soviet espionage. In Canada, the concept of allied coordination had been born; from Canada, the betrayal of those plans was reported by King. But the ultimate irony was even greater. For it had been Donald Maclean who sat silent while King breathlessly repeated Gouzenko's dreadful news to Lord Halifax. And it was Maclean who later sent an inside account to Moscow of the consequences of Gouzenko's defection—and an estimate of what the Soviets had better do about it.

In September 1945, he had recommended to his British masters that Professor May be kept from returning to London, not for the plausible and practical reasons he had then stated, but because he realized May would lead British bloodhounds to the London end of the atom-spy networks. His policy would have prevailed if Stephenson had not intervened. Otherwise, Maclean was getting away, literally, with murder.

And Burgess? Professor Wilfred Basil Mann, a distinguished British nuclear physicist, shared offices with Burgess in the cramped main chancery of the British embassy in Washington, and considered him slovenly, ill-mannered, a drunk who moved along Massachusetts Avenue like "a shambling bear in his dirty and stained duffel coat." Burgess displayed great charm when he wanted, and was a talented cartoonist. He had lampooned his former boss, a British secretary of state, during a confidential Cabinet meeting, and the drawing had been swept up with other papers and stamped TOP SECRET. Burgess recovered it and had a fancy for displaying it as an example of "spy-fever."

Early one morning, in January 1951, Professor Mann found Guy Burgess quaffing champagne in bed with the British MI6 liaison officer to the CIA and the FBI, Kim Philby. The Philbys had thrown a drunken dinner the previous night. Next day, Professor Mann called at the house on Nebraska Avenue and was told by Kim Philby's current wife, Aileen, "The boys are upstairs. . . . Go up and see them." He did, and shared a glass of champagne with them before leaving to work on intelligence estimates."*

---

*By the 1980s, Professor Mann, who had written about "atom smashing" in London during the first German blitz of 1940, was senior scientist in the nuclear radiation division of the U.S. National Bureau of Standards, defending himself against wholly unfounded accusations of having been himself a Soviet agent. In refuting the charges, Professor Mann reviewed the strange incidents of that time.

Almost a year later he reported the farcical bedroom scene to James Angleton, the CIA counterintelligence chief. It had been "distasteful and embarrassing," said the scientist. He was reluctant even then to mention it. Angleton promptly asked if he could transmit this information to London, where Philby was going through certain interrogations in the wake of the sudden disappearance of Burgess and Maclean. In England later, Professor Mann again mentioned the incident to the chief of naval intelligence, and then regretted speaking "as an outsider." He had expressed doubts about the behavior of a senior MI6 man, "a colleague to whom the code of ethics of the day demanded . . . complete loyalty."* For an outsider to suggest that a member of the club was not quite honorable was a direct invitation of scorn. The professor had a long record of contributions to British science, and he had been transferred to nuclear intelligence. Still, even he trembled inwardly at his own temerity.

To have surprised Burgess in bed with Philby did not mean, in club terms, they were in bed together as spies. Burgess had a long secret history as a Soviet recruiter, but even with clouds of suspicion gathering into one enormous thunderhead, his activities were still not thoroughly understood by the spycatchers.

Contributing to this astonishing situation was the divided loyalty that silenced those who *knew* all about Burgess.

Michael Whitney Straight, for instance. The son of rich, liberal Americans, he had been drawn into the circle of Burgess at Cambridge University before World War II, and was encouraged later to keep in touch with Soviet agents. Straight was "the most glamorous figure of the Cambridge Far Left" according to T.E.B. Howarth in *Cambridge Between the Two Wars*. One of the fixtures of the intellectual Left was the self-admiring secret society of the Apostles. Straight was in their company. Some were lured into spying for the Soviets by Anthony Blunt, the Olympian art historian who was not publicly exposed until 1979, sixteen years after Michael Straight had finally told his story to the FBI.

In March 1951, while Michael Straight was editor of his family-owned *New Republic*, he had disclosed none of his affiliations, though he later

---

*W. B. Mann, *Was There a Fifth Man?* (New York: Pergamon Press, 1982).

would claim to have broken off contact with Soviet agents. He knew that Guy Burgess continued to serve the RIS. He was surprised to see Burgess on Massachusetts Avenue. What happened next, as recounted by Straight many years later,* goes far to explain the charmed lives of Soviet-run moles. In the previous October, Straight reflected, American troops had been "ambushed by massive Chinese forces." Burgess in Washington would have known American military plans, would have passed them on to Moscow, which in turn would have handed them to Peking. Those plans were for an American advance across the 38th parallel. Four hundred thousand Chinese troops were enabled to take the Americans by surprise. Burgess therefore could have caused the deaths of many American soldiers.

That was Michael Straight's conclusion. Nevertheless, Straight records that when Burgess told him he had been in Washington at the time, "working on Far Eastern affairs," Straight merely chided him.

"You told me," Straight told Burgess, "that you were going to leave the Foreign Office. You gave me your word." When Burgess acknowledged that perhaps he had, Straight said, "Look, we're at war now! If you aren't out of government within a month from now, I swear to you I'll turn you in."

"Don't worry," replied Burgess. "I'm about to sail for England, and as soon as I return, I'm going to resign."

Burgess stayed "in government" well beyond Straight's deadline, until he ran away to Moscow.

Straight ends the anecdote: "I went back to my own work."

Had he told the FBI then what he knew, there would have been further substantiation of Gouzenko's claims—about which the FBI and CIA counterintelligence were now informed through the Russian's guarded disclosures to others in addition to the SIS interrogator, the unidentified "gentleman from England." Instead, of course, Gouzenko continued to suffer from the smears spreading like ink blots through his security records.

Burgess, meanwhile, guessed he must get out of harm's way. He had contributed to the denigration of Gouzenko, whose importance in exposing "atom spies" had been sneeringly downgraded by Donald Maclean. Both the British diplomats were under suspicion, and a third diplomat warned them of this. The protector was Kim Philby, watching the decoded

*Michael Straight, *After Long Silence* (New York: W. W. Norton, 1983).

BRIDE/VANOSA traffic for British intelligence from his Washington post. He decided Burgess had better be transferred. "Our ambassador was death on drunk drivers," Philby would say later. "I had only to draw attention, through someone else, to Burgess's drunken driving."

Philby knew that Michael Straight called regularly at the British embassy to get material for his *New Republic* editorials. Once, Philby might have considered him as a Soviet "agent of influence" who represented himself as a speechwriter and adviser to President Roosevelt. If Straight now made good his threat to turn Burgess in, the picture would change drastically.

When Philby was sure that Burgess, with Maclean, had escaped to Russia, he took all his own Soviet espionage equipment and buried it near the Potomac River. Shortly thereafter the CIA made it known to the British that Philby was no longer welcome in Washington. Philby brazened things out: it was "natural for our American cousins to feel queasy," in view of the disloyalty of his two former colleagues.

And so KGB General Harold Adrian Russell Philby would remain fallow another twelve years, with a further lease on life in the West. That was, curiously, the same period of time Michael Straight waited before going to the FBI.

TWENTY-FIVE

DANGER — MOLE AT WORK:
THE BURROWING
OF KIM PHILBY

In a way, J. Edgar Hoover had unwittingly made it possible for Kim Philby to maneuver into the position where he became involved in the Corby Case. Philby played upon Hoover's distrust of the British, and almost succeeded in killing Gouzenko.

But to blame Hoover was like faulting anxious parents for doing their best to raise children, of whom one turns out to be an assassin. The FBI and its director were convenient targets for commentators attacking the forces of law and order for their inevitable mistakes rather than looking elsewhere for the causes of catastrophe.

At one time Hoover had ambitions to expand FBI secret-intelligence operations to Latin America. This was shortly after Pearl Harbor, when there had been, to Hoover's mind, some pretty spectacular failures of intelligence. He felt his own agents had acquired a great deal of experience—not least because some had gone through the training courses in espionage and subversion provided by Camp X on the Canadian border. In January 1942, BSC was threatened with expulsion under a new law stipulating that "all records, accounts and propaganda material used by foreign agencies . . . are liable to inspections by U.S. government authorities at any time." At a Washington meeting with Hoover and Adolf Berle, the assistant secretary of state, Stephenson said the new law would mean the end of his organization.

Berle said to Stephenson, with a satisfied smile, that the demise of BSC would be regrettable but inevitable. Angry, Stephenson left before the meeting had ended and went straight to Bill Donovan, "who realized well enough that the end of BSC would at the present juncture render virtually impossible the continuance of his own organization." A direct appeal was made to President Roosevelt, who agreed the law should be modified. An amended version of the bill, excluding the crippling clause about compulsory disclosures, became law in May 1942, but still wartime SIS/London was nervous about Stephenson's vulnerability.

The jealousies within SIS were well known to Philby. In 1942 he was working for General Gubbins's Special Operations Executive. "Hyphenated agents" in America were recruited for training at Camp X. These were migrants who could be smuggled back into their occupied homelands as saboteurs and subversives. It will be seen later how useful the knowledge was to Philby in his RIS role. That same year, Philby left

SOE to help infiltrate German intelligence for MI6's Section V. He had observed the conflicts between sections, the struggle between department heads to extend control into the territories of their rivals.

Into the wartime MI5 had come an ex-policeman from India, Felix Cowgill. The man had made enemies among his colleagues, not least the cryptographers at Bletchley Park. He nursed a neurotic fear that they wished to remove him from involvement with German wireless intelligence traffic, part of ULTRA.

When Cowgill took over Section V, where Philby operated, the crisis for BSC had been averted. Cowgill concluded that "Hoover is trying to by-pass Stephenson" and characterized the FBI director as another of the evil men using intelligence as a stepladder for advancement. Hoover had appointed a liaison officer to London, who met with competition in the form of a large OSS contingent whose interests overlapped those of Hoover.

"Hoover figured he could clip Stephenson's wings by shifting the weight of liaison to London," Philby wrote later. "Like the FBI's security division, MI5 was purely a counterespionage organization. It had its worries about SIS, just as Hoover had his worries about OSS, [but] its interests could not clash with the FBI's. . . . Hoover's aim was two-fold: to move the center of cooperation away from the United States to Britain; and to get as close as possible to MI5."

Cowgill wanted all wartime exchange of counterintelligence information in his own hands. When he failed to get this, he tried to limit FBI-MI5 cooperation and toward this end regularly dispatched himself to Washington to deal directly with Hoover.

Neither man liked the other. Stephenson tried to keep them apart. His purpose was to avoid the damaging frictions that arose when London-based intelligence experts were confronted with the American way of doing things. Englishmen would comment sarcastically on Hoover's remoteness from real danger, his inexperience with real secret warfare, the hilarious discovery that large public signs pointed to the office of the Secret Service (which was the presidential bodyguard and, of course, had a different meaning in secretive London). Above all, Stephenson understood very well how to play politics in America and the necessity to pursue a seemingly open policy with the legislators. The visitors from London hardly ever showed a comprehension of American history and why it had shaped men like Hoover, whose activities had to be constantly "sold" to the political watchdogs.

Felix Cowgill, whose police experience was so totally different, hated Hoover's way of doing business. Cowgill had been a strict disciplinarian in India. If he barked an order, it got obeyed. Public opinion had been a joke. In the colonies, it had seemed unthinkable that he should pay attention to his public image. He had been answerable in India only to God and the viceroy. He had no notion of, and showed no interest in learning about, Hoover's long struggle to make the FBI first acceptable, then respectable, and finally admired as an elite force in the outspoken politics of a democracy, with all the limitations placed upon the police by the rule of law.

After the D-day invasion of Nazi-held Europe in 1944, Cowgill's attention shifted to the intelligence collected from Gestapo records. He flew to Washington to discuss with Hoover the knowledge gained of Soviet intelligence networks. The subject aroused Philby's most intense curiosity, for this was bringing the hunters close to his own trail. After one such journey, Cowgill returned in a fury over Hoover's apparent lack of discretion. Matters confided to Hoover by Cowgill had been passed, said Cowgill, to an influential senator from whom Hoover wanted a favor.

Untrue, said Stephenson. He wrote one of his famous thumbnail sketches: "Hoover is a man of great singleness of purpose. His purpose is the welfare of the FBI. . . . He became its personification [and] transformed it from a little-known federal agency into a national institution with a fabulous reputation for efficiency and achievement. . . . Hoover is in no way anti-British, but in every way pro-FBI. His job is at once his pride and his vanity. These facts are emphasized because they are fundamental to an understanding of the course of BSC's relationship with the FBI, which has not run smoothly throughout."*

Cowgill ignored it. Instead, he wrote an intemperate attack on Hoover. He drafted a letter, to be signed by the Chief, Stewart Menzies, addressed to Hoover, containing an extraordinary outburst against Hoover's alleged practice of sacrificing intelligence needs for political advantage.

Cowgill's impulsive action played into Philby's hands. Hoover had set out to annoy Cowgill, being provoked by the ex-policeman's general air of superiority and his particularly asinine inquiry, during this last visit,

*From BSC historical file and *Top Secret*, Part I, Chapter One, "Liaison with Hoover."

about the reliability of certain FBI men. Cowgill's irritated reaction was to draft a letter that no sane chief of one security service would write to another.

The letter was prepared for the Chief's signature—at the very time Philby had been instructed by Moscow Center to get rid of Cowgill! This singular order had been conveyed by Philby's regular Soviet contact in London as soon as Moscow Center learned that SIS was to create a new section operating against Moscow Center. Someone other than Philby, who also knew the British security system intimately, had presented the Russians with a simple, devastating proposition. With Nazi Germany finished, the British intended to turn attention back to secret warfare against communism. It would be convenient to have a Soviet spy in charge of the new British operation. The man for such a job was obviously Philby. But all the indications were that Cowgill would get it.

The new section, IX, had already started up and was investigating the newly captured Gestapo records. The temporary chief was "hampered by deafness and ignorance of SIS procedures," according to Philby's own later confession. Cowgill was intriguing to get rid of the man and take over himself.

"Cowgill must go!" was the simple instruction from Moscow. The RIS guidelines on how Philby should conduct his campaign to get rid of Cowgill and take his place were set forth with admirable clarity. Philby must do nothing overt. Every move must seem to come from Cowgill's enemies inside the secret agencies. If anything went wrong later, Philby must be able to show that the top post had been thrust upon him.

This Machiavellian plot was under way when Cowgill made his astonishing attack on Hoover. Essentially, the scheme involved a long-standing grudge against Cowgill held by Vivian "Vee-Vee" Valentine, another veteran of the Indian police and an old friend of Philby's father. Vee-Vee was deputy chief of SIS and Cowgill's direct superior. But Cowgill, in his overbearing way, brushed Vee-Vee aside and went directly to the Chief on matters of importance. According to Philby, this upset Vee-Vee to the point where he was soon confiding that "something has to be done about Cowgill."

This was Philby's cue to turn to the Chief's senior staff officer, a tough navy commander named Arnold-Foster, who was intensely interested in the turmoil within SIS. Again Philby played on his target's known foibles and skillfully arranged that Arnold-Foster should lunch with someone from MI5 who could be relied on to stick a knife between Cowgill's shoulder blades.

Very soon, Vee-Vee was at Philby's desk to say that the letter drafted by Cowgill could only make the Chief look ridiculous. Would Philby redraft it? Concealing what must have been dazed joy, Philby said gravely that he would, and produced a brief note that touched on the issue without giving Hoover offense.

Then Vee-Vee showed Philby a memo he had written to the Chief, listing Cowgill's many failings and arguing that drastic changes were needed in the transition to postwar operations. It ended by recommending Philby to take over Section IX. "Strangely enough," Philby confessed later, "the recital of my virtues omitted my most serious qualification for the job—*the fact that I knew something about communism.*"

The end of Philby's intrigue was not yet in sight. He had to be certain that, in the awful event of a later investigation, he could not seem to have played any part in the appointment. He was called in by the Chief, who confided that he had decided to make Philby chief of anti-Soviet operations. Philby looked suitably surprised, put on his most humble expression, and then stuttered a few words of warning. Had the Chief considered how vital it was to avoid future quarrels with MI5? Look at poor Cowgill. He'd been unable to get along with MI5 personnel. Presumably that's why he hadn't got the job. Would it not be possible to have MI5's written and formal approval of Philby's new position?

Philby's purpose was to have on record evidence that the whole plan had been worked out between MI6 and MI5 and was nothing of his own devising. The Chief took up his proposals and made them his own. Shortly afterwards, Cowgill resigned.

Thus did Philby become director of an amalgamation of Sections V and IX, with responsibility for the collection and interpretation of information concerning Soviet and Communist espionage and subversion abroad. He was also given the right to discuss intelligence matters with MI5, a priceless bonus for Moscow Center.

The final irony was the Chief's plea that Philby should draft his own charter. Philby was regarded as the expert in winning concessions, and was asked to word diplomatically a clause that he must *not* communicate information to the U.S. secret agencies! The war was not yet over. The

Chief was afraid the unreliable Americans might glean information they would pass on to the Soviets.

But by 1946, Philby was in fact schooling Americans in anti-Soviet intelligence operations. The first study by an American intelligence officer on the RIS was only produced in that year. The author then launched Special Project Division/S of the Strategic Services Unit of the Central Intelligence Group, the stopgap between OSS and CIA. The SPD/S began gathering whatever had been published on Russian intelligence and turned logically to the chief of the British anti-Soviet division of SIS. It was not long before the Americans were building rapidly and on a large scale their own counter-RIS forces. The situation, reported Philby later, was like BSC's "lending a hand to make way for the outstretched hand." Philby hoped to reap a rich harvest—in the same way Intrepid in wartime profited from American reciprocity. But whereas Intrepid passed the benefits back to London, Philby protected Russian interests by muddying the flow of information and sending duplicates of the genuine material to Moscow.

After Philby took up his MI6 position in Washington, he was assigned by SIS/London to study BRIDE/VANOSA traffic. This fell into Moscow Center's hands like a ripe plum. The Soviets had been unaware of the continuing retrieval and decoding of their most secret transmissions when the Corby Case broke. The return of purloined Soviet codebooks in 1945 had not prevented the West from monitoring secret RIS traffic. Some Soviet intelligence experts had wondered how Gouzenko could have been allowed by Moscow Center to know so much, the thought presumably not occurring that perhaps his defection had provided the West with an opportunity to make use of information squeezed out of intercepts.

Philby's position was secure. He had watched over Soviet operations, protected other moles, diverted the bloodhounds. One of his assignments in Washington seemed later to be self-invented, for it met Moscow Center's precise needs. His task was "with utmost secrecy," said his London masters with unconscious irony, to loosen Hoover's links with SIS and strengthen ties with the new CIA. This meant starving the FBI of British information on Soviet espionage. It gave Philby direct access to the heart of the CIA.

In Washington, in 1949, Philby busied himself with plans to "liberate" Albania. The Anglo-American scheme to overthrow Albania's Soviet rulers—codenamed Operation VALUABLE—depended upon the movement into the United States of pro-Nazi relics of the German occupation, among legitimate Albanian immigrants. The State Department's covert-action group had arranged for the circumvention of normal immigration procedures. Among those smuggled into the United States was the Nazis' puppet minister of the interior for German-occupied Albania, Xhafer Deva, described in a separate State Department memo as "held responsible by large numbers of Albanians for the massacres of February 4, 1944, in the capital of Tirana by the Gestapo working with Albanian gendarmarie." The reason for this leniency toward alleged war criminals was, from a secret-intelligence viewpoint, that they could assist in the anti-Communist uprisings being planned. Unfortunately, the Soviets, through moles like Philby, were arranging another fiasco like that in the Ukraine, where allied schemes to help movements of liberation ended in the betrayal and capture of anti-Soviet forces. The former president of the New York Yankees, Michael Burke, once a member of OSS, "was asked to try and create a revolution in Albania." Free Albania operations from 1949 to 1952 were compromised by Philby, it was discovered long afterwards: and as in the Ukraine, the most wanted nationalists on Stalin's execution list were conveniently parachuted into waiting RIS hands by U.S. and British aircraft on "secret" spy missions that were kept secret only from the general public.

A request for every retrievable document on Albania between 1944 and 1956, made later by U.S. Justice Department investigators, was received with some embarrassment. Only three documents still survived. One was still classified. Some files had been purged. The West and the Soviets had their own distinctive reasons for hushing up the early phases of the secret Cold War.

One suppressed piece of evidence was a letter written by Donald Maclean on the eve of his departure for the English Channel ferry, and ultimately for Moscow. It was delivered by his Soviet contact in London, sometime in June 1951, to the U.S. embassy. It was then kept secret for more than thirty years, a fact that illustrates why the public, and government leaders in many cases, had difficulty comprehending the scope and subtlety of covert Soviet operations. It was Maclean's death in Moscow in early 1983, and the return of his ashes to London, that opened the letter to public scrutiny.

Maclean wrote: "I am haunted and burdened by what I know of official secrets, especially by the content of high-level Anglo-American conversations. The British government, whom I served, have betrayed the realm to the Americans. . . . I have decided that I can discharge my duty to my country only through prompt disclosure of this material to Stalin."

It was as if the Soviets intended Maclean, even in death, to be their messenger, his letter advancing the Soviet campaign to divide the Atlantic allies. The claptrap about the betrayal of Britain to the Americans was supposed to confuse his patriotic countrymen about where their duty lay. Maclean was representing himself as the high-minded patriot who saw that Britain's real interests were with the Soviet Union, not with the United States—sentiment obviously attractive to latent anti-Americans.

And anti-Americanism wasn't entirely latent in those days.

TWENTY-SIX

A SILENCE
OF CONSPIRACY

Anti-Americanism among the other allies became a major theme of RIS disinformation after Gouzenko defected. At first, the case prompted the Soviet-controlled press to accuse Canada of creating a new *Reichstag* fire (this referred to the burning of the Parliament buildings in Berlin in 1933 as a Nazi excuse to crush the Communist party). It was Moscow's reaction to the sudden reversal of Western public opinion. Before the Gouzenko case, opinion polls showed a majority of people were well disposed toward the Soviet Union. After publication of even the sanitized version of

Gouzenko's testimony, a majority told the pollsters they felt the Russians sought world domination through communism.*

The Cold War had begun. To some Americans, the phrase had not seemed justified in 1946. Bernard Baruch, for instance, dropped it from a speech. But a year later, he conceded that Soviet behavior warranted the new description for a conflict in which both sides shrank from outright hostilities of a conventional sort.

In Europe, which Churchill said was "a rubble heap, a charnel house, a breeding ground of pestilence and hate," the winter of 1946–47 had stormed like another blitzkrieg across the twenty-four countries laid low by World War II. A presidential survey claimed the civilian populations could be saved only through massive U.S. aid. A congressional committee heard that there was a real danger of "losing Western Europe." The gigantic rescue operation mounted by the U.S. government met with renewed Soviet intransigence.

Stalin's 1946 policy statements were studied by the Kremlinologist George F. Kennan, who concluded that the Soviet leaders were bent upon a crusade to convert weaker societies to their faith. No convert ever had the chance to recant. Therefore, as Kennan had said in his famous *Foreign Affairs* article, the way to deal with the Soviets was to "contain" them within the frontiers to which they had advanced already.

Those new frontiers were formidable. For two hundred years Russia had pushed at the eastern gates between the Baltic and the Black Sea. She had been ejected after the Napoleonic Wars, again after the Treaty of San Stefano, and again after the Congress of Berlin. Now "the Turks of the North were in," and Winston Churchill foresaw a deadly hiatus. He pressed upon President Truman the need to take up a challenge that Britain alone could do little about. "With an aching heart and a mind oppressed by forebodings," Churchill viewed the United States as standing on the scene of victory, "master of world fortunes, but without a true or coherent design."

Immediately after the war, on the outrageous basis of his secret deal with Hitler, Stalin had imposed his cult on Estonia, Latvia, Lithuania,

---

*Shortly before Gouzenko defected, the Canadian Institute of Public Opinion had asked Canadians if they thought Russia could be trusted to cooperate; in Ontario, 62 percent trusted the Soviets. Similar results were reported by pollsters in the U.S. and Britain. By June 1946, Canadians were asked if Russia sought world domination: 58 percent thought they did. Again, the figures were typical of how people generally felt.

part of Finland, a third of Austria, Poland, east and central Germany, Yugoslavia, Rumania, Bulgaria, and Albania. "The vertebrae of Europe are his," wrote military historian Major General J. F. C. Fuller. "A thousand years of European history has been rolled back." This was a reality that Truman opposed with the Marshall Plan, named after former Chief of Staff George C. Marshall, who had replaced Byrnes as secretary of state. It became part of a Truman "doctrine of containment," and it would eventually pour $12.5 billion worth of aid into shattered Europe. "The most unsordid act in history," Churchill called it.

Western Europe began to be transformed: industrial regions sprang back to life, and the people saw the first real hope of future prosperity. The Soviets were livid—their plans had rested upon the "inevitable" economic collapse of the effete West. Stalin's apologists called the infusion of capital "the Martial Plan," alleging that it was aimed at encircling the Soviet Union. It seemed a peculiar encirclement. In 1948, it was the Soviets who took over Czechoslovakia and imposed a blockade of Berlin.

The West's response was the Berlin Airlift, an extraordinary morale-boosting accomplishment. The city, a Western island in the sea of Communist East Germany, was cut off by the blockade of rail and road routes by Soviet armed forces. The airlift meant supplying two and a half million Berliners with the necessities of daily life by the split-second rotation of American and British aircraft through West Berlin's two airports. The original cause was a currency row. The Soviets had flooded West Germany with paper money to fuel inflation. The Western allies responded by printing new money. Moscow's avowed purpose was to prevent a resurgence of German militarism, and the Russians began a series of harassments to delay a constitution for the new West Germans. To the Soviets, it seemed an easy matter to take Berlin hostage by applying the blockade, but they were unprepared for the unity of the Western allies and the response of Berliners, who submitted to a tightly disciplined existence rather than surrender to Stalin's bullying. The airlift lasted through 1948–49, operated by pilots trained in faraway Montana, where the approach lanes and navigational systems of the Berlin region were simulated so there would be less danger of aircrews straying into Soviet airspace. A third airfield was improvised in West Berlin with the voluntary help of teenage Berliners. By December 1948 there were variations of the airlift, including Operation Santa Claus, during which small parachutes came down by the thousand with gifts purchased by the aircrews out of their own pay. Stalin's attempt to evict the West from Berlin was frustrated by a technological triumph that also saw an uplifting of the human spirit. The Soviets would try again, with demands that Berlin be made a demilitarized "free city" under their actual control; but they had already admitted defeat when they began relaxing the blockade in 1949. By then, their behavior had succeeded in bringing about the birth, on April 4, of the North Atlantic Treaty Organization (NATO). The phrase "Cold War" became the handy way to measure the advances and retreats of Western engagement with Soviet intrigues.

A blanket of silence lay over the most costly of these intrigues: Soviet espionage and its powerful arm of disinformation. The Western public was told little about the RIS campaigns to sow mistrust and confusion. The silence was useful to those bureaucrats who had private reasons for claiming that "national interests" would be hurt by disclosure.

For Gouzenko, that same silence meant that he continued to preach in the wilderness. If he was right, then what he said about Soviet infiltrators in Western security was suppressed by those he accused. It was a vicious circle.

Donald Maclean had pretended that the only disclosure that would save his country was "to Stalin." It was inexplicable, to those unfamiliar with Gouzenko's theories of conspiracy, that a privileged Englishman could say this. Maclean was wellborn, had earned a Cambridge degree in modern languages, and was a member of the secretive Cambridge "Apostles." If for example, Michael Straight had spoken up earlier, the notion that the highly educated and wellborn were to be trusted *above all others* might have undergone some healthy revision.

In such an event, Philby might have been exposed much sooner. Instead, it was a great many years before the *whole* Philby story exploded the biggest of the lies invented to discredit Gouzenko.

So much evidence had been suppressed that it was hard to trace all the betrayals made possible because Gouzenko's warnings were ignored. It was easier to join the skeptics. They refused to believe that Soviet intelligence would go to such absurd lengths to kill a defector, or to assassinate his character.

We did not consider the full, devastating account of Philby's operations in this field until 1983, when Stephenson read the unsupported statement in a *New York Times* book review that his wartime aide, Dick Ellis, was a traitor.

The name of Ellis had been linked already with Gouzenko, and also with Philby. Yet Ellis had been in Singapore, as chief of British intelligence in Asia, at the time he was supposedly suppressing Gouzenko's testimony about Soviet-run agents in SIS. So far as Stephenson knew, Ellis had nothing to do with Philby.

The *Times* was reviewing a book about Stephenson's old wartime partner General Donovan, *The Last Hero*, by Anthony Cave Brown. The reviewer faulted Brown for giving little space to

the crucial case of Colonel Ellis, a British intelligence officer who worked at the heart of the OSS. According to the secret CIA history of the OSS written by Thomas F. Troy—a history that was eventually declassified and published—Colonel Ellis was detailed by British intelligence in 1940 to Donovan to assist him in the task of creating his secret-intelligence organization. In this capacity, Colonel Ellis worked out the organization plan and personally selected a friend of his, an ex-officer in the Czarist Russian army, to be chief of operations for spying and special activities. Colonel Ellis's contribution and assistance were deemed so important to the fledgling organization that David Bruce, later Donovan's intelligence chief, stated that "without [Ellis's] assistance, American intelligence could not have gotten off the ground in World War II." Colonel Ellis remained an *éminence grise* in the OSS throughout most of the war.

But the real importance of Colonel Ellis emerged only in 1965, long after Donovan had died and his microfilmed files had gathered dust in his executor's office. Under grueling interrogation by a team of British intelligence investigators, Colonel Ellis broke down and confessed that before World War II began, he had been recruited as a double agent by the Germans and then blackmailed into service by the Soviet Union. Thus the man who really organized American secret intelligence was a German-Soviet mole. Situated at the core of the OSS, he was in a perfect position to expose and compromise every secret agent, operation and modus operandi of the agency. (Indeed, in 1963 Ellis even wrote a history of the wartime Anglo-American intelligence collaboration that was based on secret-intelligence documents.) While the British government suppressed any mention of the Ellis betrayal until 1981, possibly to avoid damaging its intelligence relationships with the United States, his story is an additional lens through which it would surely be productive to view the chain of OSS failures brought to light by Mr. Brown.

The reviewer, Edward Jay Epstein, seemed unaware that the British government had never released the relevant material, not in 1981, nor at any time. No proof had ever been offered to substantiate such grave accusations.

In reviewing the Gouzenko case, Stephenson and I had fully discussed the Ellis question with the appropriate authorities. If Ellis was held responsible for the failure to proceed on Gouzenko's original disclosures, bigger issues arose. It might be concluded that this high-ranking British intelligence officer had betrayed secret resistance to the Nazis, a tormenting thought. Western Europe's unity in the face of the Soviet challenge was founded upon the trust and goodwill created by the ABC wartime alliance, and by the Fourth Arm experts who led the struggle against tyranny. Damage now to this trust would add further recrimination to the victories gained through the conscientious labors of KGB disinformation.

We went back over the Gouzenko case, in the light of all that was known by this time. It was possible to see certain processes by which Soviet intelligence and disinformation turned Western secrecy to Moscow's own advantage. The secrets that had surfaced in the intervening years confirmed Gouzenko's warnings, so frequently and publicly ridiculed, and amply justified Gouzenko's lively fears for himself, Svetlana and their growing family—fears for which he suffered public derision.

Kim Philby, holding a position similar to that of the second ELLI, had arranged for the execution of another Russian whose attempt to defect was handled exclusively by SIS. The methods used by Philby were precisely those feared by Gouzenko. By the time Gouzenko dared talk more openly about those fears, Philby and his fellow Soviet intelligence officers had transformed the second ELLI into a ludicrous myth. They had also prepared the groundwork for destroying the reputation of Dick Ellis, thus casting doubts even on the wartime successes of Intrepid, BSC, and the vital coordination of Western intelligence.

TWENTY-SEVEN

A DEFECTOR BETRAYED: PHILBY'S TURKISH CAPER

Kim Philby had been powerful enough in September 1945 that he could have assigned himself to the Gouzenko problem and salvaged a great deal for Moscow Center. We knew now that he planned later to have Gouzenko killed. However, at the time of the Hiroshima bomb, while still basking in the approval of his SIS chief in London, Philby had been stunned by a direct threat to himself. In his office in the Broadway Building, he was brought up with a jerk by a report crossing his desk from the British embassy in Turkey. The report stated flatly that a Soviet vice-consul in Istanbul wanted asylum in Britain in exchange for details of Soviet networks and agents, including two Moscow-run spies in the British Foreign Office and another "directing a *counter-espionage organization in London* [italics added]."

The Chief, Stewart Menzies, turned over the entire business to Philby. It seems never to have crossed the Chief's mind that the man "directing a counter-espionage organization in London" was sitting right there.

Konstantin Volkov, the local NKVD chief in Turkey, operating under the cover of vice-consul, had worked at NKVD headquarters and Moscow Center for many years. He was now approaching his opposite number in the British consulate-general.

The reports were delivered into Philby's hands because he was regarded by the Chief as the expert in these matters. The material had been dispatched by courier, each package chained and padlocked to a king's messenger. Volkov insisted the Russians had broken several British ciphers and therefore nothing regarding his case must be sent through the British diplomatic wireless service. Volkov's stipulation resulted in the much slower method of communication. This gave Philby his first break.

Delay, he was fond of observing, is the chief weapon in the bureaucrat's armory. It also happened to be the RIS weapon in such situations. Philby saw that his best hope of cutting down Volkov and disposing of the danger was to warn Moscow Center, then assign himself to the case and drag things out long enough for SMERSH to liquidate Volkov, whose irritating wife was asking asylum too. So she must go. Otherwise, she would be witness to the fate of her husband, who had also given incriminating documents to her so she could negotiate her own freedom if anything happened to him.

Ten days' delay were won by Volkov's demand that nothing be communicated by cable or radio. Philby asked for time to study the background of Volkov. This was nonsense. He knew it was almost certain Volkov had no SIS dossier. But it allowed Philby that same night to contact his Soviet control. He hoped Moscow would soon have a disposal squad on its way to Turkey. No effort would be made to warn NKVD watchdogs in the Soviet embassy because Volkov might see the telltale message. The Russian SMERSH team would have difficulties at the Turkish frontier, however. If they decided to travel as a trade mission, their sudden appearance would take some explaining. Sanitizing Volkov was going to be awkward. Terminating him would be more hazardous still. The longer Philby dallied, the more time for the Soviets to organize Volkov's liquidation. He did not want to arrive in Istanbul before the killing of Volkov, and thus risk being suspected of involvement in that gruesome operation.

But Philby had to fly to Istanbul to maintain his masquerade. The case was being managed now through the normal but slow diplomatic-bag route. The "bag" closed once a week and traveled overland and by sea, fastened to the messenger whose protection was the insignia of a silver greyhound, and diplomatic immunity. Once London decided to act, it would be logical for SIS in Istanbul to collect Volkov. The British might very well hustle Volkov into one of the Istanbul safe houses. The fat would be in the fire if Volkov then blew the whistle on the moles in

British intelligence. If SIS/Istanbul knew a case officer of superior rank was flying out from London, they might delay action. Then Volkov would continue to follow his Soviet embassy routine.

Philby reported to the Chief next day. He had searched through files, he said. Nothing seemed to fit this man. The case was potentially very harmful to Soviet espionage and enormously valuable to SIS. Philby did not wish to downgrade the qualifications of Englishmen on the spot, but Konstantin Volkov needed to be handled with great delicacy. One clumsy move, and either the Soviets or the Turkish authorities might intervene. The trick would be to get Volkov and his wife into a safe house. A preliminary debriefing there would reveal if there was any need for urgent action. He should then be slipped out of Turkey to Egypt, the nearest British-held territory.

The Chief jumped at the idea that someone fully briefed on the case should take control. Philby had overdone the self-effacement, however. In his anxiety to avoid appearing over-eager, Philby hinted at the dispatch to Istanbul of a case-hardened senior officer. The Chief said he'd been thinking the same thing. He proposed the director of Mideast Security Intelligence, Douglas Roberts, who was home on leave from Cairo. Roberts spoke fluent Russian, had worked closely with the Turkish secret service, and would be ideal for the always delicate task of throwing the harness over a defector.

Philby was confronted now with the hair-raising prospect of Volkov delivering the goods on his shopping list to Roberts, who would see at once, in what promised to be a formidable "product," the name, sticking up like a sore thumb, of H. A. R. Philby, Esquire.

Philby, nimble-witted and familiar with SIS nooks and crannies in the way that a small, scheming schoolboy knows where naughty uncles hide the evidence of their weaknesses, set to work to knock Roberts out of the running. Nowhere in his later confession was this apparent. Instead, Roberts, as if by some miracle, is seen suddenly discovering "an unconquerable distaste for flying." Roberts sailed back to Cairo a week later. Philby was left free to take direct action. A KGB-approved version of events, by Philby, claimed: "I had originally hoped I could so maneuver the discussion with the Chief that he himself would suggest my flying to Istanbul." This was Philby's style: planting ideas that spurred others into action, manipulating others to risk their lives, then betraying the idealists as naive children. Only during reexamination of the Corby Case did the totality of Philby's betrayals, the cold-blooded treachery leading to mass murder, begin to become clear at this stage. But Philby was careful not to betray others who shared his devotion to Moscow. Thus he skirted around his consultations, during this critical moment before he sent himself to Turkey: "I said, in view of [Roberts's] defection, I could only suggest I should go out in his place. . . . With obvious relief, the Chief agreed."

Three days' delay followed: delay that provided sundry SMERSH thugs with time to prepare Volkov's murder and his wife's subsequent execution by firing squad. Some of the delay was secured through the SIS coding section after Philby professed ignorance of coding procedures. This entailed the services of an expert to instruct Philby on certain complex measures by which onetime cipher pads can be made impregnable. Philby won further delay by pretending to brief his deputy on the section's workload. Then, when he finally did leave, on a Tuesday, it was for Cairo.

Why Cairo? Well, the SIS station chief in Istanbul had not yet been let into the secret of Volkov's proposed defection, which Volkov had confided to a British embassy official with no SIS connections. There was no love lost between SIS and these untainted diplomats. So Philby brightly offered to steer himself through Cairo, the Mideast regional headquarters covering, among other places, Turkey. This would involve making a kowtow to the regional chief and thus serve diplomatic ends, ensuring no hard feelings in Istanbul. It also gave Philby another twenty-four hours' delay that, with the Devil's own luck, he stretched into a further day and night of delay, for the plane to Cairo was diverted to Tunis by a storm. It then refueled in Malta. When it reached Cairo, there was no time for Philby to complete his business there and continue on to Turkey by the connecting flight. Looking suitably chagrined, he wasted another few hours with another SIS officer.

It was Friday when he landed in Istanbul. He had passed most of the week dawdling, yet giving the impression of a professional case officer in a hurry. In his other manifestation as a foreign correspondent, Philby knew that he would have been hounded by editors' cables; and that if his explanations were unsatisfactory, and were not followed by results, he would be, by the week's end, fired from his newspaper.

But for Philby in this diplomatic guise, the weekend began very comfortingly. He was met at the airport by the station chief, who showed a proper sense of priority and took him home for a stiff drink. Philby filled him in with London gossip. Then, to keep the Foreign Office happy, the pair sauntered off to see the minister at the British embassy, Knox Helm, known to be stuffy about status and protocol. Helm was much put out by Philby's explanation of why he was there, and insisted that the ambassador must be consulted. Ambassadors being busy people, the consultation would have to take place the next day.

Another twenty-four hours for SMERSH.

The following morning Knox Helm saw the ambassador, Sir Maurice Peterson, then returned to Philby with further cause for annoyance. Philby had failed to mention that he knew Peterson already. In any case, today being Saturday, it would be best all round if Philby would delay seeing the ambassador until tomorrow at the ambassador's Sunday cruise on the *Mahouk*, the ambassadorial yacht. This was most agreeable to Philby, who spent another evening enjoying embassy hospitality—all chargeable, of course, to British taxpayers slogging through their first month of postwar bankruptcy.

Ambassador Peterson attended to his slightly seasick guests that Sunday morning on board the *Mahouk*, a flat-bottomed riverboat built for the gentle Nile and now rolling unevenly in the heaving waters of Marmara. After a queasy lunch, the ambassador still had not opened up the topic of Volkov. Philby waited for guests to take a swim and then murmured politely that he believed Sir Maurice had some reservations about the plans he had brought from London. What plans? asked the ambassador, looking blank.

Nothing had been done to prepare Ambassador Peterson. Philby was granted another delay. He undertook to brief Sir Maurice. The next question from the diplomat was one of protocol: Had SIS informed the Foreign Office in London? Philby must have been tempted to answer no, with the chance of having to dawdle all the way back to London on this new errand. Unfortunately for Philby and Moscow Center, however, the answer had to be yes. Philby had actually delivered a letter from the Foreign Office to Knox Helm requesting the ambassador's help. Evidently, Helm had not shown the letter to Sir Maurice, who told Philby that nothing more need be discussed: "Go ahead."

Time had run out. Or so it seemed. On Sunday evening Philby finally got around to discussing with others the procedure for putting Volkov in the bag. Philby was not about to simplify matters with a straightforward plan. He offered, with the grave courtesy that a man from head office must display to the fellows on the spot, a number of options. Should the Turks be involved? If so, to what extent? Or was there too great a danger that someone in the Turkish secret police would tip off the Russians? The needless debate swung to and fro. When it appeared to be settling on a definite course of action, Philby set it swinging again. By the early hours of Monday morning, the embassy men were proposing what Philby had wanted all along. Before *any* decision was made about how to handle Volkov, the would-be defector should be put into contact with Philby; only in this way could the British find out his particular circumstances— how much freedom he had to leave the embassy, what hours he worked, where he lived with his wife. . . .

One more postponement was available to Philby. He had been instructed in London to make use of a British embassy first secretary, John Read, who spoke Russian. This meant explaining to Read what was about to happen. Philby spent an enjoyable Monday morning with him, spelling out the situation at prodigious length. Now all that remained was to enlist the services of the British consulate-general officer who had been approached in the first instance by Volkov—*twenty days earlier.*

If SMERSH had failed by now to get its act together, after nearly three weeks of continued delay, then Philby would have thought Moscow Center and the cause scarcely worth the trouble. He ate a hearty lunch, speculating to himself on the expression on the face of John Read if worse should come to worst: if Volkov proved to be still in circulation and able to keep an appointment that afternoon with John Read. It had to be that afternoon. Any further delay might someday turn suspicion on Philby. Yet if the meeting did take place, there would be something more substantial than suspicion—there would be Konstantin Volkov naming the Soviet spies circulating freely among John Read's closest colleagues— Philby among them.

No such meeting was held. Volkov had vanished into thin air. Attempts to reach him failed. Once someone in the Soviet consular office answered his telephone and claimed that *he* was Volkov, but the British diplomat who had made the call stated firmly that he was very familiar with Volkov's voice and that the voice he had heard was not it. Another call was answered with the message "Volkov's in Moscow." Finally someone from the British embassy called formally upon the Russians and was told that nobody in the Soviet mission had ever heard the name Volkov.

Much later, reports trickled through to London that Volkov had been seen at the Istanbul airport, strapped to a stretcher, being loaded into a Soviet aircraft. Later still, an account reached the outside world of Volkov's wife's execution by SMERSH.

Philby, in an extended Russian version of his memoir, published in 1981, omitted some details related here. He did not mention that Volkov was bargaining for prize money, the equivalent of about $100,000 in those days, in exchange for the address and the key to the box where he had deposited documents disclosing all he knew about Moscow Center's operations and who served Soviet intelligence inside Western security agencies. The existence of Volkov's box was one of Philby's nightmares.

Philby emerges from all versions of the episode as considerably less than heroic. Nearly forty years later, it was revealed that Volkov had never been about to finger Philby at all. At first it seemed that carelessness in translation or interpretation had given the impression that the Soviet mole was in MI6, Philby's crowd. With the new insight, Volkov was seen to have been talking about "an acting chief of a department of the British counterintelligence directorate." This was MI5.

The revised version first came from Gouzenko, who was shown the relevant passage in the original Russian written by Volkov when he had opened negotiations with the British in Istanbul.

But Gouzenko did not see Volkov's shopping list until 1966. Why not earlier? Volkov had handed it over to a Russian-speaking British diplomat. Why was the disparity never noticed? Even allowing for the absence of distrust in those clubbish days, why did SIS never take seriously Volkov's claims to know Soviet agents in the secret services?

The failure to take Volkov's accusations seriously was partly because Istanbul in those days was a choke point for Jewish refugees trying to reach Palestine. "It colors the views of our people [the Foreign Office] excessively," said Churchill. The prevention of any large Jewish migration to Palestine occupied the military and the Foreign Office, it sometimes seemed, more than Hitler. Efforts were made to stop the Jewish treks, between 1939 and 1945, by diplomacy, deportation, and the interception of ships carrying illegal immigrants. The exodus *after* the war represented the pitiful remnants from Nazi death camps. Still, British diplomats in Turkey and the surrounding region devoted a great deal of time to asking that the refugee traffic to Palestine be stopped. When the *Salvador* was sunk in Turkish waters with the loss of two hundred Jewish lives in 1940, the chief of the British Foreign Office refugee department wrote that the event was "an opportune disaster." Philby, with his special and personal knowledge of British Arabists, knew very well the preoccupation of the Foreign Office and SIME (Security Intelligence/Middle East). He had an advantage over the general public. Only by the 1980s did much of the truth about this fatal bias emerge from declassified records.

President Truman had caught a whiff of British preoccupations in the early stages of the Corby Case. The man who virtually ran the British Foreign Office throughout the war, Alexander George Montagu Cadogan, suddenly recommended that a dragnet be put out for Soviet agents, following Gouzenko's revelations. It seemed an about-face. The British had previously wanted to move cautiously against PRIMROSE and proceed from there to tail other Soviet contacts. Then Cadogan had taken an opposite stand and expressed the strongest feelings that "publicity attendant on the arrests [of Soviet agents] will *not* have an adverse effect on Soviet policy towards the Americans."

Cadogan's turnaround followed Soviet support for the Jewish underground, smuggling refugees through the British blockade into Palestine. Stalin put his conspiratorial powers behind the movement for establishing Israel, not from any sympathy for the Jews, but to embarrass the British at a time when they were blocking some of his moves in Eastern Europe. Cadogan's position was expressed early in World War II, when, resisting offers of help from Zionist agencies, he wrote, "Jew control of British propaganda would be a disaster." Six years later, Cadogan's strong line on the Corby Case was linked with the British foreign secretary's anger over Soviet foreign policy. Cadogan "had become exasperated at Molotov's behavior at the Council of Foreign Ministers," declared Mackenzie King, referring to Molotov's proclamation of Soviet support for a future Israel.

•   •   •

In this atmosphere, a would-be Russian defector seemed irrelevant to British concerns when money was represented as being his motive and he talked wildly about sensational disclosures. Volkov made a fatal mistake in requesting that negotiations should be conducted through the secure diplomatic bag, because the result was that his proposals landed on Philby's desk, were delayed, and blocked from becoming more widely known.

After Philby's cold-blooded disposal of Volkov, he had to deal with Gouzenko. Philby saw that Gouzenko presented a greater potential danger than Volkov, but the SIS officer dared not leave his London office again until his own tracks were covered.

What action did Philby take? He was questioned on this, in the interrogations preceding his escape into Russia. But nothing was available from the files, even thirty-eight years later. Hearsay evidence in the 1980s could pass unchallenged. And the London files on Gouzenko were missing. Presumably, all these records would between them indicate the steps Philby took to make sure that, if Gouzenko could not be killed, he could be discredited.

Hearsay evidence made it seem, instead, that Dick Ellis interfered in the Corby Case, allowing Soviet penetrations to continue. Ellis's accusers, after he himself was dead, tried to show that he took up the super-secret part of Gouzenko's interrogation and made sure it led nowhere. Gouzenko had gone through questioning by Canadian security specialists, but they had left to the British the task of pursuing Gouzenko's specific charges regarding Soviet moles in British intelligence.

"Whoever that British interrogator was," Gouzenko would later insist, "was himself working for the Russians, because when I finally saw his reports on my alleged statements, they were nonsense, and distorted to make me look an idiot, greedy for fame and money." But the mysterious interrogator had never identified himself to Gouzenko.

Philby became MI6 chief in Turkey, the year after he suppressed Volkov. In 1949, he took up the Washington post, making frequent journeys to Canada. He persuaded his Ottawa cronies to try to launch their own external-affairs intelligence service. This, he suggested disarmingly, would be best structured by himself. He was, after all, the expert in these matters. Had they succeeded, Moscow Center would have controlled an organ-

ization legitimately collecting secret intelligence from its ABC allies.*
Fortunately, the RCMP insisted, at that time, on running its own security
service. Philby had to be content with knowing that he was safe from
any suspicion, and that he was in a position to help those busy with
emasculating Gouzenko as a source of information on Soviet espionage.

*This was not as outlandish as it first seemed. Communist China used such a device to control
the Indonesia foreign office: and President Sukarno was induced, in 1964, to declare a "confrontation
war" against Malaysia. It was China's second attempt to destabilize the Malay states by waging
unconventional warfare. The first was the jungle war waged by Chinese guerrillas. The second was
a war conducted through a third government whose foreign-intelligence service was virtually run
from Peking.

THE POWER OF SECRECY

TWENTY-EIGHT

GOUZENKO'S
TWO <u>ELLIS</u> AND
THE RED ORCHESTRA

Someone from British SIS did see Gouzenko early in 1946, and discussed the Russian mole in London codenamed ELLI. Gouzenko stuck to this story in 1981 when it was pointed out that the SIS man could not conceal Gouzenko's statements about moles because already this testimony had been reported through men of probity like Mackenzie King. "But Mackenzie King's men were not interested," retorted Gouzenko. "It was only when someone I knew as 'a gentleman from England' arrived that I got full and undivided attention on the subject of Russian double agents. And it was to this man alone that I divulged information I felt was especially sensitive."

It did not at first occur to Gouzenko that he had talked to the very Soviet mole he feared, when he confided to "the gentleman from England" in 1946. He had opened up the possibilities of RIS agents within Western security when he testified to the royal commission and briefly discussed the possibility of there being two double agents codenamed ELLI. But that part of his evidence was kept out of the published commission report. Gouzenko assumed there was good reason for this, and that investigations were proceeding. He had been reassured by Stephenson, and knew nothing about the termination of BSC.

By 1952, however, more than bemused by events, he had appeared before one committee of inquiry after another in Washington and Ottawa. He was regarded as an interesting source on matters already disclosed in the commission report. But he was not encouraged to talk about his chief preoccupation, that the RIS had as its chief target *glavni protivnik*, the main enemy, the Western intelligence agencies. To his RCMP contacts, he seemed obsessive in insisting that the RIS was not the bungling, inexperienced service depicted in spy fiction. He drew up a detailed plan to lure defectors from the Soviet services. He said the best source of information about extensive RIS operations was those inside the RIS, which was almost impossible to penetrate by outside agents. RIS defectors should be encouraged by five guarantees—of friendly protection, immediate citizenship, financial support, meaningful employment, and some form of recognition for their services.

Gouzenko's "five-point plan" coincided with subterranean rumblings among the Western intelligence agencies. Maclean and Burgess had escaped. Philby had been recalled from Washington and was undergoing intermittent interrogation that would lead nowhere. Very belatedly, Gouzenko was asked by the RCMP to recall his earlier allegations about Russian double agents.

He wrote on May 6, 1952, to Superintendent George McClellan (soon to become Canada's security chief, but at the time making inquiries on behalf of U.S. and British security): "At the very first moment when I gave Canadian authorities information from a great number of other agents . . . I repeated just what I had heard from cipher clerk Kulakov [who] had just come from Moscow where he was working in the cipher branch of Intelligence HQ." Gouzenko then dealt with other native-born U.S. and British agents serving Moscow and continued:

I was not told *but saw the telegram myself* concerning this person [a Soviet agent in MI5]. And then as second confirmation I was told by Lieut. Lubimov. The telegram I saw in Moscow during the latter part of 1942 or the beginning of 1943 dealt with a contact through a *dubok* [hiding-place] with the man from MI5. . . . [Later] Zabotin [the chief of the GRANT network] in Ottawa received from Moscow a warning that a representative of British 'greens' [counterintelligence] was to arrive to help the RCMP strengthen work against Soviet agents.

Zabotin was given a detailed list of special precautions against this British countermove.

Gouzenko concluded his lengthy statement with a summary of what he believed had gone wrong, as McClellan had requested: "The first mistake was that the task of finding the agent was given to MI5 itself. . . . If an agent is so powerful and has influence, he could make such investigations more complicated and fruitless. My humble suggestion is (and I think it is not too late yet) to entrust this job to some people outside MI5. . . . If, during the last six years, British authorities had established a twenty-four-hour watch, month after month, on the movements of members of the Soviet embassy—a real check, not just token—they would have not just one but dozens of agents in their hands by now."

This Gouzenko letter was never removed from its top-secret classification. No action was taken on it in London. Again, the nagging fears multiplied with the passage of time because, as Gouzenko himself had written, an agent of power and influence at the top could suppress precisely the kinds of informed concern he was expressing. If it is remembered that Gouzenko wrote of this concern in 1952, when Philby still had another eleven years' life ahead as a top Soviet mole, and at a time when the whole idea of treachery *inside* Western intelligence was unthinkable, it becomes apparent that Gouzenko was still a man of acute perceptions, despite living in relative isolation. None of his ideas at the time could have been picked up from published literature on espionage.

He contacted Stephenson to further voice his apprehensions. The man who had saved his life stirred up the RCMP once more, and again discussed the puzzle with the FBI. Already, some of the CIA's counterintelligence experts were convinced that Gouzenko's worries were well founded.

But though Gouzenko might win individual support from a retired intelligence chief like Stephenson, he was still tightly ringed by the peacetime bureaucracy. He would have to wait another two years, until 1954, to get a serious hearing. By then, the evidence of betrayal was accumulating too rapidly to be ignored. By then, Gouzenko might have been dead, for already an assassin had been assigned by the RIS to get rid of him. The assassin would later surrender to the RCMP after being activated by Moscow. Gouzenko depended on the security agencies for his life and found it difficult to circumvent bureaucratic channels, even though he suspected his own enemies used the same channels to stifle his protests. It was a catch-22 situation.

Some American and Canadian counterintelligence men at the top knew by now that Gouzenko had not exaggerated in depicting the RIS as an organization with a long history of burrowing into the key bureaucracies of the West. Not only was the evidence available through BRIDE/VANOSA "cryptops" and Nazi files; it was implicit in the odd failures in liaison and in the attempts by SIS/London to bury what was known now about Red Orchestra* operations in England.

Mrs. Brewer—the disguised GRU colonel Ruth Kuczynski, who had run Red Orchestra networks in Britain—had been appointed by the "Grand Chef" of the Red Orchestra, Leopold Trepper. One of Hitler's aides would later say that Trepper cost the lives of 200,000 German soldiers by his wartime operations in Nazi-held Europe. But the question now was: How much damage had Trepper's Red Orchestra inflicted on the West? Trepper was fighting for Stalin, whose enemies were first the Atlantic allies, and then Hitler's Germany. The war against Hitler had been only an interruption of Lenin's "neither war nor peace" operations against the Soviets' capitalist enemies. Nevertheless, Trepper had champions in the West who would eventually extract him from Soviet control and convey him to Israel where he proved "an intelligence bonanza"— illustrating precisely Gouzenko's arguments about RIS defectors and also the futility of adopting a McCarthy-like attitude to sinners who might, with encouragement, confess all.

Trepper was "papered" before the war with a Canadian passport taken, as was the custom, from a man killed in Spain's civil war. He arrived in Belgium to tighten control of Russian networks and recruit new agents and saboteurs, using the identity of Adam Mikler of Quebec, a businessman setting up a chain of European stores as owner of the Foreign Excellent Raincoat Company. His "raincoats" sheltered his agents, posing as shareholders, business managers, and salesmen. His Polish-born wife used a Canadian passport issued to a member of the Dutch Communist party under a false name. Their son, traveling on her passport as Ed Mikler of 131 rue St. Louis, Quebec City, had in fact been born in Moscow.

Belgium, it became apparent from postwar inquiries, had been a training ground for Red Army GRU intelligence officers in the 1930s, as well as a depot for agents and recruits. Canada was the chief source of their falsified documents.

Once again, Gouzenko's warnings were being more than fully justified. The wholesale doctoring of Canadian papers indicated collusion in

---

*Originally known as "Rote Kapelle," the codename was applied by Nazi counterintelligence to a single element of World War II Soviet espionage against Germany. It was distended to encompass *all* Soviet espionage in Western Europe from 1936 to 1945, and is here used in that sense.

Ottawa. The difficulty in piecing together events before a world war that had destroyed so much of Western Europe, including police records, was made even more complex by the extraordinary lengths to which a man like Trepper went to cover his tracks. He had mingled in Paris with the family of Dick Ellis's White Russian wife, using the name Herbst of German intelligence. Moreover, Trepper had entered France as Sommer, a Swiss businessman, and he left France as Majeris, a Yugoslav clothier. While in Paris, he managed also to supervise the local branch of the Foreign Excellent Raincoat Company in his other guise as Adam Mikler. Many of his movements remained obscure until, in his true persona of Leopold Trepper, he escaped Soviet control in 1973, and finished up in Israel, where he died in 1982.

As a free man, Trepper helped bring some pieces together. Soviet intelligence had targeted the British intelligence services since the 1920s, and until World War II gave priority to the penetration of American and British centers of influence. Networks had been run from Brussels and Paris into Britain. Soviet agents had thrown their energies behind the British war effort against Hitler only *after* the Nazi invasion of Russia. Before then, their job had been to sabotage that effort and report on pro-Nazi factions in Britain. The name Red Orchestra had originated with Nazi security services after the 1941 invasion of Russia. (It is used here for convenience to describe Soviet operations under "Uncle" Trepper.) From 1940 to 1942, Trepper commanded seven Soviet networks, each active in its own field and subordinate to its own chief, who reported to Trepper. In 1942, Trepper was betrayed in France. He pretended to collaborate with his German captors, and then escaped. He stayed underground in Paris until the city's liberation, and then he returned to Moscow. For his trouble, he was sent to a Siberian work camp. Stalin could not believe Trepper had not really collaborated with the Nazis. "One must never forget," Trepper said later, "that Stalin had worked hand-in-glove with the Nazi intelligence agencies, which meant I kept in close contact with Nazi agents right up to 1941. Stalin found that suspicious. He expected everyone to be as treacherous as he was." Khrushchev, when he replaced Stalin, rehabilitated Trepper, who returned to his native Poland in the mid-1950s. There, he challenged the Polish Communist government for its anti-Semitic policies. His two sons launched hunger strikes on behalf of Jews. Trepper's career had taken a sudden turn, and he was now fighting for his fellow Jews. Sympathizers in Britain put such pressure on Warsaw that the old man was finally allowed to leave in 1973. He settled in Israel, where he died at the age of seventy-seven, after providing invaluable firsthand information on the RIS. Not the least valuable, in view of the missing records, was his account of the White Russian exiles in Paris and the dangerous game they had sometimes played between Soviet and German intelligence.

An old spymaster who crosses the lines, like "Uncle" Trepper, is the bane of moles, long-term agents, "sleepers," and their controllers. The Soviets never know what small and ancient tidbit will provide enemies with the missing piece in a jigsaw, as the veteran searches his memory under the tactful prompting of his new friends. Trepper had remembered that one of his most resourceful agents was codenamed GISEL—the same name used by Moscow Center for the Ottawa spy ring and already disclosed by Gouzenko. GISEL was also a codename recurring in RIS traffic intercepted by BRIDE/VANOSA.

So now there were several GISELs. The one in Switzerland was Marie Josefovna Poliakova. Like Gouzenko when he was a bright young student, she had been picked out by party talent-spotters who sent her, at twenty-one, to the Higher Intelligence School on Arbatskaya Ploschad in Moscow. She had spent the 1930s as an "illegal resident" in Germany, Belgium, France, and Switzerland, serving the GRU operations technical-intelligence unit. During World War II she had been acting chief of a special GRU section and at one time recruited agents for the Far East through New York. She had moved through wartime Nazi Germany while organizing the legendary Lucy Ring, and was Moscow Center's representative who met Leopold Trepper when he made his ill-advised journey back to Russia, and jail.

But why would Moscow Center give her the cryptonym GISEL when she could be confused with others?

The answer would demolish the arguments used to ridicule Gouzenko's claims that there had been two ELLIS. The ridicule was readily swallowed because there had been a widespread underestimation of RIS capabilities. An official CIA report on the Red Orchestra described "a structure built too late and in haste . . . only some of the parts skillfully formed and adequately tested . . . overloaded, bound to come tumbling down." This may have been true to the extent, as the CIA believed, that "the sheer bulk of intelligence traffic became a hazard in itself" during the war and confused the Moscow Center analysts. Yet the constant purges within the RIS also rectified its failings. Now, some of the new RIS methods were becoming known. Gouzenko's claims seemed less melodramatic.

The far-flung networks of RIS telegraphists and secret transmitters were becoming familiar to Western monitors. The skills of the Soviet telegraphists were recognized as formidable. "Burst transmissions" of ultra-high-speed Morse were technically within reach. Clandestine operators were locked into their own Moscow controllers, who divided the world into regions. Each agent reported from his own region to the regional director. There was no possibility of crossed lines. Cryptonyms were used on the basis of brevity and ease of transmission. They were often duplicated, *not* within a geographical region, but from one region to another. GISEL in Switzerland was handled quite independently of GISEL somewhere in another region.

Now Gouzenko's insistence that there were two ELLIs made sense: one in Canada, already uncovered, and another in London. ELLI was a group of letters easily transmitted.

Gouzenko had talked about a Soviet agent, identified as Hermina Rabinowitz of the International Labor Office in Montreal, taking orders from GISEL. Investigators had assumed this meant GRU military intelligence command. It proved instead to be the Swiss GISEL: confusing to anyone trying to break Soviet secrets, but perfectly clear to Moscow Center. Hermina had obtained funds for spies in North America through the acting Soviet consul in New York, Pavel Mikhailov, who had his own separate espionage ring—quite apart from Yakovlev, whose "hospital" handled the Rosenberg papers and other atom-spy products.

The evidence was mounting.

REPUTATION AND
DISINFORMATION

> The Germans have a good intelligence corps. But look what a narrow base they have: Germans. In England—Germans. In America—Germans. Even in Japan—Germans! Suppose there was war tomorrow, all these Germans would be in a concentration camp the first day and the whole of German intelligence would fly apart in soap bubbles. . . . Anybody can be a Soviet agent, as you have already learned: English, Italians, Eskimos and even millionaires.

Thus speaks a Soviet RIS instructor in Igor Gouzenko's first novel, *The Fall of a Titan*.

He had finally completed his long novel. It revealed the interplay between Soviet citizens and the ruling bureaucrats, rather as if Tolstoy were chronicling a drama of life under Stalin instead of under the czars. His characters were rich and subtly drawn. Several stories were woven through the main plot concerning the Soviet bureaucracy's resolve to make use of the popular writer Mikhail Gorin, "the conscience of the people."

Gorin at first is deceived by flattery. His seducers are ambitious academics. His family becomes caught up in the conspiracy. Beautiful young women are inspired, fall in love, suffer betrayal. Some are sent to labor camps. The author moves into his contrasting settings with confidence, leading to the climax: the murder of Gorin, who has become increasingly intractable; and the final ceremony when the ashes of Gorin are immured in the dark red walls of the Kremlin while Stalin salutes and Molotov pays cynical tribute to "our companion in arms, friend of Lenin and Stalin, founder of Socialist literature. . . . Great and fertile was the friendship of the two Titans working on the one patriotic effort. . . ." The dreadful joke is that Gorin has become Stalin's enemy. But safely dead, he can be reconstituted, and his popular works made to serve the party.

This was the reality, Gouzenko believed, behind George Orwell's anti-utopian novel, *1984*. In that novel, published in 1949, Orwell had anticipated a time when the supreme bureaucracy would rewrite history to suit itself, purging newspaper files, reprinting material to alter the daily chronicling of history, to fix the image of Party infallibility.

Gouzenko had experienced all this in real life. He had seen how the dictators depended upon the collaboration of the bureaucrats. In his mind, the structure of bureaucratic life lent itself to the fascist methods of the Communist party. He had also seen that within democratic societies, the bureaucracy became the instrument of a ruling party's resolve to make facts fit policy.

In 1950, he supported his family by writing and by selling his paintings; he had developed his artistic talents to a professional level. (It would be another eight years before the ruling Liberal party in Canada was overturned by a Conservative leader, John Diefenbaker, who promptly decided that his new government should award Gouzenko with a pension of $500 a month. "It is utterly shameful," said Diefenbaker, "that this courageous Russian should have been left to struggle alone in a strange, difficult environment. It's no wonder he feels the West *must* understand the need for a settled policy toward defectors who have acted from conviction.")

Gouzenko's enemies were depicting him as a drunk who had squandered "something like $7 million." The truth—that he could not drink alcohol for medical reasons, and that his income was so modest it could not be taxed—was not acknowledged. When he was accused of having *The Fall of a Titan* ghostwritten, he showed the elaborate series of "architectural drawings" with which he had planned the book. Through these scenes, he had moved his characters, each one drawn and identified, so that he knew at a glance where the figments of his imagination might be at any stage in the writing of each chapter.

Some of his frustration seemed to come out in the words of one character: "I feel myself a pauper, a man spiritually robbed. I have found only emptiness; I am in a frightful wilderness! Right now I want to cry out to the whole world: 'Give me a reason for living . . . .' Do you hear the frightful moaning? It's everywhere—it's in us and around us. That's the world writhing in inexpressible pain. They're tearing the soul out of the earth with the bloody forceps of hate. . . . Deprived of love, mankind is becoming hardened like a faraway planet forgotten by the sun."

But the real irony in this passage becomes clear to the reader only later, when the speaker proves to be the NKVD agent instructed to trick the writer Gorin into betraying his true disenchantment with communism. The NKVD agent has taken this opportunity, as a well-informed scholar, to voice his own real feelings about the Party.

Gouzenko's story shows Orwellian insight. It ends on a note of hope. Here he is identifying with the three survivors: a man, his wife, and their baby Andrei. "The thin white clouds parted for an instant. . . . The sun shone—springlike, friendly, long wished for. Its strong caressing rays struck the three people on the hill, burned their outline in gold and fused the river in front of them. Little Andrei tore himself away from the mother's breast and, turning toward the sun, extended his arms to it. Then he looked into his little palms—had he caught it?"

When Gouzenko finally published his novel in 1954, the ruling Liberals still directed that there should be no financial reward for "a turncoat mentality." Luckily for the Gouzenkos, this hardhearted attitude did not infect the RCMP, which continued to keep a watchful eye on them.

Meanwhile, Gouzenko's credibility seemed on the rise among both Canadian and U.S. security agencies. He was invited to give secret testimony in 1954 to a U.S. Senate subcommittee on internal security. But obstacles were put in the way. British security seemed to be discouraging Gouzenko's appearance on the grounds that it might hurt ongoing investigations. These objections came through the grapevine; the FBI, and the CIA's counterintelligence chief, James Angleton, had grave doubts about their origin. Had they come from a mole in British intelligence?

Angleton was worried by the dilatory action taken against Kim Philby: the Soviet mole had been put through a secret SIS "trial" conducted by the Chief and a tough-minded queen's counsellor, Helenus Milmo. Philby survived recurrent questioning between 1952 and 1955. When the dean of inquisitors, Jim Skardon, took up the interrogation, Philby later described the ordeal at the hands of "unquestionably the trickiest cross-examiner I ever met. . . . Skardon was scrupulously correct, his manner verging on the exquisite; nothing could have been more flattering than the cozy warmth of his interviews."*

*For once, a KGB general and a CIA chief agreed. Allen Dulles commented: "The very existence of a specialist in government employ like Skardon, who is called in to confront and 'break' a special category of high-level traitors and turncoats, is a phenomenon of the times in which we live." *Great True Spy Stories* (New York: Ballantine Books, 1982).

But even Skardon's snake-eyed courtesy was no match for Philby's suave denials of any wrongdoing. The British Foreign Office recommended the spy to the *Observer* and the *Economist* of London as a likely chap to be their foreign correspondent in the Middle East. There he remained from 1956 to 1963, still feeding intelligence to SIS that later proved to be chickenfeed, meanwhile pumping the real stuff to Moscow Center.

Philby was still in a position to damage Gouzenko. He knew he was under scrutiny, but he could still save the Soviet's second ELLI within SIS by laying a trail of false clues in the direction of someone that Moscow Center would happily destroy anyway.

Rivalry between MI5 and MI6, however, worked to Gouzenko's advantage. Philby's old service, MI6, failed to prevent MI5's move to help the FBI put Gouzenko before the Washington subcommittee on internal security. "A defector is like a vintage wine; the first pressing is the best," a counterintelligence officer had once said. MI6 had tried to show that after an entire series of pressings Gouzenko would prove pretty third-rate stuff for the connoisseur.

As a result of Gouzenko's secret testimony, a new series of investigations started. A general term for them was Operation Featherbed, from "birds of a feather flock together." This sounded uncomfortably like McCarthyism's charges of guilt by association.

But the tide of opinion had turned against McCarthy after a portly sixty-three-year-old Republican, Joseph N. Welch, demolished the senator before a nationwide audience. Welch, the U.S. Army's special counsel, had grown angry listening to an account of the subcommittee's hunt for subversives among employees of the Army Signal Corps. His words of contempt became a refrain: "Until this moment, Senator, I think I never really gauged your cruelty or your recklessness," he said at one point. Then: "I like to think I am a gentle man, but your forgiveness will have to come from someone other than me." And finally, when McCarthy's bullying led to a fatal stumble, Welch's words would ring through America for many years to come: "Have you no sense of decency, sir, at long last? Have you no sense of decency?"

The end of McCarthy was a triumph for decency. The panic button had been hit. American emotions had exploded. Now, the destructive effects of the witch-hunts, the blacklists, and the huge diversion of FBI manpower were becoming the stuff of drama.* A sense of the fragility of America was still part of every citizen's heritage, and all had been required to close ranks in the face of the threat defined by Senator McCarthy. The House Un-American Activities Committee (HUAC) hearings were only theater, like the ritual removal of a condemned soldier's buttons. The real issue became HUAC itself. The Constitution gave it no license to trample on the freedoms of any American. Most commentators agreed with the view that "every witness who cooperated enhanced its illegitimate authority." As a result, there were "no villains and no heroes—only victims."

This made it difficult to convince decent Americans, especially those among the victims, that there were nevertheless sound reasons for action against Soviet subversion. Polltakers in August 1954 recorded a steep decline in support for Senator McCarthy: about 22 percent of adult Americans revised their opinion of McCarthy downward, and 24 million Americans were said to regard him with distaste.** Hostility rubbed off on FBI and CIA counterintelligence officers, and the revulsion from McCarthyism spread into Canada and Britain, helping in the coverup of real traitors.

Stephenson tried to redress the balance. He had not made a public appearance since before World War II, when he had warned against Hitler and Nazi Germany's preparations for war. "I was called, for my pains, a warmonger." On May 31, 1954, he chose a publishers' conference in Canada to affirm the importance of a free press, the need "to keep up a flow of accurate, timely information." Totalitarian states controlled information, and it was difficult sometimes for newsmen to get at the truth. So that democracy could defend itself against secret dangers, the first line of security was information gathered by the media—or, if that failed, by the intelligence experts. The Soviets had been waging a secret war, about which the West was as uninformed as it had been about Hitler's secret preparations.

*David Caute's *The Great Fear* is perhaps the best contemporary account.

**In 1950, according to Gallup polls, 50 percent of Americans had been favorably disposed toward McCarthy; only 29 percent expressed disapproval.

Stephenson disclosed for the first time, but with such care that the reference passed unnoticed, the breaking of wartime codes. He was speaking long before the public disclosures about ULTRA or the BRIDE/VANOSA "cryptops," and so his comments were cryptic. The interpretation of enemy coded traffic, he said, was vital to success in secret warfare.

He added, however, a warning against secret knowledge. The known facts about the Soviet Union were that "at the summit are fourteen men who live in a state of power and luxury not excelled by any tyrants in the history of mankind. Their henchmen are given special privileges far beyond the ordinary, including the secret power to impose death. . . ."

It was this secret power, and its powerful eroticism, that most troubled Stephenson. To resist it, the use of an equal and opposite secret power was a tempting idea. But the only safe counterweapon was freedom of ideas, freedom of expression, and a belief in the good sense of an informed citizenry.

Stephenson was challenging the RIS disinformation experts, while he was also refusing to endorse gestapo-like methods in the West. He took the view that Western strength lay in the absence of police controls.

He had spoken just as a "gestapo-versus-liberals" conflict approached a peak within the security services: a battle in which the reputations of men like Dick Ellis would get mangled.

CONFLICT IN THE WESTERN RANKS: "GESTAPO" versus "LIBERALS" or SPY vs. SPY vs. SPY

On one side of this conflict were the "gestapo-minded" counterintelligence officers, who were far from resembling Hitler's Gestapo, but who played into the hands of some critics by seeming to push their suspicions of Soviet penetration too far. They were disliked by the "liberals" in the secret-intelligence branches like MI6 and the CIA. The spycatchers were by nature disenchanted with the human race. Their profession obliged them to assume the worst. Their training was largely technical, with brilliant exceptions like the CIA's James Angleton—but Angleton had moved over to counterintelligence from an academic background. This "cross-fertilization" was in theory what secret-service chiefs on both sides of the Atlantic felt to be desirable.

Dick Ellis fell into the "liberals" category. He was not tied to institutional rigidities. As an SIS chief in Asia, after 1946, he saw "the power of the peasant" and glimpsed Mao's vision of millions of human atoms making an explosion of their own, shaking the world as much as nuclear bombs. The Fourth Arm had become the peasantry. Ellis was not popular among those who still believed that the way to deal with rebellious peasants was to beat sense into them. He preferred "to fight subversives but negotiate with honest patriots" who might have turned to communism in desperation. His critics thought in terms of sledgehammers.

Such a sledgehammer was the explosion of the second American hydrogen bomb, which ripped through Bikini atoll with the force of a thousand Hiroschima bombs, as the Afro-Asian nations gathered for a conference at the Indonesia hill town of Bandung in 1955.

Another American bomb, no larger than a ballpoint pen, set off a chain reaction at Bandung more damaging to American interests. It was slipped into the Air India airliner *Kashmir Princess*, chartered to fly Communist China's foreign minister to the first Third World conference at Bandung. The foreign minister still used the traditional English rendition of his name: Chou En-lai. Chou warned Hong Kong's British governor of a plot to sabotage the plane, alleging the bomb was to be planted by "counterrevolutionary forces" while the airliner refueled in the colony. The governor dismissed Chou's fears. The *Kashmir Princess* blew up over the Java Sea, and all the Communist Chinese delegates on board were killed. Chou, however, had prudently taken another route.

Chou made a speech playing on all the emotional issues. The Air India plane had been sabotaged, he said. India, then exercising enormous influence in Asia, had been victimized by the West. Western imperialists had conspired to stifle China's voice at its first appearance in neutral territory. The speech, Dick Ellis correctly predicted, would help swing Indonesia into China's camp. Meanwhile, Ellis's successors tried to repair some of the damage by searching the seabed with navy divers. They recovered evidence that the pencil-bomb came from the CIA through a Taiwan front.

The Bikini H-bomb introduced strontium-90 to the vocabulary of death. Chou knew how to exploit that, too. The test explosion dusted the Japanese trawler *Lucky Dragon-5*, whose fishermen faced death from cancer. Ralph Lapp, head of the U.S. Office of Naval Research nuclear branch, predicted that before the 1980s there would be enough radioactive material in the stratosphere from such tests to affect not just one ship's crew but the health of every living thing on earth. Communist propaganda replied that the victims of these bombs were always Afro-Asians because the white-faced minority regarded them as inferior. Chou echoed *The Thoughts of Mao*: No matter how powerful these new weapons, they could not prevail against the rising tide of the poor and the oppressed. It sounded like the announcement of a new version of the Fourth Arm, now sponsored by China—the colored races against the imperialist West.

But racism could divide the Communist camp, too. Gouzenko had always maintained that Russian racial arrogance would alienate Asian communism. It was a view shared by Dick Ellis, who had become an expert in Communist Chinese methods of guerrilla warfare in Malaysia. What both Gouzenko and Ellis understood was that a new form of secret Fourth Arm was evolving in Asia and that, despite its pretense of following Soviet ideological leadership, it would ultimately challenge the Soviet Union.

This rivalry began to become evident to a wider audience at about the time the Russians launched the first man-made space satellite, *Sputnik*, in 1957.* The Soviets were worried about Communist Asia's rival leaders and wanted to demonstrate their technological progress. In New Delhi, Khrushchev dazzled Nehru and a vast Indian audience with boasts about Soviet scientific achievements.

He wanted to woo India from China as divisions widened between Russia and China. Evidence of the coming split had been reported to Stephenson from inside China. He believed the tensions would lead to a break, but in Washington, the CIA's James Angleton insisted that talk of a split was deliberate Moscow propaganda.

The Soviets were in fact preoccupied with the creation of a Maoist Fourth Arm. Like the ABC Fourth Arm outlined in 1941–42, it mobilized unarmed and oppressed peasants for the overthrow of their well-armed masters.

The tiny pencil-bomb in the *Kashmir Princess* was politically more explosive than the new monster weapons. It was a model for the terrorism to come. Looking back from the 1980s, it was clear why the Soviets would wish to destroy those who, like Dick Ellis, perfectly understood the symbolism.

After 1950, Ellis was doing contract work for the Australian Security Intelligence Organization (ASIO), which felt itself deeply involved in the wars on its Asian doorstep. He did not know it, but a Washington dossier

---

*A year before the launching, in October 1956, nuclear physicist Niels Bohr went to see the president of the Soviet Academy of Science in the Ukraine. (Bohr had played a major role, of course, in producing the first atom bomb after his escape from Nazi control.) Bohr's Soviet friend described the projected satellite. "It will be called *Sputnik*," he said. "That is a joke. The word means 'fellow traveler.' " He gave details and a specific date for the launching, still a year away. There was derision among Stephenson's intelligence contacts when this was reported, though Stephenson took it seriously. On cue, *Sputnik* went up on October 5, 1957. "An outer-space raspberry," said Clare Booth Luce, "to a decade of American pretensions that the American way of life is a giltedged guarantee of our national security."

was being built up against him under the codename EMERTON, based upon what certain Nazis said about his prewar connections. Was he a KGB agent who, like other Stalinist operators, plugged into Hitler's prewar espionage agencies? In London, MI5 hardliners wanted to look at Ellis's record. They were refused access by his outraged MI6 colleagues.

The masters of deception had created a frightening world. Magic mirrors could distort or flatter, trapdoors were sprung under the unwary, puppets danced through false exits. The portrait of EMERTON twisted on its string. Was he a spy who, after years of danger, found more in common with his enemies? Was he like the soldier who shares so many hardships and dangers with those he fights that both finally share a secret contempt for civilians? Nazi German intelligence, spiced by Soviet agents, made Ellis out to be corruptible. It seemed strange to see a man's career threatened by old Nazi-Soviet intrigues.

Stranger still, nobody consulted Stephenson about the suspicions gathering around Ellis. General Donovan was still alive then, and nobody had questioned him either. Ellis's five years as Intrepid's deputy had been firmly fixed in the memories of both OSS and BSC directors, and Ellis's accusers could have looked to them for guidance. They did not. Perhaps they knew that a study of OSS and BSC files would have been more likely to support the view that Soviet intelligence had always wanted to get Stalin's old enemy, Dick Ellis. The opportunity arose, as it happened, when Moscow needed to divert attention from the second ELLI, whose existence, with other Russian moles, had been disclosed by Gouzenko.

In the 1960s, a decade of deception, the master of the craft was being set up as a victim. Ellis was the subject of an investigation, the background of which had been secretly obscured by the Soviet twisting of the Gouzenko case.

Washington's counterintelligence chiefs had picked over wartime records, hunting other prey through microfilm and worn documents, smudged telecom sheets and ancient telegrams. They found that a "welcome source of Soviet intelligence," according to one KGB report, had been the official SOE man in Moscow, supplier of Anglo-American sabotage and assassination "toys," and the victim of entrapment by a *mozhno* "permitted" prostitute under Moscow Center control. They also found that Donald Maclean had been followed to Washington in 1944 by a Soviet intelligence chief, Anatoly Grimov, using diplomatic cover to set up operations linked to the Corby Case networks.

A prize mole had been acquired by another RIS chief on a similar mission in London. In this case, there was not much Washington could do but turn over its evidence to the British, who conducted another inquiry that was hushed up. This mole was Surveyor of the Queen's Pictures, ex-member of Her Majesty's Secret Service, Sir Anthony Blunt, who continued to enjoy honors and to be valued by the art institutions of America as an adviser. His task was to sustain the loyalty of British intellectuals recruited by the resident RIS director.

Israeli counterintelligence, screening immigrants for RIS backgrounds, began to produce independent reports. Philby came under closer Israeli scrutiny after he bobbed up in Beirut as a foreign correspondent, with good British Foreign Office references. He had been officially cleared of suspicion that he was a Soviet agent by the then prime minister, Harold Macmillan. But in 1963 he confessed to a colleague before vanishing into the Soviet Union. Someone had warned him that the game was up—and Ellis's accusers said it was Ellis.

When told that Philby, after all, was a Soviet agent, Harold Macmillan commented, "You should never, you know, *catch* a spy! Discover him and then control him, but never catch him. A spy causes far more trouble caught than uncaught."

This attitude might have protected Ellis from further suspicion if Britain had still bedazzled the Americans who had first learned the black arts of secret warfare from men like Ellis and Philby. As Dick Ellis had once said, speaking with an Australian's keen objectivity in these matters, "They're very good at *duchessing* you, the British Establishment. You're duchessed when you get bowled over by invitations to take tea with a duchess—or a duke, baron, bishop or king. You've entered the magic circle, and after that you're frightened to say something that shows you don't belong inside the circle."

In Washington, Hoover had never been duchessed, and FBI counterintelligence was, like the plodding British constabulary, outside its influence.

And so, now, was James Angleton of the CIA. As a member of X-2, the counterintelligence branch of the wartime OSS, Angleton had listened respectfully to Philby lecture on the art of cultivating double agents. He remembered this with a cold rage.

James Jesus Angleton was said to have two obsessions, trout fishing and poetry: "coaxing forth the secret life that lurked beneath the water's surface, unraveling the enigmas of Ezra Pound's *Cantos.*"* Angleton, a product of Yale and Harvard Law School, had a mind of infinite complexity that searched beneath the surface of things. He had always believed that Igor Gouzenko was too lightly dismissed. Investigations had been cleverly cut off. By whom?

Angleton's admirers in London also felt Gouzenko had been poorly used. Searching through the recollections of Gouzenko and other defectors, and, matching them with new material from BRIDE/VANOSA, they traced links between Soviet prewar operations and the specific evidence in captured German documents of SIS leakages in Paris. Old German intelligence sources claimed that high-grade information had come from a British SIS officer through a White Russian family. One source named a Captain Ellis, an Australian with a Russian wife. From this Captain Ellis the Germans were said to have bought organizational tables of SIS and information on the way a line was tapped between Hitler's headquarters and his prewar German ambassador in London. The real Dick Ellis, it was now learned, had been one of very few SIS officers associated with the tap. Circumstantial evidence piled up.

To his friends, it seemed Dick Ellis was being framed, in a service where a scapegoat was easily created to take the blame for otherwise serious and unexplained breaches of security. The Soviets had an interest in helping this along. Manifestly, they had intimate knowledge of SIS weaknesses and knew through their moles precisely how to plant false evidence and play on prejudice. Philby had maneuvered and manipulated, as we have seen, in just such a way to get rid of senior SIS officers.

In 1963, though, Ellis enjoyed a brief resurgence as Ellis-the-enemy-of-Bolshevism, with a book attacking the Soviet version of an affair in

*David C. Martin, *A Wilderness of Mirrors* (New York: Harper & Row, 1980; Ballantine Books, 1981).

which Ellis got his first British intelligence experience. In 1957 Moscow had published *The Shooting of the Twenty-Six Commissars*,* repeating old Stalinist charges against the British that they had committed deliberate acts of aggression to gain territory in Central Asia, at the birth of the Russian Revolution. Ellis responded with a scrupulously researched volume, *The Transcaspian Episode*.** His sources read like an explorers' *Who's Who* from the days of empire: Captain Preston of Dunsterforce, Longstaff of Baku, Colonel Bailey of Tashkent and Bukhara. . . . "At a time when Soviet diatribes against 'imperialism' and 'colonialism' are the substance of propaganda in the Third World," wrote Ellis, "it seems urgent to set the record straight." He concluded the book: "Afghanistan has become an object of Soviet penetration. . . . The initial Communist attempt to seize control of Iraq met with a setback which may turn out to be a case of retreating, the better to advance later." He warned that the focus of Soviet attention was on the Islamic world: "The region has acquired a new importance . . . transcending the comparatively simple conflicts of Anglo-Russian rivalry . . . under the impact of the new Russian and Chinese imperialism that is masked by slogans of world communism, operating as instruments of Russian and Chinese great-power policies."

These were strange sentiments from a supposed "Soviet spy." But by now the students of Soviet deception had become giddy with suspicion. They found it possible to dismiss Dick Ellis's book as a devilishly clever piece of Soviet disinformation designed to make Ellis appear hostile to Moscow. "Nobody much will read the book," went the argument. "Meanwhile Ellis comes out looking like an unrepentant anti-Bolshevik capitalist. That's what Philby did at the outset—wrote anti-Communist stuff to cover his Soviet intelligence operations."

Another way of looking at it was that Ellis had always been Moscow's archenemy. Stalin's Chekists remembered him for Baku and later Fourth Arm schemes to defeat tyranny. Ellis could be a target for assassination— if not physically, then in reputation by Soviet disinformation.

The operational methods of KGB disinformation had been disclosed by two more recent defectors, Anatoly Golitsin and Michael Goleniewski. The latter claimed to be the son of Czar Nicholas and rightful heir to

*Istoriva Grazhdanskoy Voyny S.S.R. (Moscow, 1957).

**London: Hutchinson, 1963.

the throne of Russia; his critics used this boast to discredit him. Golitsin had his detractors, too, who said this former KGB agent had refused to deal with a succession of CIA case officers and at one point insisted he must talk only to the President of the United States. The more accusations were made against the two men, the more James Angleton became convinced they were disinformation targets.

Golitsin insisted that the Soviet Union's disinformation methods were based on forty years' experience dating back to the days of Dick Ellis at Baku. "For the next ten years," reported a British intelligence source later, "Angleton and some high-powered CIA people devoted themselves to breaking Russian defectors that Golitsin said were KGB disinformation agents, and to discovering Golitsin's 'super-mole' in the CIA. This obsession filtered back into the British services. It was like a poison. We couldn't prevent its spreading because there was renewed closeness between SIS and the CIA." It was only in 1974 that a new director of the CIA, William Colby, said he must fire Angleton rather than watch the agency continue to tear itself apart.

Others excused Angleton's obsession on the grounds that Kim Philby's defection was a traumatic experience for the CIA man who had for a time listened respectfully to Philby. Nothing after such a betrayal of friendship could be taken for granted: neither assertions of loyalty by colleagues nor security clearances offered by the sister services. It had been enough, before the great disenchantment, if a trusted colleague said, "I vouch for this man." Now, even the colleague was not necessarily to be trusted.

Those who shared Angleton's alarm egged on a faction of young rebels within British security questioning why some operations had gone wrong. Fatal errors had occurred. Conflict arose when the failures became the subject of criticism. Interdepartmental hostilities, always present, multiplied. If the KGB had hoped to see Western intelligence agencies wound themselves, it could not have done so more competently than by inciting such distrust.

The full story of Dick Ellis revealed how susceptible a professional intelligence officer was to Soviet disinformation. Ellis had matured in another age, innocent by comparison. Even his contemporary, Lawrence of Arabia, could have been "proved" a British traitor in the service of the enemy, if modern methods of deceit had been available to those who wanted to destroy his reputation.

Gouzenko had said that the Soviet bureaucracies of intelligence created an infinite variety of opportunities for rival officers to damage one another. If the RIS set out to neutralize an enemy abroad, there was no shortage of veterans experienced in Moscow Center's internal struggles. Once again, Gouzenko was proved right, though not in a way he could have anticipated. His own evidence was turned against one of the Soviet regime's longest-surviving enemies: Ellis.

Ellis had always refused to take part in factional strife. He was called a "social misfit" because he stayed aloof from the self-destructive squabbles between departments.

What he did not fit into was the prim Victorian world of the man known to the RIS as the Chief and to Intrepid as C. In 1964, C was revealed to be General Sir Stewart Menzies. Until then, he had enjoyed the traditional secrecy in which British security chiefs dwelt.* Suddenly he stood naked to the public gaze. His reaction exemplified the curiously archaic standards, the ossified social concerns of those who thought Ellis a misfit. How did Menzies feel, stripped of his cloak of secrecy? "Well," he replied. "I'm rather prominent in the county Hunt, y'know. I do rather wonder how people there will take it." As to national security: "Oh, I don't really think it will be hurt by this, I just worry that the people in my *county* will say I misled them."

Philby wrote of Menzies: "The Chief's eccentricity is what first impressed the visitor. His stationery was a vivid blue, his ink green. He wrote an execrable hand. . . . His official symbol was CSS, but in official correspondence between overseas stations and Broadway, he could be designated by any three successive letters of the alphabet, ABC, XYZ, etc. In government circles outside SIS, he was known as 'C.' "

Whether such rigmarole convulsed Moscow Center with laughter, Philby never said. He dwelt upon the peculiarities of this secret British

---

*Until then, the British Official Secrets Act intimidated all who might reveal the identities of CSS or, for that matter, wartime BSC and Intrepid. Anonymity began to crumble after Americans made such secrecy seem absurd by naming their directors of intelligence in conformity with a strong democratic dislike of concealment. Anonymity seemed to benefit the bureaucrats only, disguising from taxpayers any abuse of trust.

enclave instead. Rickety stairs, creaking elevators, low ceilings, and a gentle snowfall of plaster remain part of the general impression. As to Menzies:

> He was not, in any sense of the words, a great intelligence officer. His intellectual equipment was unimpressive, and his knowledge of the world, and views about it, were just what one would expect from a fairly cloistered son of the upper levels of the British Establishment. . . . His attitudes were schoolboyish—bars, beards and blondes. But it was this persistent boyish streak shining through the horrible responsibilities that world war placed on his shoulders . . . that was his charm. His real strength lay in a sensitive perception of the currents of Whitehall politics, in an ability to feel his way through the mazy corridors of power.

This Alice-in-Wonderland figure, whose identity could change from CSS to ABC, fought running battles with the directors of intelligence of the three armed services. Their attacks were based on "a lack of adequate intelligence from SIS." Senior officers were after Menzies's job, and it would be a brave man who would swear on the Bible that their complaints were exaggerated. Certainly the RIS was fully informed about the strife; their own General Philby was reporting it from inside. What the RIS released later for general consumption, however, was designed to bring Western security into disrepute.

A FINE DISREGARD FOR THE RULES: DICK ELLIS'S STORY

Ellis was one SIS officer whose intelligence career had earned him the doubtful distinction of an extensive file in Moscow Center. Because of the various interpretations put upon Ellis's part in the story of Gouzenko, it was illuminating to examine in greater detail how he came into Intrepid's "last case."

There was a wayward quality about Dick Ellis. It stemmed, perhaps, from an ancestor, William Webb Ellis, said to have unwittingly created a new game named after his high school at Rugby. "With a fine disregard for the rules of football," according to the eighteenth-century account, William Ellis "took the ball in his arms and ran with it."

His descendant, Dick Ellis, was distinguished throughout his life for taking the ball and running with it. He displayed his own fine disregard for the rules from the time he left his native Australia to fight on the Western Front in World War I as a teenager. Like Bill Stephenson, he was a soldier in the trenches and was lucky to survive the slaughter. He saw 400,000 British-led troops sacrificed to the folly of the Battle of the Somme, and he never lost his skepticism about military claims of infallibility. He was transferred to the Middle East, where he soaked up the nineteenth-century concept of "the Great Game" played by Britain to prevent the Russian bear from descending through Afghanistan and Persia into British India. That, too, was a game in need of change. Ellis did not think according to traditional imperial rules.

"He was a volunteer when the British crossed into Bolshevik Russia in 1918, and the young Communist leader opposing them was none less than Stalin," wrote Ernie Cuneo.* The Washington lawyer got to know

---

*A loyal friend, Cuneo wrote his recollections of Ellis for an American veterans' organization soon after the 1981 charges were made. "Ellis," wrote Cuneo, "amassed one of the most brilliant records in the long history of British intelligence."

Ellis very well during World War II when they worked together with
BSC, and after Cuneo had been appointed by Donovan of the OSS to
represent him at the State and Justice departments. "With the fall of the
czars, the Turkestan Moslems had established an autonomous Turkestan
government subject to the control of the central Soviet. When they
refused to obey, the Turkestan Soviet organized a Red Army to crush
it. . . . When Stalin sent the commissars to organize the contested areas,
they were executed."

Stalin regarded these twenty-six commissars as victims of a British-led
execution squad at Baku, on the Caspian's western shore. A Soviet painting showed Ellis helping to direct the shooting party. A memorial, erected
on Stalin's orders, still proclaims that on this spot the commissars were
"slain by the British."

What really happened, according to Ellis, was this: There had been
a reign of terror. An anti-Soviet rebellion among workers had replaced
the Baku government, whose commissars were arrested. A British mission under Major-General W. Malleson attempted to help stem a
German advance through the region toward Indian and British-held
Afghanistan. The overthrow of the czars had been followed by Russia's
abrupt withdrawal from World War I, and the British forces marched
from northwest Persia to occupy the strategically important oil city of
Baku. When the anti-Soviet Baku government refused to hand over
the commissars for British protection, as Malleson requested, there was
a row. "You're all alike!" raged Malleson. "If we don't take the commissars to safety, you'll shoot them." This is exactly what the Baku
government had already done. Stalin refused to believe the official British
denials of complicity. It became Stalinist dogma that offical British
support was given to all counterrevolutionary groups in Russian Central Asia, although Soviet rule had been established. Later, "historical
documents" were faked to prove the British had intended to capitalize
on the unrest and colonize the area. The Caucasus and Central Asia
were weak fronts along Soviet borders. Baku, a key port and large
oil city, once occupied by British troops, seemed to Stalin the target of future secret British operations. This became an obsession, and
in the next world war Ellis would appear to confirm Stalin's worst
suspicions.

Ellis had come away from World War I, like Stephenson and Donovan,
marked for life. All who survived the incredible bloodshed of the Western

Front were changed. Those who died found a voice through one of their numberless legions, a Major McCrae:

> We are the dead. Short days ago
> We lived, felt dawn, saw sunset glow,
> Loved and were loved, and now we lie
> In Flanders Fields. . . .
> Take up our quarrel with the foe:
> To you from failing hands we throw
> The torch; be yours to hold it high
> If ye break faith with us who die
> We shall not sleep, though poppies grow
> In Flanders Fields.

Bright red poppies appear like drops of blood on lapels each year to mark the remembrance of Flanders, in Washington, London, Ottawa, and Canberra—wherever the English language is spoken. Close to sixty years after McCrae was killed, it was Dick Ellis who remarked on a cold Armistice Day in London that he had often wondered about those haunting lines: "If ye break faith . . . we shall not sleep." What was meant, he wondered, by *breaking faith*? Was it failing to keep the peace? Or bringing about war through the neglect of our defenses? Ellis was a stickler for getting the facts straight.

His work under cover for British SIS between the two world wars made him expert in two major areas of concern, the politics and languages of Germany and Russia. As an agent in Istanbul, Berlin, and Paris, he watched the growth of an unholy alliance between defeated German generals and the infant Soviet Union, a strange realm of whirling political fogs and shifting loyalties. A "Black German army" was created in the vast hidden spaces of Russia, the result of a treaty signed by Germany and the Soviets at the ancient watering place of Rapallo on the Italian Riviera in 1922. Ellis later described what he called a collaboration:

Germany had lost the Great War, was plunged into economic chaos, and was killed militarily by the Treaty of Versailles. The Soviet Union had been cut off from the rest of the world since the revolution. They needed each other. The Red Army lacked troops, and no foreign military organization would give it training. Germany was denied heavy guns, tanks, an air force and a navy; and its small army of 100,000 men was of no consequence.

The bargain was this. If Germany's military commanders were put at Soviet disposal, and helped rebuild Russia's war machine, the Soviet Union would manufacture the arms and provide the training and testing grounds for the German forces.

Junkers set up a bomber factory near Moscow. By 1926, the shells produced inside the Soviet Union for Germany could be counted by the hundreds of thousands per year. . . . There was even a plan for the combined invasion of Poland. A third of the annual German budget plus substantial sums of money in stabilized marks went each year until 1930 into a business cartel through which the cash flowed into Russia. This paid for poison gas manufactured at Kresnovgardeisk, submarines and battleships made in the Leningrad shipyards, bombers built in Central Siberia. A German tank corps was provided with training facilities in the central Volga, where the "Black *Reichswehr*" exercised its 20,000 officers and men. Their names had been erased from the official army lists in Germany. . . . They were future officers of the secret army. Prototypes of new weapons were disassembled and shipped through the free port of Stettin on the Baltic. The prototypes of the Stuka dive-bomber and the long-range Fockewulff bombers were developed on the banks of the Don. This illegal re-arming of Germany took place under various kinds of commercial cover. It was extremely difficult to penetrate because the Germans had the tremendous advantage of operating in territory cut off from our view.

There were industrialists in Britain and France who later urged an alliance with Germany that would take the business away from Russia and at the same time create an Anglo-French-German front against "godless communism." Ellis, working in this climate, felt no obligation to limit his own exploration of Nazi and Soviet reactions. The times were strange. Cynical men seized whatever opportunities were offered. Stalin himself had directed the German Communist party to regard the Social Democrats, not the Nazis, as the enemy. Stalin recognized in Hitler a fellow dictator and, Ellis reported at the time, "Stalin was confident that German Communists would give him ultimate control of the Fascist state." In 1938, Ellis worked with Stephenson in London, helping to arm Winston

Churchill, then in the political wilderness, with the facts of Hitler's buildup for war. Ellis was known as a specialist in the histories of the ancient Persian, Babylonian, and Egyptian empires. He had, it was said, an encyclopaedic knowledge of Islam. He became a friend of H. G. Wells, who was writing his classic *Outline of History*. They both, like Stephenson, attended a weekly luncheon meeting of the creative eccentrics who would assist in irregular warfare if Hitler's Soviet-supported armies continued their aggressive course.

This was more than a period of appeasement. Fascists had infiltrated the British ruling elite. They might well have seen Ellis as guilty of treacherous conduct for passing information to help these unofficial military preparations while he was still the servant of an antiwar, appeasement-minded government. Bound by the oath of secrecy, he was leaking secret intelligence that the men in power wished to ignore. Admiral Barry Domville, for instance, recruited influential Britons for his movement, LINK. If Hitler had conquered Britain, a collaborationist government would have seen anti-Nazi activities like those of Ellis as evidence of treason. Ellis believed there were Englishmen in high places ready to serve such a government, and said so. Long after the event, there were still powerful men alive who resented Ellis for his condemnation of the potential friends of Hitler—and in their eagerness to wound Ellis, then seized on the stories that he had helped German intelligence.

In the years before the war, Berlin had become, after Moscow, the center of Communist intelligence operations. On one level there was an integration of Nazi and Soviet intelligence; on another level, involving German workers with Communist affiliations, there could be no cooperation, since the Soviet intent was to exercise secret control. Ellis saw his job as one that required him to keep in contact with overt Stalinist and Nazi agents. He was searched out by Moscow's men for whatever he might disclose about British ambitions in Central Asia. Stalin still feared being outmaneuvered through secret Anglo-German understandings, and his suspicions were aired again in 1938 when the revolutionary Nikolai Bukharin was accused of helping the British try to annex Soviet territory.

◆　◆　◆

A year later, in August 1939, came the nonagression pact between the Nazis and the Soviet Union, and the Secret Additional Protocol (the Ribbentrop-Molotov agreement) to divide Eastern Europe into Nazi and Soviet spheres of influence. Poland was to be carved up. In September 1939 the Germans marched. From the first day of the Nazi invasion, Moscow furnished military intelligence to Berlin. When Britain and France met their obligations to Poland and declared war on Germany, anyone who worked in the secret world of spies would have had difficulty separating true from false.

Ellis put on military uniform and early in 1940 visited Little Bill Stephenson in his business office on St. James's Street, between Piccadilly and Buckingham Palace. One of the few pieces of art decorating Stephenson's private quarters was a short-barreled pistol. Ellis had obtained it from Cossacks fighting around Baku in 1918, though it had been fashioned for the imperial Persian cavalry. Now Ellis indicated that he might soon be back in those exotic parts.

Ellis had become involved in the so-called Baku Project. In 1940, this was part of a study for the British Chiefs of Staff, officially entitled "Military Implications of Hostilities with Russia." If Baku was knocked out, ninety percent of Soviet oil resources would be unavailable to Stalin's customers, Hitler and the Nazi war machine. Sixty thousand British troops in the Mideast were earmarked for an expedition into Soviet territory. RAF bomber pilots were secretly briefed on the approaches to Baku. A spy plane had already flown across the Caspian Sea to photograph Baku port and oil facilities. The photo-reconnaissance aircraft of 84 Squadron had produced a mosaic that revealed inadequate Russian defenses. The British Fourth Arm expert, Colin Gubbins, working with Poland's underground, was to back Caucasian separatists in PROMETHEUS, an operation to spread subversion and sabotage among "the oppressed nations of the Caucasus and Soviet Central Asia living under unspeakably savage repression." All of this was seen as undermining Hitler's preparations to strike in the West, following Poland's collapse and the subsequent months of "phony war."

On the other side, a peculiar alliance continued. The German-Soviet Commercial Agreement of February 11, 1940, circumvented the British blockade of Germany. The Soviets would supply huge quantities of metals and raw materials needed by the Nazi arms industry: Russian oil and cotton, crucial to German military campaigns; 100,000 tons of chrome,

500,000 tons of iron ore, 300,000 tons of pigiron, 500,000 tons of phosphates, a million tons of cattle grain. The agreement meant that Germany could import through the Soviet Union the necessities that normally came across seas patrolled by the Royal Navy. It meant that the German lifeline in rubber would be maintained intact. It meant, as it turned out, that Soviet aid to Germany would exceed that of the United States to Britain in the critical period ahead when Britain would be standing suddenly alone.

Few could foresee the speed and success of the approaching Nazi blitzkrieg in the West. But already, Ellis reported, Stalin's propagandists had done an astonishing job of undermining the resolve of the allies. The New York *Daily Worker* declared in August 1939, it was "a filthy, dirty falsehood" that the U.S.S.R. was considering an agreement with "the most vicious enemy, the bestial Nazis"—only a few days before such an agreement became official, clearing the way for the Nazi invasion of Poland. Faith undeterred, the *Daily Worker* a few weeks later proclaimed the war "imperialist" while Poland was still in the process of being savaged and divided up; and Communist trade-union workers were called upon to delay aid for Britain and sabotage arms production. Soviet acquisition of territory (in addition to eastern Poland, Russia was to have "influence" over Finland, Estonia, Latvia, Lithuania, and Bessarabia) would be later justified on the grounds of the Soviet need to establish a forward strategic line of defense. The acquisition was allowed for in the Germany-Soviet Boundary and Friendship Treaty. Its real purpose was made clear after Hitler finally did attack Russia some eighteen months later. Stalin had been concerned only with control over border peoples who might be subverted; he was preparing for irregular warfare, forced upon him by his enemy, Britain, and was totally unready for the blitzkrieg launched by his ally, Hitler. All over the world, he had orchestrated the Communist call to support the Nazis.

The Baku Project never materialized. A British diplomat, Fitzroy Maclean, reported that Stalin had asked the U.S. embassy in Moscow for an assessment of the damage that might result from any British bombing of Baku. The American experts, when called upon, said Baku would become a sheet of flame, the refineries out of action for years.

• • •

What had prompted Stalin to ask such an odd question? Was the Baku Project leaked? As a project considered to be too risky, it still had deception value. At that stage in the war—the two months prior to the Nazi blitz-kriegs in the West that swept from Norway to France during April and early May 1940—Churchill was not yet Prime Minister and Neville Chamberlain was still nervously discouraging the dropping of real bombs on the real estate of his fellow property owners in Germany (propaganda leaflets were unsporting but, in Chamberlain's view, permissible). Secret warfare schemes were even more heavily frowned upon. The Political Warfare Executive discussed flooding Nazi Germany's markets in South America with counterfeit German currency and bonds. Even after Churchill took power, Frank Pick of London Transport (the public bus and general transport service) said he could not support the idea "because it was putting ourselves on the same level as the Germans." Churchill stood up and said, "Mr. Pick! Shake my hand." Bewildered, Pick did so. Churchill then explained that he was on his way to Dover, then under bombard-ment, and "should I be killed I shall be proud, when I shake hands with my Maker, to tell him the last man with whom I shook hands on earth was a *righteous* man." Pick left, and Churchill turned to the remaining company and said, "Never ask me to see that impeccable busman again."

Ellis learned to conceal such plans from overscrupulous, sanctimo-nious, or timid political bosses. He might well have leaked the Baku Project, which this time was rejected as simply beyond British resources, in an effort to frighten Stalin into reducing aid to the Nazis.

Such a leak could be made to seem sinister if there should be no paperwork proving official sanction. In those days, very little was put on paper. Ellis often quoted the old defense of his fellow Austra-lians: "I've signed nothing, you can prove nothing." He signed nothing, avoided all written commitments. That was the mark of a good agent. Later, more prudent bureaucrats of intelligence went to the opposite extreme of putting everything on paper and having it signed by all. Ellis was easy to hit if he became a later RIS target, because he left himself unprotected by memos. He seemed a likely target because he was associated with Churchill—in Stalinist history, the arch-conspirator who wanted "to strangle Bolshevism in the cradle." Ellis had helped resistance to Soviet rule. He had reported on the way the secret police provided the sources of power. He knew where Stalin's physical weaknesses were to be found along the borders, dating from the first mission to Baku.

Ellis had been receiving advance information in exchange for "chickenfeed" offered to convince the other side he was corruptible. Later, his enemies would claim he was paid for solid secrets, not only chickenfeed, which is unimportant intelligence. Later still, his service chiefs would admit paying him a salary that was ridiculously low, in keeping with prewar custom, when British agents were expected to have private incomes. "Of course Ellis would take the enemy's money," one retired chief commented. "Agents used to be encouraged to empty the opposition's pockets if they could. The old-fashioned Secret Service view was that you screw the bastards any way you can. A good agent often had to take the opposition's money to keep his credibility. We've lost cases through damnfool morality."*

Ellis was sent to New York in August 1940 to help restore close contact between SIS and the FBI. Britain had just lost any foothold in Europe to the Nazis, who had blitzed their way to the English Channel with tanks fueled by Soviet gasoline, bombs ignited by Soviet guncotton, and bullets sheathed in Soviet cupro-nickel. Across the Atlantic, the Soviets demonstrated their long reach by the "legal execution" of Stalin's archenemy, Trotsky. If anyone could have helped the FBI, it would have been Ellis with his knowledge of Russian terrorism. No Soviet law had been broken by the murder, since Trotsky had been found guilty *in absentia* of treason, and sentenced to death. Ellis explained that Trotsky's greatest offense had been to tell the truth—he had described Stalin as an accomplice of Hitler.

A specific RAF plan to bomb Baku was certainly leaked to the Soviets later, in Air Ministry papers betrayed by a former leader of the British Young Communist League, Douglas Springhall, who was tried for espionage and jailed in 1942. The Baku Project angered Stalin but the light punishment handed out to his agent was a useful pointer for future Soviet intelligence operations. It indicated that espionage on behalf of the Soviet Union was regarded more tolerantly now the Soviets were

---

*The case of double agent TRICYCLE is often quoted as an example of the FBI's Hoover objecting on moral grounds to working with a man who had used Nazi funds even though it was to secure intelligence for the allies. In this case, the intelligence concerned Pearl Harbor.

allies. Soviet propagandists in Britain from 1942 onward daubed the walls of bombed cities, demanding SECOND FRONT NOW! The paint pots were carried, often, by those who prior to the Nazi invasion of Russia had opposed the war. It was difficult to talk of treachery in a time when secret arrangements were being made to supply the NKVD with British intelligence on bombing targets like Baku, and with details of secret warfare projects.

After the Baku Project was aborted, the Soviet leader's fears were fed by strategic policy decisions at the secret 1941–42 ABC war talks in Washington. This saw the Joint Chiefs of Staff for the first time endorse the inclusion of unconventional guerrilla and terrorist warfare as part of a grand strategy. The Fourth Arm would provide "leadership for insurrection against tyranny," in Dick Ellis's words. His presence at the talks was reported to Moscow by a Soviet-run agent in Washington—identified as agent Number 19 in messages later decoded. Stalin saw at once the revival of the old threat from the capitalist West. He wanted an immediate allied frontal assault against Hitler's Europe. The alternative, a buildup of Fourth Arm secret armies in Europe, might spread into the Soviet empire. *

While Ellis and others discussed guerrilla warfare at the 1941–42 Washington conference, the GRU Military Intelligence Directorate had established an operational base in North America, using the convenient Canadian back door into the United States. In Ottawa, the NKVD and GRU set up their missions under diplomatic cover.

Hoover, as we know, stopped any open wartime NKVD or GRU presence in Washington. His FBI resources were stretched thin by the war. The director suspected clandestine Soviet activities, but he could never prove them. One of his sources was an important defector, Walter Krivitsky. While directing Soviet secret operations in Europe, said Krivitsky, he had seen information that came through a White Russian family

---

*Stalin's obsession with internal security, with eradicating dissent, runs like a bright thread through the twisting fortunes of the Soviet secret police, providing such continuity that when the KGB deputy chief, General Semon Kuzmich Tsvigun, died in 1982, it came as no surprise to Western observers that he had started his career forty-three years earlier. The recipe for longevity in the job was to suppress ruthlessly any dissent that might be fanned into a brushfire of revolt. His sudden death preceded the final move of Yuri V. Andropov to leadership of the Soviet Union after fifteen years at the head of the KGB. The history of KGB chieftains was one of lives abruptly terminated, not by the oppressed peasants, but by violent rivals.

exiled in Paris. A member of that family bought information from a senior British SIS officer. Ellis had married into a White Russian family, had even used the family connections while based in Paris to gather SIS intelligence.

But Ellis gave a perfectly plausible explanation for all this. Yes, he had married into the Zilenskis family, White Russians living in Paris. Ellis's brother-in-law knew a White Russian general who kept in contact with a Nazi German intelligence officer. The Russian general fed intelligence to the Nazis that was, in fact, fake. He got back whatever intelligence the Germans wanted to give the White Russians, and this German intelligence was useful because it was designed to lure some of the White Russians into collaboration with the Nazis when they invaded Russia.* Ellis, aware of both sides, plugged into the traffic and took out whatever intelligence seemed valid and useful to London.

It should have been possible to check some of this with Krivitsky. But Krivitsky had been killed in Washington in 1941, after his extensive talks with the FBI and with SIS in London. He had been shot in the head. The suicide note was faked. When Dick Ellis heard the details, he pointed out that the killing bore the SMERSH trademark. The defector's head had been blown apart with a soft-nosed bullet.

Who killed Krivitsky? There was never any doubt in Ellis's mind that the defector was assassinated. Not only was Krivitsky the equivalent of a KGB general and one of those "witnesses against communism" so feared by Stalin; he was also, while alive, an encouragement to others.

When Ellis was transferred back to London and then to Cairo from his post at Intrepid's side in 1944, he was earmarked to become third man in the SIS hierarchy, controller of Far East and Western Hemisphere operations. He had been at the top of the vertical flow of secret intelligence by virtue of being Intrepid's deputy in charge of an agency whose task was to coordinate information. "He was a remarkable and unpublicized individual without whose help the CIA, as successor to OSS, would never have gotten off the ground," wrote David Bruce, who had directed OSS in London and who completed a long and unusual career of service to the U.S. government as its first representative in Communist China.

---

*Stalin had infiltrated White Russian exiles, fearing Hitler might use their military men to lead a "liberation army." The Nazis did, in fact, raise a Russian Army of Liberation. It was never used directly against the Soviets because Ellis's general convinced German intelligence that the army would change sides at the first opportunity. The general was working, in fact, for Moscow Center.

President Truman in 1946 awarded Ellis the U.S. Legion of Merit for "giving unreservedly of his talent and wealth of knowledge toward the development of certain of our intelligence organizations and methods. . . . His superior foresight and diplomacy were responsible in large measure for the success of highly important operations. . . ." The liaison officer and legal adviser to General Donovan of OSS, Ernie Cuneo, later wrote:

> Ellis instructed the fledgling OSS on techniques of clandestine communications, in which he was the foremost expert . . . the very lifeline of any intelligence system. . . . When OSS desperately needed instructors, Stephenson summoned Britain's best: Major-General Colin Gubbins of SOE, whose mission was armed action behind enemy lines . . . and from the other branch, SIS, one of its commanding officers, Dick Ellis.

Cuneo pointed out that Ellis "uncovered one of the great spies of all time, Harry Dexter White, then virtually in command of the U.S. Treasury, compared with whom Philby was small fry . . . like having ourselves an American agent at the top of the Politburo, for White was a prime factor in the formation of American policy."

The allegations against White were not at first believed. It was some time before the damage he did to American interests was known. The Soviets lost a powerful agent, but their loss would have been greater if Ellis and BSC had commanded more attention. Instead, Ellis became unpopular among those who thought White incapable of treachery; and meanwhile, Moscow blamed him for uncovering White. So Ellis stood in double jeopardy.

Ellis, like the ancestor who launched a new game by breaking the rules of the old, had no regard for old-boy ties, nor for coziness of the kind that would have exempted someone like White from public punishment. Let the upper classes protect their own from exposure for lesser crimes. For treachery, Ellis was not prepared to make a distinction between ordinary men and those who claimed an intellectual superiority that somehow exonerated them.

THE PHOENIX FOUNDERS: DICK ELLIS'S LATER YEARS

Although he had made some enemies in Washington, Ellis also won respect for his professional competence. His postwar work in Asia took him into a region where British and American perceptions differed. Washington had little interest in the first guerrilla wars launched in the Malay archipelago which, from 1945 to 1950, was viewed usually as a colony resisting a national movement for independence. Ellis was the first of his breed to be caught up in the new struggles inspired by Asian communism, using "national independence" as a front. He helped create Phoenix Park in Singapore as a base against terrorism. The image of the phoenix attracted Ellis. It was a bird that consumed itself by fire and rose from the ashes.

Guerrilla warfare was widespread in the twin peninsulas of Malaysia and French Indochina, soon to be better known as Vietnam. Ellis's knowledge of front organizations was firsthand, and unrivaled. He had dealt with them since 1920, when the International Workers' Aid set the pattern. The brainchild of German Communist Willi Muenzenberg, the IWA spread Communist propaganda in Britain, Germany, and Japan. Muenzenberg, who had traveled with Lenin to Russia during World War I, "carrying the incubus of revolution," later drew up the Comintern program for "patriotic fronts" that Ellis had long ago reported to SIS, warning that Muenzenberg in the 1930s was forming "innocents' clubs" with harmless-sounding titles to conceal their real purpose of exploiting genuine discontent on Moscow's behalf. By the 1950s, Ellis had counted literally hundreds of Communist-front organizations in Asia.

His colleagues in Singapore were a closemouthed lot. "These guys are really nuts about security," reported Bob Jantzen, the CIA station chief in Singapore. "They won't even tell each other what they're doing, much less us. MI5 is just not talking to MI6 and vice-versa. . . . It's a thousand times worse than wartime."*

Ellis became a specialist in antiterrorist operations long before terrorism became a household word in the West. He had knowledge of secret Fourth Arm methods practiced by the West against the Nazis and he understood how to counter such methods.

His career had been obscured by the mystery surrounding intelligence work. In piecing it together, his attackers had failed to notice that he knew Gouzenko only through the reports of interrogators. He had never himself seen Gouzenko, much less spoken with him. Not only did his attackers at home jump to wrong conclusions; so did Moscow Center.

It would be later alleged against Ellis that he took cover behind diplomatic illness—"heart trouble," sneered his critics—after Western counterintelligence pursued him during the investigation of links between Philby, Burgess, and Maclean. Certainly he returned to his native Australia in 1954, but in order to advise the Australian Security Intelligence Organization (ASIO). Officially retired from SIS, he was nonetheless engaged to work at Secret Service headquarters in London in 1963 to sterilize SIS records. Yet this was after he was said by his enemies to have admitted to treacherous conduct.

His new SIS task was to weed, or edit, secret records and to put them "in order." This, of course, would render them useless for the official historian who, Ellis was informed, would be working from the files after Ellis had finished his cosmetic operations on them.

In a report to a retired intelligence chief, Ellis wrote in 1963:

I hope to show you some items which I am extracting and copying and which would interest [Stephenson]. Despite all the efforts of the denigrators, the frauds, the incompetents, and the downright fearful (SM was one**), BSC shines brightly in retrospect and [Stephenson] emerges from the mass of paper with dignity, amazing foresight, initiative and much patience with fools in their folly. . . .

*Quoted by former CIA agent Joseph B. Smith in *Portrait of a Cold Warrior* (New York: Putnam, 1976).

**Stewart Menzies, director-general of the Secret Service.

Ellis continued with thumbnail sketches of the personalities of secret intelligence chieftains. His portraits were not always flattering. Many MI5 counterintelligence figures "came out badly" from his perusal of their memos and correspondence. Claude Dancey, a controversial British opponent of Allen Dulles's American intelligence operations for the wartime OSS, clearly failed to pass muster.

On the other hand, Ellis had good words for the "doers" like Lord Louis ("Dicky") Mountbatten and General Sir Colin Gubbins of Special Operations. His letter implied that these supporters of Intrepid had failed, however, to outmaneuver Intrepid's enemies within the bureaucracy:

> I have found top-level recommendations for top honours [for Stephenson] . . . sidetracked—not clear by whom. Anyhow, when the "official history" comes to be written—in five years' (?) time, BSC and its chief will come out well. At present, the first draft of the history is only finished up to the outbreak of war. *I am taking the opportunity to slip a few bits of paper into the files.* [Author's italics.]

Clearly, Ellis had extraordinary freedom. He was being left alone with super-secret files, entrusted with the task of "arranging" them for future historians.

Then came an even more significant passage. It referred to William John Vassall, a clerk in the office of the civil lord of the British admiralty. Vassall had been arrested as a KGB informer, following warnings to MI5 from the CIA after it debriefed Anatoly Golitsin. Later, the Russian defector was questioned in London, where he offered "more than two hundred examples" of KGB penetration into the British security services. Vassall was among those investigated and found (through confession under interrogation) to be guilty of passing secret documents to the Soviets. In 1962 he was sentenced to eighteen years in jail. A report in the following year by an official tribunal caused such political repercussions that Prime Minister Macmillan wrote later about the problems when a spy is captured: "Unhappily, you can't bury him out of sight, as keepers do with foxes."*

In his letter, Ellis commented: "The Vassall report is causing a certain amount of flap. It is an extraordinary document; evidently nobody was

---

*Quoted from his diary by Harold Macmillan in his memoirs, *At the End of the Day.*

to blame except an obscure Admiralty Security Officer—now dead!"

Ellis implied that the simplest way to dispose of a spy scandal was to blame somebody already dead. If he believed his own security services would lend themselves to this deceit, he was foreshadowing his own posthumous role as a sacrificial lamb. His lifelong enemies in Moscow knew about this convenient method of coverup. They could anticipate the readiness of a faction inside allied counterintelligence to fasten on disinformation leading to Ellis's condemnation as a Soviet agent, once Ellis was also safely dead.

In his revealing report, Ellis made reference to such enemies within the British Foreign Office. He had been recommended by Menzies to the organization known as INTERDOC, which specialized in distributing accurate versions of Communist-inspired news reports. INTERDOC, in effect, fought KGB disinformation with facts. It was work with which Ellis was familiar. Now, when he was supposedly undergoing trial by suspicion, Menzies was urging his employment in a similar enterprise in Europe.

I am kept busy with this INTERDOC organization. And together with other chaps, I have formed a working committee which is organizing an international conference at Oxford in September. We have raised money from —, —, —, and some professional groups, much to the astonishment of the Foreign Office who said it couldn't be done. They are now wondering if it was a good thing to kick me out of . . . [reference to a branch of secret intelligence] as several of us are now doing privately what they have never succeeded in doing—getting an "action group" going. We are keeping it "private and confidential," as publicity could kill it.

Ellis wrote a covering letter from Travellers', then his club on Pall Mall. Defying modernization, the club's telephone number still appeared on his borrowed stationery as WHITEHALL 8688, an intentional reminder that it was where Whitehall's mandarins congregated. It was the preferred luncheon meeting-place for Ellis's old friends and enemies within the world of diplomacy and intelligence.

◆   ◆   ◆

Ellis was later obliged to move from the Travellers' "for reasons of economy," he said. At his new cubbyhole, the Royal Automobile Club, farther along Pall Mall in the direction of Trafalgar Square, he gave the author in 1972 his version of the pressures building up around him. These I took at face value. He was then in his mid-seventies, remarkably spry despite his complaints about "a dicky heart." He was dressed like a man of modest means who had known better times: dark suit carefully pressed and brushed, striped shirt a little frayed at the cuffs, shoes highly polished. He had taken the train up from his temporary "digs" in Eastbourne. A cable from Stephenson had directed him to me. We discussed his contribution to a new book going deeper into wartime intelligence operations, *A Man Called Intrepid*. "The powers that be," said Ellis, "think this is a good time to show how those operations saved us."

But he did not care for "the powers that be." Bureaucrats were a lot of old grannies using secrecy to cloak their mistakes. These "nervous nellies" had frowned upon the help he had given Montgomery Hyde,* who was "not a man they can fool around with," because of his additional distinction as a member of the British and European parliaments. Ellis had been reprimanded for abusing the oath of secrecy, and his pension had been reduced. ("The train fares keep going up," he reflected mournfully. "God knows how old men manage on fixed pensions, and the Devil knows how I manage. But that's how they keep a whip hand, you see. There's always a technical device handy for cutting your pension, miserable enough that it is.")

We settled on very modest terms of remuneration. Ellis provided me with research. Often, when I arrived to talk about someone's secret wartime role, the interviewee would flourish a telegram from Ellis saying, in effect, "It's okay to tell all." General Gubbins, a ruthless man in battle, showed me his handwritten preface to a book Ellis was writing about American Lend-Lease. Gubbins endorsed Ellis's historical sense and recommended Ellis as a man of integrity and as a reliable observer of events.

Gubbins wrote his laudatory preface for Ellis and discussed him with me in admiring terms, *seven years after* the alleged written confession to

---

*Montgomery Hyde wrote *The Quiet Canadian*, about Stephenson, in 1962. Despite the reprimand, Ellis then went to work on the secret files that SIS wanted to have weeded. Hyde, a distinguished London barrister and historian, stoutly defended Ellis against charges of treachery when these began to surface in 1981. It was significant that although he worked in BSC with Ellis, and knew him very well, none of the anonymous investigators ever questioned Hyde.

spying for the enemy. It was unthinkable that Gubbins would *not* have been discreetly warned. And if Gubbins had been told of an Ellis confession, his fiery temperament and his devotion to his old wartime Resistance leaders in Europe would have made it impossible to disguise this. He most certainly would not have collaborated with Ellis by writing a warm introduction to Ellis's own book on wartime matters. *

Were the charges against Ellis a form of Soviet revenge? Stephenson thought so. Ellis had been a personal enemy of Stalin when the Soviets first used terror in 1918–20. Ellis had been engaged in a secret war with Stalin, who thereafter linked him with subversion, real or imagined. The new evidence, considered in reopening the Gouzenko case in the 1980s, made it clear that Philby, when he sat down in Washington to sift through the monitored RIS traffic, saw how to play on interdepartmental feuds to build a case against Ellis. It would serve Moscow's purpose to label as one of their super-moles a man Philby professed not to know when they had offices in the same SIS building on Broadway in London.

There seem to have been two groups, nominally in fierce conflict with each other, who for different reasons wanted to nail Ellis. First, the Soviets. We have seen how Philby made himself a suspect in order to divert attention away from other Russian moles. It would be simple to perform a similar operation, with similar aims, on Ellis. The other group, in head-on collision with Moscow, was Western counterintelligence. At some point, as Ellis had told me before he died in 1975, he did fall foul of a British security investigation. By 1981 alleged details of such investigations had made newspaper headlines. Stories of Soviet double agents threatened public trust, caused confusion within the security services, and seriously damaged relations between agencies. One faction was scoring off another faction within the Atlantic alliance's intelligence groups. Ellis could be seen as a convenient scapegoat.

If Dick Ellis were to be hung with the ELLI rope, it was a dangerously convenient way to answer ugly questions raised by the new disclosures.

---

*The prestigious Royal Central Asian Society, under the presidency of the Earl of Selkirk, announced in 1970 that Ellis had been awarded the coveted Sir Percy Sykes Memorial Medal "for any distinguished traveler . . . deemed to have increased man's knowledge of, and stimulated man's interest in, Asiatic countries." Later that year, Ellis addressed the London Society of Antiquaries, also a rare honor. The men behind these tributes to Ellis, who was then seventy-five years old, were well within the British Establishment and would have been warned at some time in the previous five years if Ellis had been judged a traitor.

It disposed of the suspicion hanging over the entire Corby Case that the intelligence services had been careless, if nothing worse. The charges against Ellis played the KGB game, too, by reviving both the public doubts about integrated intelligence and the armed services' doubts about the Fourth Arm role into which CIA and SIS were unavoidably moving. The charges left the Soviets free to concentrate on the task described by the younger Winston Churchill, reflecting the widespread anger of the 1981 disclosures:

> Ever since the secret of how to build the atom bomb was betrayed to the Russians, the principal efforts of Soviet intelligence have been to place or procure agents of influence—through ideology, blackmail or hard cash—in key positions from which at decisive moments they can influence decisions or take courses of action in the interests of their Soviet masters. . . . Not only does Russia today have fifteen times as many tanks facing Western Europe as Hitler had when he invaded France, Belgium, and the Low Countries; she has a Fifth Column and a Fourth Arm which in power and influence make the Nazis look like a vicarage tea-party.*

*Winston S. Churchill, Jr., in The *Sunday Express*, London, March 29, 1981.

WHO WILL WATCH THE WATCHERS?

THIRTY-THREE

MOLES, AND BUREAUCRATS, COVER THEIR TRACKS

Washington was shocked by the admission in 1981 that no records existed anywhere of immunities and inducements offered prior to 1964 to spies to secure their confessions. Identities of moles and informers, true and false, haunted the London headlines. In the New York Public Library, an investigator reported that the rare tag MFOC, "Missing from Our Collection," popped up when works embarrassing to the Soviets were requested in the reference section, one of the most complete and efficiently supervised in the world. The Trotsky assassination, for instance, might as well never have occurred, for MFOC appeared on the standard studies: General Leandro Sanchez Salazar's *Murder in Mexico*, Isaac Don Levine's *The Mind of an Assassin*, and others, including a work on Trotsky by the "father of the Canadian public service," O. D. Skelton, who had been among many investigated during Operation Featherbed. This security operation concluded that the public services were riddled with Soviet sympathizers, naming twelve in the Canadian hierarchy, four deputy ministers, and 245 secret members of the Communist Party International in government employ.

But any publicity would challenge a policy of granting permanent anonymity to some who confessed to being Soviet agents. James Angleton, the former CIA counterintelligence chief, voiced the fear that unmasking self-confessed traitors really served Moscow's interests: "The nagging question that continues to cloud the central meaning of these cases is whether the confidential arrangements made by sovereign governments in granting immunity from prosecution have been flagrantly violated. The culprit is the leaker. He has in effect jeopardized the fiduciary relationship which at times is indispensable if we are to contain and neutralize the steady deployment of Soviet agents and assassins now operating in the West."

"The Secret Service," said Sir Michael Havers, the British attorney general, "achieves a bonus, that it might otherwise not have, by receiving detailed confessions in exchange for permanent anonymity." It was the KGB who gained advantage from the flurry of revelations in the early

1980s. They made confessions harder to extract from ex-Soviet agents in the future, if it seemed that, despite guarantee of confidentiality, identities would later be publicized.

There was another professional view, however: one of outrage that accessories to Soviet assassination and mass murder should be given promises of any kind simply in order to extract confessions from them. Most career officers were afraid to speak out on this score, fearing they would have their pensions cut or their jobs threatened. The RCMP, however, was confronted with a new Ottawa plan to create an independent security force. Threatened with extinction, at least in their counterintelligence role, some Mounties were prompted by the new Gouzenko revelations to speak more openly. "There are no safeguards against security serving the policies of the government in power, and no guarantees that Moscow Center won't control the new service," said one RCMP veteran. "It's really too easy. The moles climb to the top, ingratiate themselves with the government and do its bidding. They would only assert Moscow policy in a crisis."

A bizarre trial arose from the leakage of a secret RCMP report. The patriotic editor-in-chief of a daily Canadian newspaper, Peter Worthington of the Toronto *Sun*, an outspoken critic of the federal government, suddenly found himself and his newspaper charged with breaking the Official Secrets Act. It was an extraordinary situation, involving a man whose credentials were beyond reproach. Worthington had served as a naval flier in World War II and as a paratrooper in Korea. His father was a distinguished army general who had fought bureaucratic stodginess to meet Hitler's challenge. The younger Worthington had been a rebel too. Then he served as a correspondent inside the Soviet Union, as well as covering brushfire wars in Asia and Africa. He had arrived at an outspokenly critical view of the Soviets, and especially the RIS, for the best of reasons: his experience as a reporter led him to facts that led to the only conclusion, that Moscow was history's greatest enemy of the working man's freedom. He had become the close confidant of Gouzenko. Now, he was accused of *publishing examples of Soviet espionage.*

It was a disturbing example of what could happen when a vengeful government perversely mobilized its security powers, not to protect society but to silence a shrewd and knowledgeable critic. The security powers had seemed safe enough, but only so long as they were in the hands of trustworthy leaders. Now they were being abused. Fortunately, the rule of law proved impervious to government interference. The charges were eventually dismissed, but only after more than a year of harassing hearings.

Worthington and the *Sun* were said to have leaked RCMP reports on Soviet spies. He was able to show that the reports had been distributed to three governments and a variety of individuals. Nevertheless, his office was raided by RCMP officers. Later, embarrassed counterintelligence agents confided that the whole operation realized, however briefly, their worst fears: the use of the security machine by a politically motivated group acting on behalf of an essentially undemocratic government. Those responsible in Ottawa quickly withdrew once they had measured public awareness and resistance. The incident reminded Gouzenko of the hazardous conditions in which he still survived, thirty-five years after an earlier federal government had tried and failed to return him to Moscow.

What was it this later government apparently wished to keep from the public? Apart from specific examples of Soviet espionage, all involving cases now terminated, the RCMP had reviewed "The Vulnerability of Public Services to Foreign Intelligence." It stated:

The KGB is still the prime enemy but the nature of the homegrown Far Left has changed radically. A clandestine member of the Communist party photographing confidential material in a government office is one problem. Quite another is followers of splinter factions who take as malign a view of Western governments as they do of some Communist governments. The Trotskyite fringe is unlikely to produce senior civil servants like [name omitted] passing state secrets to the KGB controller in New York's UN building, but there is the possibility of militants photocopying sensitive documents for publication in anti-Western magazines.

A second change is the routine fabrication of documents by the KGB, based on real official papers, but distorted in order to damage the reputation of a Western government or individual.

A third change is the shift in public attitudes towards homosexuality. This is no longer regarded as a character defect barring a civil servant from sensitive posts. The high percentage of homosexuals in departments like foreign-affairs, as noted, coincided with the uncovering of five officials of ambassadorial rank whose homosexual activities placed them at the mercy of the KGB, which had photographed them in compromising situations. The argument today is that the blackmail element would have been removed if homosexuality were regarded with greater tolerance in this society.

The highly placed "sleeper" planted by the RIS in the upper levels of the civil services remains the major threat, and is the most difficult to counter. Without the cooperation of defectors from the other side, "sleepers" are hard to detect. They are motivated less by ideology. . . .

Many enjoy the secret power, or the sense of it, as a counter to their feelings of frustration. Career diplomats are especially vulnerable, since recent surveys suggest fully fifty percent of those in the diplomatic service admit they are frustrated by bureaucratic procedures and would leave if similar conditions could be found outside. . . .

The highly trained Soviet sleeper moving diligently up the ladder of promotion, trusted and efficient, covering his or her tracks with conscientious memos that reflect obedience and loyalty to the department, remains the major threat.

The Corby Case had sparked FBI investigations leading in turn to Operation Featherbed, which confirmed fears that security investigations could be Soviet-influenced. Featherbed grew out of the U.S. Senate internal-security committee hearings, linked with the FBI discovery of the so-called Silvermaster atom spy ring, and with the execution of the Rosenbergs. Two subdivisions of RCMP investigation teams worked under codenames MERCURY and APACHE. They studied the monitored BRIDE/ VANOSA traffic of Soviet agents and the statements of Russian defectors. They pursued suspects through fourteen years of detective work. For five of those years, the effective controller of security, and chairman of the Canadian government security panel, was himself under scrutiny. This was Robert Bryce, clerk to the Privy Council and secretary to the Cabinet in the late 1950s and early 1960s, a period when American and British counterintelligence was trying to measure the damage done by known Soviet moles.

So far as the public was concerned, Bryce had loyally served his country. Canadians disliked smears, hearsay evidence, guilt by association.

Bryce had been a friend of Herbert Norman, the Canadian ambassador in Cairo who committed suicide there after the Suez crisis of 1956. Both names had come up during the U.S. hearings involving the spy-courier Elizabeth Bentley. The FBI's inquiries revived doubts about Norman that had first been aroused during World War II. Norman was at Harvard with a Japanese Marxist to whom Bryce had introduced him. When the FBI came to deport the Japanese scholar after Pearl Harbor, they found Norman apparently trying to rescue the other man's papers, which included U.S. defense plans.

In reviewing all this in the early 1980s, Norman's suicide and the questions surrounding it were once again examined. Norman's first request for a public statement of confidence in himself had been refused by Prime Minister Lester Pearson. Later, in Cairo as Canadian ambassador, Norman said he could not face another U.S.-instigated investigation. He jumped to his death there after weeks of soul-searching. Much later, one of Anthony Blunt's recruits to the Soviet cause admitted that Norman was one of many Soviet sympathizers he had denounced to the FBI when offered immunity from prosecution.

The Toronto *Globe and Mail* noted in 1981 that a surprising number of suspects had died suddenly. The newspaper ran a series on "the missing Gouzenko papers," and was in a reflective mood. "Heart attacks" had been the cause of death in some peculiar cases, it observed. Tom Wylie, homosexual friend of Guy Burgess, who was a senior Whitehall official . . . a former Canadian ambassador and former chief of a military college . . . Sir Andrew Cohen, a friend of the self-confessed spy Sir Anthony Blunt . . . and John Watkins.

Watkins had been Canadian ambassador in Moscow. During a Featherbed interrogation, he was told that his successor, David Johnson, had been secretly photographed in homosexual activities by the KGB. Similar photographs had been taken, said the RCMP, of Watkins.

A few facts were forced into the public domain by renewed demands for the truth. Watkins had died from "a heart attack" on October 12, 1964. He had been rousted from retirement in Paris and was being examined by the then director of Canadian counterintelligence, Leslie James Bennett, and the future chief of RCMP "B" Operations, Harold W. Brandeis. A coroner's report at the time was confined to a yellowing sheet of paper, handwritten in eccentric English, stating that Watkins's death was sudden, unexpected and "not imputable to the crime of whomsoever, neither to the negligence of anybody . . . no need for inquest." The need for an inquest was suddenly admitted, almost two decades later, because of the associated publicity; but it was conducted as quietly as possible, attracted little media attention, and was opened and closed swiftly, without notice. *

Watkins had been hauled in for questioning in the first instance because his Soviet connections had been confirmed from three sources: two Russian defectors and the BRIDE/VANOSA cryptops. Watkins had suddenly dropped dead just before returning from Montreal to be with the Canadian ambassador in France, Jules Leger, a future governor-general of Canada. Neither the doctor who rendered the medical verdict nor the judge who wrote the original report found themselves able to remember anything of the case by 1982. The truth was that Watkins had been offered immunity in exchange for cooperating in the exposure of more Soviet agents.

These belated disclosures might seem to have self-destructive results. Bennett, the counterintelligence chief, had been interrogated and prematurely retired in 1972, but the details took ten years to reach the public. It then emerged that the self-inflicted wounds among ABC intelligence services, following Philby's exposure, had not left the Canadian security service unscathed. When an Ottawa newspaper ran a photograph of Philby in Red Square, a copy was pinned on the RCMP headquarters noticeboard. Philby bore a resemblance to Bennett, and some anonymous hand had written underneath: *"Is this our Jim?"* * *

One RCMP veteran, looking into the question "Why do our counterintelligence operations keep failing?" reported that, far from digging up a double agent from the files, he could scarcely comprehend "the vast and windy reports and needless accounts of routine surveillances

---

*ROCKBOTTOM had been the codename given Watkins, the "special inquest" was told in 1981 by the then chief of Canadian counterintelligence, who turned out to be . . . Harold Brandeis. The chief "stepped out of the shadows to declare that his involvement in the death of John Watkins was kept secret for 17 years for 'security reasons,' " reported the Toronto *Star*. SECURITY PROMPTED COVERUP headlined the *Globe and Mail*, Canada's national daily. A former head of counterintelligence in Quebec told the coroner, "We had information on the KGB [about] which, if it had been made public, the KGB could take countermeasures." The inquest was resumed in 1982, and left the public none the wiser.

**For Services Rendered, by John Sawatsky (New York: Doubleday, 1983), provides a remarkable examination of this counterintelligence puzzle.

that came to nothing." Bennett himself accused the chief investigator, director-general John Starnes of counterintelligence, of "believing a traitor over somebody [Bennett] who could not be proved a traitor." Nevertheless, Bennett was sent into limbo on "medical grounds." Doubts about him continued to pile up, until in 1983 the awful suspicion took root that the only beneficiary had been the KGB. By then, to Moscow Center's undoubted satisfaction, the RCMP faced being stripped of all responsibility for national security. An investigating commission claimed, in its 1,800-page report, that the Mounties considered themselves above the civic control to which they were properly responsible.

A new Canadian Intelligence Service was proposed. Some experts predicted it would be five years before the new agency would be organized to fight the KGB, and that Moscow would have lots of time to make use of this "window of vulnerability." Others argued that the new civilian agency would wield "tremendous powers that go beyond the needs of the country," to quote the Canadian Civil Liberties Association.

Stephenson lent his experience to the debate. In 1982, he had been made an honorary commandant of the intelligence branch of the Canadian Defense Forces. Even at his advanced age, it was felt that he was the man who could weigh security needs against the rights of the private citizen.

The conflict was familiar. In an ideal world, security measures would be seen as directly threatening the individual. But in a world of terrorism, in which one side encouraged secret warfare of an increasingly sophisticated nature, it seemed necessary to ask the individual to surrender some rights in order to preserve his general freedom.

There were bizarre consequences to the failure to see the world as it really was. In 1981–82, Anthony Blunt, though supposedly in disgrace as a Soviet spy, was found to be coolly scrutinizing the work of amateur sleuths in pursuit of more Soviet spies. He was still functioning openly as an art expert, writing away merrily for intellectual journals whose editors showed considerable delicacy by omitting to mention his chief qualification: traitor. Blunt was one source of allegations against Dick Ellis, and through him some minor Soviet informers surfaced. Leo Long was forced into publicly confessing that he had passed wartime information to Blunt. Long was an unimportant British military intelligence officer whose significance was greatly enriched by the newspapers that played ball with Blunt. The possibility now had to be considered that Blunt was still serving his old Soviet masters. The RIS had nothing to lose in the public scandals. And Blunt made espionage seem respectable when done for idealistic reasons. "Anyway," he said with ill-concealed satisfaction, "it's amusing to see the security services spinning round like mad dogs chewing their own tails."

His relationships had led to the interrogation of many, like Stuart Hampshire, the Warden of Wadham College, Oxford. Hampshire wrote to the *Times* of London on November 28, 1981, an indignant denunciation of "genteel British McCarthyism, playing on guilt by association and with dark allusions to sources in the secret service." He had been shown the draft of an article "which insinuated that I was plausibly suspected of having been a Soviet agent. . . . The writer omitted to say that nearly everyone who had been associated with secret military intelligence in the war, and with Professor Blunt, had been interrogated, and this was a very large class."

A French filmmaker who had worked on James Bond movies, Louis Dolivet, wrote from Paris to the *Times*: "My name was headlined and linked to Britain's latest sport: spy hunting. . . . It becomes a dangerous sport if the hunters lose their heads, shoot in all directions, hunting and wounding the innocent and in their frenzy almost forget the game they were after."

The impulse among bureaucracies to prove themselves always right could have disastrous consequences, as the Corby Case proved. Stephenson had always deplored the institutionalizing of intelligence. This encouraged elitists who made their own secret organizations, engaged in separate diplomacy, followed their own laws. Whatever didn't fit those laws was condemned. They were like ancient monastic orders in a medieval church claiming a monopoly on truth. The equivalent of being "in grievous error" today was to question the wisdom of the secret agencies. Defectors like Gouzenko had been unable to challenge the reliability of their interrogators in that atmosphere of infallibility.

The religious quality of this faith was carved in stone inside CIA headquarters: AND YE SHALL KNOW THE TRUTH AND THE TRUTH SHALL MAKE YOU FREE. Stephenson remembered a crusty old journalist who

reflected the healthy skepticism of the media, and who would have decorated the CIA's portals with the additional proviso he had once proposed
nailing up outside every church: IMPORTANT—IF TRUE.

The reputation of Dick Ellis had been turned inside out. He had broken
the rules—Soviet rules, or Nazi rules, or the West's own rules, it didn't
much matter; they were rules made by the priests of intelligence to protect
their special interests. Intrepid's wartime aide was represented as a Soviet
spy who destroyed Gouzenko's leads to future Soviet intelligence operations. It was the most surprising of the many reversals of image since
the Corby Case had been prematurely closed so long before. It was
important, said Stephenson, if true. And if it wasn't true, then the reason
for the reversal became even more important.

Dick Ellis was in a special situation, challenging to Stephenson's disciplined mind. The charge that Ellis tampered with the Corby Case, or
with Gouzenko's later evidence, was untrue. But somewhere, someone
clearly had a reason for stirring up the consequent distrust. It was idiotic
to suppose the KGB remained ignorant of some serious sources of friction
between the Western allies. The official CIA history, appearing in the
1980s, disclosed American wartime anxieties about the encroachment of
British intelligence operations upon the sovereign territory of the United
States. Mischief-makers could fan suspicion today by claiming that these
British operations benefited the Soviets. "A full-size secret police and
intelligence agency . . . run by the British on American soil" was one
of the allegations made against Stephenson's organization during World
War II. The CIA history merely quoted, and certainly did not endorse,
the charge. But it was the kind of thing that hostile propaganda could
exploit.

The secret report on the Corby Case was still secret; but in 1981 an
appendix appeared in Ottawa, one which made it appear that Stephenson
had advocated the continuation of BSC operations in a way that would
justify early State Department fears. The truth was, Stephenson *had*
argued for the extension of the wartime alliance; but this was all on
record, and it had been a view shared with Donovan of OSS. He had
not written, however, "The Influencing of American Opinion by Covert
Means." This openly suggested that the United States was a nation of
mongrels, with no commonly held beliefs to unite them against a new
enemy. It would have reinforced the lingering suspicion that Britain still
nursed an imperial attitude to its old colonies in America, reviving mem-

ories of earlier days when Britain purchased newspapers to plant propaganda against the leaders of independence. It was not likely to amuse Americans. They had tolerated the *chutzpah* of the Secret Occupation of Manhattan, because it was a desperate gamble, with survival at stake. The forgery could have only one purpose, therefore—to spread bad feeling between old allies.

Dick Ellis had been credited with drafting the secret Corby Case report, distributed on a strictly classified basis when he was SIS controller for the Western Hemisphere and Asia, before the emphasis of the post shifted to the Far East. But he knew nothing about this appendix, with its advocacy of clandestine British operations in peacetime America. Its potential for making mischief between allies rendered it suspect. It bore the date June 1946, and read in part:

> Sir Winston S. Churchill rightly said the chief moral to be drawn from the Corby Case is that Soviet espionage is dangerous because it can recruit its agents from native Communist "fifth-columnists." But it should also be pointed out that Soviet *propaganda* in the United States is equally dangerous—and for the same reason. . . . The defeat of such propaganda necessitates the re-employment of those [covert] methods outlined in that part of the BSC official history dealing with political warfare. . . . His Majesty's government . . . should also have resort to undercover means. . . .

It was true that Stephenson had urged Churchill to make the statement about Communist fifth columns to Parliament. But from a distance of thirty-five years it was impossible now to detect where false insertions in the appendix had been made or subtle distortions introduced. It was tempting to blame the KGB, intent on destroying Ellis's reputation and the ABC alliance. There were others on Ellis's side of the game, however, who might well have had their own reasons to do so. Had they been standing on the sidelines at his funeral?

LONELY FUNERALS AND
WEEDED FILES

It was another of those spymaster funerals. An owl-faced man stood at the back of the church, which was gloomy and damp. He wore a dark Scotland Yard macintosh and thick-rimmed spectacles. When he removed the spectacles, his face seemed flat, without character, and vulnerable. He resembled Smiley in a spy novel by John Le Carré, whom he knew. His name was Sir Maurice Oldfield, catcher and master of spies. He had been forty years in espionage. The CIA had its own dossier on him, dating back to the days in Singapore when Oldfield and Ellis were colleagues but—as a CIA station chief noted—so security-minded "they never told each other what they were doing." If they communicated, it was by bureaucratic memo.

Long after he was said to have confessed to treason, Ellis enjoyed Oldfield's support and trust. Then, in 1974, a year before Ellis's death, Oldfield had telegraphed Ellis his congratulations. It was Ellis's eightieth birthday, and Oldfield neither minced his words nor worried how they might look to some top bureaucrat. He was the junior saluting the Grand Old Man of British espionage: Ellis was the oldest living professional agent.

Now Ellis was dead and no longer able to defend himself against character assassins. "The mortuary backstabbers," Oldfield called them. At the funeral, Oldfield looked donnish, tidily dressed, yet somehow scruffy: a striped shirt with an old-fashioned detachable collar, a stringy necktie faintly evocative of some obscure public school, an ancient black suit, very large black shoes.

He had become deeply religious and indicated that he suffered agonies over "the freedom to dish out violence and death." As SIS director-general, he forbade agents to use violence, after a report that British infiltrators into the Irish Republican Army had been supplied with explosives. Ironically, he fought the IRA later as Coordinator of Security in Northern Ireland. Some of his men wondered if he had turned soft.

Oldfield seemed like a decent man trying to keep his balance in a dirty business. He had been several rungs below Ellis on the promotion ladder. Then something, for Ellis, went wrong. He faltered while Oldfield overtook him, plodded upward, and became the expert on KGB disinformation, remarking how cleverly Moscow peppered false documents with red herrings and mischief.

He trod softly behind the procession of mourners to the open grave in the burial grounds dark under the damp elms, and stood back beside a gravedigger among the dripping shrubs. During the past ten years, he and other security-service chiefs had helped Ellis find small tasks to earn a few honest coppers and augment his reduced pension. When asked why, if Ellis committed treason in wartime, he wasn't hanged, Ellis's enemies would beat around the bush. Some said the job exposed Ellis to more temptations than mortal man could bear. Some said he broke department rules and should have pumped out self-serving desk reports. Oldfield called such desk reports "fodder for the committees writing about committees to be read by committees and presented as history."

The only game Ellis had admitted to playing was the Great Game against the Russian bear. Like his Rugby ancestor, he played the game with "a fine disregard for the rules."

But *what* rules? Inside his wooden box, forever laid, Ellis was lowered into the ground. After a lifetime of concealment he had wanted to go to his grave in style, neat as a pin. By contrast, Oldfield revealed ill-fitting jacket and unpressed trousers as he thrust back the wings of his raincoat and clasped his hands behind him. A shovel turned. The first clod of earth dropped upon the coffin with a thud.

What rules? Who defined them? Oldfield turned and saw, beyond the cemetery's iron gates, the familiar baggy shapes of the silent watchers who had waited for Ellis to be buried and who now drifted back to their unmarked cars.

Oldfield caught up with one of Ellis's children. "If there's anything I can do—?" He handed her his card, and hesitated. The service had been so simple and austere. He shivered. The woman led him gently to the edge of the grave.

Already, the coffin was vanishing under the shoveled earth. Oldfield stared down. He was clearly not talking about Ellis's corpse when he said softly, "There, but for the grace of God, go I."

◆   ◆   ◆

Oldfield died, in his turn, suddenly. The Security Service scavenged around his hospital bed before the body was cold, turned his bachelor residence upside-down, scooped up every scrap of paper from penciled notes to grocery bills. Were they striking before an enemy got there? And who was the enemy?

In 1982, a year after his own lonely funeral, Oldfield was the subject of a magazine column by Auberon Waugh, who wrote:

> It was officially announced that he had died for health reasons. . . . I thought the old boy had been murdered by members of the Secret Intelligence Service. . . . Normally, when SIS officers murder each other it is the result of some poofish quarrel or lover's tiff. On this occasion, it may have been a misguided desire to protect the good name of the Old Firm. I gather that members of the rival—and slightly more respectable—Home Security Service had been breathing down the necks of their glamorous colleagues in the SIS about various wild allegations. . . . If these had received a thorough airing and Maurice Oldfield's name had been dragged through the mud, it would have been a poetic revenge for what the SIS pooftahs had done to the reputation of my old chief Roger Hollis.

Waugh was a satirist and the magazine had a reputation for scurrility. But the writer was also known to be well informed. The *Christian Science Monitor* queried its own writer on intelligence, William V. Kennedy. He reported that the United States also suffered from killingly competitive intelligence bureaucracies. "Despite the expenditure of literally hundreds of billions of dollars during the past 30 years," wrote Kennedy in the May 7, 1982, *Monitor*, "the United States does not have a reliable intelligence service." What Americans had were rival agencies of which the most questionable were the covert-action staffs of the CIA. Whether or not they would stoop to bumping one another off, he did not say, but they certainly kept a jealous watch over one another. And they, too, knew how to weed the files.

The rules for one agency were not necessarily the rules of another, although they had a common interest in maintaining a common dignity. Scandals should be concealed in the interests of all. One was brewing over a West German security chief's alleged request to the CIA to suppress documents in the United States about ex-Chancellor Kurt Georg Kiesinger's Nazi connections. The Bavarian Interior Ministry suspended a department chief while it investigated his negotiations with a CIA director "to make it difficult" for journalists to discover in the U.S. national archives the papers hurtful to Kiesinger. The difficulties had been created simply enough. The guide to the captured documents was taken out of circulation. "Anyone who has searched for documents in America's immense archives will know how impossible this becomes without the guiding papers," said a Bonn official. "The guide was the key, and vanished."

The gentle art of extracting key information from secret files had its skilled practitioners in World War II. The truth was surfacing now only because there had been times when the records kept by one government were *not* in alignment with the records of its allies.

Take the case of Poland's government-in-exile in London. An outstandingly heroic courier between Warsaw and London was Jan Nowak, who settled later near Washington. As a consultant to the U.S. National Security Council, Jan Nowak had access to files. He was curious about allegations that the wartime allies failed to act on information regarding Nazi death camps. The allied excuses included the plea that little was known about the camps. But Nowak had made hair-raising journeys at the end of which he had always "introduced the subject of the extermination of the Jews and the destruction of the Warsaw ghetto . . . genocide . . . the scale and methods." His predecessor, Jan Karski, had arrived in London from Poland in 1942 with extensive eyewitness reports, even risking his life to get into one death camp to see things with his own eyes. Karski personally reported all he had seen and knew to the British foreign secretary, Anthony Eden. Eden circulated his account among the war cabinet.

Jan Nowak went to the Public Record Office outside London long afterwards and was shocked to find that everything from Karski and himself with regard to the extermination of the Jews had been omitted.

Eventually, Jan Nowak wrote a book, *Courier from Warsaw,* * recording this and other examples of how history could be rewritten in secret files. Those he had examined in London were supposedly declassified under the thirty-year rule protecting state secrets for a reasonable time. It hap-

*Wayne State University Press, 1982.

pened that he had an alternative source, however: the records kept by the Polish exile government. He demonstrated that statements he had made to Churchill's intelligence adviser, Desmond Morton, were reported in two totally contrasting ways. The Polish prime minister's office had rendered an account, with which Jan Nowak agreed, of his intelligence summaries of Polish resistance to the Nazis. Desmond Morton was on record as dismissing Nowak's reports out of hand, and changing their meaning. Quite clearly, for reasons of policy, the British version had been doctored.

What reasons of policy? Nowak had been told the British did not want to hear about mass slaughter of Jews. Any flow of refugees to Palestine would cause serious difficulties with Arab allies at that point in the war. As to the Polish resistance, the Western allies had no wish to tangle with Stalin later by preventing a Russian occupation of Poland.

Whatever motives prevailed then, this distortion of intelligence had evil repercussions later. As the security adviser to President Jimmy Carter, Zbigniew Brzezinski, wrote in a foreword to Nowak's book: "He sheds new light on major events little known or poorly understood." Nowak's discoveries could hardly fail to alarm friendly governments about the reliability of their allies.

Anyone searching for the most significant volume of Canadian Prime Minister Mackenzie King's diaries, kept after his unique lunch with the NKVD in London at the end of October 1945, would have discovered that it was totally missing. It was not a question of "guiding papers" having disappeared, nor of such a weight of vast and windy reports that an investigator lost his way. King's diaries were a national treasure. But those recording his busy Gouzenko bustlings during most of November and December were gone.

The paper-handlers scavenged for incriminating papers to burn when a spymaster died. They removed the diary notes of a prime minister who had consulted privately with Soviet intelligence. They tampered with reports supposedly supportive of the written history of wartime espionage. They deleted, they disguised, they distorted in accordance with their own changing rules. Stephenson's BSC history, while subject to the self-censorship of 1946, remained unaltered for a typically silly, bureaucratic reason: Stephenson was not subject to the secrecy laws that gagged other men of good conscience. He was the gifted amateur. He was his own boss, and he kept his own bits of paper. Now, those papers indicated that Dick Ellis might have become a victim of the very procedures Ellis himself had followed as a professional spy chief who doctored his own service's files.

THE MI5 CHIEF WHO DESTROYED VITAL FILES was the headline in the London *Daily Mail* in early 1982 over a report by the tireless Chapman Pincher. It referred to Ellis's "weeding," and to the destruction of records on those who confessed in return for immunity. "The British prime minister does not know," Pincher wrote, "that even Kim Philby, that most monstrous of traitors, was assured in 1963 that he would be granted immunity from prosecution if he assisted MI5 with a full confession . . . despite the fact that the authorities knew full well that Philby had been an accessory to the murder of many anti-Soviet agents working for Britain and America. . . ."

Accessory to murder?

Yes. In his SIS capacity of directing anti-Soviet operations, Philby had backed Western plans for "civil wars" within the Soviet empire. Nobody realized until long afterwards that the Soviets *wanted* the West to squander intelligence resources by chasing will-o'-the-wisps and small-fry Soviet operators who Moscow Center calculated might be "wasted" in return for larger, long-term gains.

All this might seem trivial in a world haunted by fears of a nuclear disaster far exceeding the horrors of Hiroshima. It was often forgotten that the secret weapons of terror and the Fourth Arm had advanced at a great pace too, but with less publicity about design and strategy. Scarcely a day passed without discussion in the newspapers of how the world might continue to prevent the further use of nuclear weapons—side by side with reports of actual, increasingly sophisticated, acts of terrorism.

The knowledge of Fourth Arm technology, like that of the atom bomb, once acquired could not be cast aside. Weapons were improved to meet each new challenge. The secret Fourth Arm of the West was officially abandoned after Hitler's defeat. Then Gouzenko crossed over with news of Soviet secret warfare against wartime allies. Even though his disclosures were limited, other evidence contributed to the West's reaction. There was a scramble to model counter-operations on World War II experience, but often without experienced officers. Leftover OSS covert-action new-comers were shifted to what would become the CIA. They were up against a seasoned Soviet system, however. The civilians and military officers hastily drafted in the West began to compete for experts on Soviet secret warfare. All too often, the "experts" proved to be German or other European Nazis whose common denominator was their fervent proclamation of dedicated anticommunism that often shrouded an expedient adoption of the most convenient political philosophy.

This became apparent in the 1980s when the U.S. Department of Justice began its search for information on the smuggling of Nazis into the Western Hemisphere in exchange for help in the undeclared secret war with the Soviet Union. Justice was spurred by the return to France of Klaus Barbie, wanted for war crimes he allegedly committed when he was Gestapo chief in Nazi-held Lyons. Barbie had taken refuge in Bolivia, where it was reported he had enjoyed special protection until the French government took action in 1983. Some Nazis were helped to migrate to Latin America and some resurfaced in the Middle East to resume their war against the Jews. From dubious sources sprang fake accusations against men of probity, wherever the Soviet Union had infiltrated the ranks of Nazis with its own disinformation specialists.

The advocates of Western covert action argued that the Soviets had taken over the Fourth Arm concept. Like those who called for more nuclear arms to match Soviet strength, they pointed to the Soviets' sponsorship of terrorism, guerrilla wars, and political assassins and called for an equivalent force. By the 1980s, one Russian version of a Fourth Arm fighting group was the *Spetsnaz* (an acronym from the Russian words for "special purpose"), trained and controlled by the KGB for undercover operations from Afghanistan to Zanzibar. They were murderous, tough, evasive. A few had been caught in South African raids into Angola, but they were hard to identify. A member of *Spetsnaz* had his own "legend," a false biography that might identify him as a civilian-aid adviser, say, or the local man from Aeroflot.

Which came first: the West's covert action or *Spetsnaz*? The Russians would point to the days of Western intervention in the Bolshevik revolution, to Baku and Dick Ellis in 1918. The West insisted there had been no intervention since the establishment of the USSR—indeed there had been such a determination to stick to the letter of agreements with Stalin after the war that two million Russian expatriates had been returned, though it was obvious many were anti-Communists marked for prison or execution.

American reluctance to launch CIA covert-action operations to meet the *Spetsnaz* challenge was expressed in the *Christian Science Monitor's* 1982 intelligence review: "Covert action was first institutionalized in the OSS, involving sabotage, execution of opposition leaders, and psychological warfare. . . . For a democratic society to pursue such activities short of a state of war is to risk corrupting our own free institutions."

Gouzenko, now close to death, still argued from his hideout that the West must pursue such activities to protect itself against the far more extensive operations of the KGB and its *Spetsnaz*. But he was no closer to being sympathetically heard than he had been in 1946.

The Corby Case had been followed in 1946 by Western covert-action operations that proved disastrous to their sponsors. One operation involved parachuting agents into what used to be called White Russia, a region of Ellis's expertise. Despite Gouzenko's warnings of RIS double agents, among those involved in the operation were agents planted by Moscow. The covert-action teams were to spark rebellion *against* Moscow. Instead, the KGB collected and executed all—except, of course, its own *agents-provocateurs*.

This postwar attempt to loosen part of the Soviet empire drew upon Nazi collaborators and war criminals, in turn betrayed by the Soviet doubles. It took Dick Ellis back to the prewar White Russian conspiracies whose dangerous games with Nazi and Soviet intelligence he had exploited. Out of such a cesspool came later "evidence" that Ellis spied for and against them all.

Covert operations had backfired, sometimes betrayed by the very men hired for their sound anti-Communist views. The facts were suppressed. Ellis had opposed these particular covert-action operations as being doomed from the start. His opposition was interpreted by his attackers as proof of his dubious loyalties.

On May 16, 1982, a former U.S. Justice Department investigator made allegations of a general coverup. Files had been withheld. Details had been deleted from intelligence documents on the familiar grounds of "national security." Papers were "lost."

Who was impeding the investigations? A mole, apparently—but who was it? The question refused to be answered.

THIRTY-FIVE

WHEN THE CAT'S AWAY, THE MOLES WILL PLAY

Then Igor Gouzenko died. The *Times* of London made the announcement on July 2, 1982, after a funeral variously estimated as having taken place in an unnamed location somewhere between June 27 and June 30. "Gouzenko's death, while *apparently* of natural causes, was in some ways as mysterious as his life since September 1945 had been," wrote the editors of the additional Gouzenko testimony, released by the Canadian government.*

For the first time, newspapers printed photographs of Gouzenko unmasked. A Washington newsletter edited by the retired CIA historian Thomas F. Troy published one picture of Gouzenko, "shown here as he was never shown in life . . . without the hood which has become his symbol, the hood he wore against the possibility of identification by the Soviets and retaliation."

The *Times* obituary said: "Mr. Igor Gouzenko, who died last week near Toronto at the age of 63, will be remembered as the most famous cipher clerk in the history of intelligence. . . . He lived for the rest of his life in fear of KGB retribution."

*Robert Bothwell and J. L. Granatstein, *The Gouzenko Transcripts* (Ottawa: 1982).

The death of Igor Gouzenko and the disposal of his remains were shrouded in mystery. He had never really been out of protective custody. The preacher's oration spoke only of "Mr. Brown who came to us from Prague," though the mourners were limited to his family and the closest of his few close friends, all of whom knew perfectly well it was not Mr. Brown who was being eulogized.

The funeral revealed one more closely guarded secret. His children had multiplied to ten. One daughter was herself having a baby. Grandchildren were there. The new life of Svetlana and Igor had been exceedingly fruitful. But the size of the family would have provided the Soviets with a clue to his new identity. "He'd had a very hard life here," said Peter Worthington, editor of the Toronto *Sun*, who was at the funeral. "Gouzenko had to stay under cover, and work for every bean. But he gave his children a magnificent start in the world he'd dreamed about. They achieved the best in education, in professions. They symbolized his final victory. They were around him when he died, in peace— and not as the Soviets wanted, in violence. The KGB hadn't been able to kill him. He beat them at their own game. And in all the hard times, he'd never once had a qualm about his decision."

The *Times* described Gouzenko as "devoted to the royal family." The irony was that he died in obscurity while traitors he had tried to expose still seemed to bask in elitist approval. King George VI had awarded Gouzenko and his family with British citizenship, but nothing else. A knighthood had gone to Anthony Blunt; and although Blunt had been exposed in 1979 as a spy and a traitor of Gouzenko's ELLI type, he was still blandly writing in the *Times* on matters artistic. Blunt had been publicly dishonored, but only because persistent citizens demanded answers to the sort of questions Gouzenko kept asking. Blunt would have still been *Sir Anthony* when Gouzenko died, if a section of public opinion had not forced an official admission that Blunt had long before been granted immunity from prosecution.

Why was Blunt allowed to continue in the royal service after he made his confession in 1964 in exchange for immunity? Why was he granted that immunity when less exalted (and perhaps less guilty) spies suffered due punishment?

More important still, did Blunt know who the London ELLI was? Could he have saved Gouzenko from years of anguish?

The last time I had spoken with Gouzenko, he wanted desperately to be seen for what he was: a loyal citizen of the West, perceptive as a writer and a painter, and consistent in his concern about the formidable Soviet challenge to the way of life he had chosen. He did not think himself obsessive, but he was familiar with Soviet psychiatry and its devotion to making dissidents seem to be the victims of mental disorder. He had described this secret-police assault on the senses in *The Fall of a Titan*, when the writer Gorin loses his mental balance in trying to keep his independence.

He had no answers to the questions plaguing his later life. If only he had been wiser, he might have found some way to identify "the gentleman from England" who had quietly destroyed his most sensitive disclosures. He had been talking into a microphone that had been unplugged, so that what he said was never heard by those he intended to warn. If others had started to doubt the existence of the Soviet agent who had achieved this, Gouzenko himself never yielded. Yes, there was a London ELLI. Yes, there was widespread Soviet penetration of Western intelligence. Yes, he had believed these particular matters to be so secret that he had confided them only to the single debriefing officer, "the gentleman from England," whom he had trusted to take further action.

Why was Gouzenko never given the opportunity to look at the suspects who were flushed out near the end of his life? Why was he never shown photographs of Dick Ellis in 1981, when the public accusations were first made? Couldn't Gouzenko have identified, even after all these years, the anonymous interrogator?

A confrontation might have silenced the critics who said Gouzenko's evidence of Russian moles could never be suppressed by one treacherous questioner. His contention was that a traitor high in the service could dissipate the effect of Gouzenko's general statements and keep to himself all details revealed exclusively in that single key interrogation. Philby had demonstrated how easy this was; and a similar confession might have resulted from the exposure of the Russian mole or moles who gagged Gouzenko.

So why wasn't he given the chance to scrutinize the suspects or their photographs, once the publicity of the 1980s started the reinvestigation of the Corby Case?

The answer was simple. Gouzenko was blind.

Gouzenko's blindness was one of the secrets of his closely guarded life. He had started to go blind during the period of the spy scandals in 1973. It was then he got the first hard evidence of a conspiracy against him, when he was finally allowed to hear a version of his alleged statement to "the gentleman from England." An attempt was made by the KGB to prevent Gouzenko from exposing this report's falsity. A KGB agent was called in to kill Gouzenko, but Moscow's plans were thwarted.

There were obvious reasons, then, why his deteriorating eyesight had to be kept secret. Blindness made him more easily identifiable. It would also tell the KGB there was less chance of Gouzenko's picking out the man he suspected of betraying him.

Perhaps the news did leak out. By 1981, the stories about the mysterious ELLI were linked with accusations against men whose photographs Gouzenko might once have recognized.

Now that he was dead, anyone might be said to be ELLI who was approximately in the right place at the right time. "Approximately" described the movements of intelligence officers like Dick Ellis. It seemed urgent to pull together all we now knew, and I summed up these conclusions for Stephenson:

The second ELLI is now a total mystery. If he was Philby, we shall never know. It is clear Philby had time and opportunity to secretly take down Gouzenko's testimony on moles, then distort that testimony, and later create havoc (even from his final retreat in Moscow) by planting false clues to damage the Soviet's real enemies. The chaos in the aftermath of World War II created perfect conditions for confusing the issues raised by Gouzenko. There were secret arrangements made without your knowledge for close liaison during the war between OSS and SOE with the NKVD. When Gouzenko's defection made it impossible for Philby and other Soviet sympathizers to exploit this liaison, there followed a form of covert warfare between the Soviets and ourselves in which the Soviets had the enormous advantage of continuing operations with their existing organizations. Ours—BSC and OSS—were dissolved.

If we knew more about how the charges were built up against Dick Ellis, we might understand more about Gouzenko's fate. The defection and its immediate consequences occurred in a period when U.S. covert actions in Europe changed dramatically. These are only now coming to light as a result of an investigation by the U.S. Department of Justice.

One reaction (to the report issued as a result of this investigation) is that of Massachusetts Congressman Barney Frank, who said publicly: "I thought it was the kind of thing people make up. There was a form of mad hysteria. . . . The U.S. had more intelligence agencies than there were countries to spy on."

Let's reconstruct the chain of events.

A: BEFORE WORLD WAR II, Dick Ellis dealt with anti-Communist exiles in Europe. He was the SIS expert on what Stalin called the nationalities question—the euphemism for unrest among non-Russians making up half the population of the USSR. Stalin regarded White Russians as potential leaders of revolt. Ellis dealt with the best known of the White Russian leaders in Paris, General Andrei Turkhul—and encouraged him to keep up his powerful Nazi connections. The Nazi Germans had secret plans for using White Russians and Ukrainians to overthrow Stalin, although during the 1930s they were still working clandestinely with Soviet military intelligence.

B. AFTER THE OUTBREAK OF WORLD WAR II, Turkhul disappeared. Many Ukrainians thought that if Moscow were defeated by the Germans, they would have a free Ukraine. So they donned German uniform and fought against the Red Army. . . .

GENERAL TURKHUL showed up unexpectedly in Central Europe, having been traced through a secret transmitter which provided the Germans with intelligence on Soviet military formations and movements. Turkhul was in fact a Soviet agent sending chickenfeed to the Nazis to maintain his credibility. So . . . Turkhul had been in reality loyal to Moscow Center while posing as a White Russian to Dick Ellis! The Ellis connection with Turkhul has been twisted into damning evidence of his disloyalty.

C. AT THE END OF WORLD WAR II, the forcible return of two million citizens of non-Communist countries wanted by the Soviet Union was secretly arranged by the U.S. State Department and the British Foreign Office. These tragic victims of Stalin's vengeance were for the most part Ukrainians and White Russians who were legally no longer Soviet citizens, as Stalin claimed. There was never any doubt that they faced execution or imprisonment.

Yet former Nazis were entering America under a secret arrangement known as The-One-Hundred-a-Year CIA Act. Immigrants were smuggled into the U.S. (a fact made known *only now* through Congressman Frank, a member of the House subcommittee on immigration). The Nazis had been recruited in the desperate effort to learn, almost from scratch, about Soviet intelligence methods.

ENTER PHILBY. He had considerable influence as the SIS chief of anti-Soviet operations in 1945–46. His recommendations on joint U.S.-British secret missions carried weight. His real bosses in Moscow Center instructed him to arrange the return of more anti-Communists. This was not so difficult to arrange as it first sounds.*

THERE HAD BEEN A NAZI GOVERNMENT OF BYELORUSSIA, with local Russians appointed by the German invaders in 1941. These Nazi collaborators exterminated twenty-five percent of the population, including nearly all of the country's Jewish population—three or four hundred thousand Jews. The entire Nazi government of Byelorussia, the president, the vice presidents, cabinet ministers, governors and mayors and police chiefs moved to America, the Justice Department report now shows.

---

*Operation VALUABLE was sponsored and then betrayed by Philby, by his own confession. The plan was to overthrow the Soviets' puppet government in Albania. The airlift of anti-Communist guerrillas by U.S. and British aircraft resulted in the capture of the Albanian patriots. But it was only in June of 1982 that declassified State Department documents disclosed another part of Soviet scheming—the unrecorded movement into the United States of Albanians who had collaborated with the Nazis, but among whom were infiltrated Soviet agents professing "anti-Communist" fervor. Philby's "Free Albanians" had a voice in American policy, according to the now-declassified account of a meeting between Secretary of State Dean Acheson and British Foreign Minister Ernest Bevin. Acheson says: "Bevin asked if we would basically agree that we try to bring down the Hoxha (Communist) government. . . . I said yes, but if this were precipitated now, the Greeks and Yugoslavs might touch off serious trouble. . . . [Bevin] asked, 'What government would replace Hoxha? Are there any kings around that could be put in?' "

Their Byelorussian scheme to "liberate" territory from the Soviets *had been pushed by Philby.* "Every one of the operations had been penetrated by the Soviets. . . . The parachute teams that were sent in had an astounding fatality rate. Nearly all the paratroopers were caught and killed within minutes after they landed. . . . Their program was assassination. . . . They were hit teams. . . . They were to start a civil war. . . . Many were later identified as having been double agents. The Soviets had penetrated both the British and German intelligence services."

THE SOPHISTICATION of this Soviet double cross now makes it less difficult to see how Dick Ellis was framed. He had been associated with "imperialist interventions" among the non-Russian nationalities, and with Fourth Arm planning *against* dictators. Philby knew all about Ellis. It should have been child's play to shift onto Ellis the blame for Gouzenko's elimination from Western intelligence councils.

CONCLUSION: When Gouzenko raised doubts, somebody had to be made the scapegoat. Philby was familiar with the Ellis case. He knew that accusations had been made against Ellis as far back as 1946, when a German intelligence officer, eager to prove his anticommunism, claimed that Ellis spied for both Nazis and Soviets. (Possibly the German informer was already serving Moscow Center. A contemporary, Heinz Felfe, made similar accusations against Americans in order to win U.S. confidence. Felfe finished up as senior intelligence adviser to the West German government until discovered to be a Soviet agent, whereupon he confessed.)

After Philby's escape to Moscow, a panic search for moles began. U.S. counterintelligence sought a British investigation, which included a review of Ellis's activities. SIS refused to let MI5 counterintelligence carry out the scrutiny of Ellis's record. When Soviet moles like Sir Anthony Blunt confessed, the gestapo-versus-liberals row became acute. Ellis was interrogated in the mid-1960s. Nothing was ever released to show him guilty of anything. But he did feel that Western intelligence mandarins were self-serving. They disliked the creative eccentricity of the old-style spy: the style that before World War II got Ellis into that snakepit of double and triple agents selling their virtue like whores.

Nevertheless, the nine-month inquiry has just ended, and the British security commission under Lord Diplock now reports to Prime Minister

Thatcher that the government is mole-proof. Nothing more is said about Ellis. The *Economist* described the sanitized version of the Diplock report as "smacking the smugness, given Britain's sorry record of high-level Communist penetration." If Ellis was targeted by the Soviets, what had the RIS to gain? The clogging of Western security channels. The Diplock commission has created an anti-mole machine of departmental complexity. Security vetting is to be carried out through a network of interlocking committees. The blueprint looks like a plumbing system, badly plugged. Every branch of government comes under scrutiny. What better way to constipate a nation's defense system? Who wants to become a Dick Ellis of the future, publicly humiliated, because he or she exercised personal initiative? Who wants to risk pension, promotion or career for the doubtful distinction of being labeled a "creative eccentric?" Yet the most troublesome of the KGB's adversaries are the creative eccentrics who leave no bits of paper in bureaucratic files for the moles to discover.

The Soviet bureaucracy demands that everything be signed in triplicate. Our biggest advantage is the American democratic spirit, which allows for informality, the breaking of rules in emergencies, and resistance to the signing of official forms.

But a piece of paper bearing the codename ELLI in Moscow, and the burial of papers concerning Gouzenko and the aftermath of his defection, threaten to kill the spirit of creative eccentricity characterizing the successful secret warfare waged against Hitler. If that spirit is destroyed, the Soviets will win a notable victory.*

---

*Anything that serves the ultimate truth [of Soviet communism] is not really false," states a KGB 1981 report, *The Practise of Recruiting Americans*. It names "government officials with access to secret papers," then journalists, in a list of ten priority targets, playing a part in undermining confidence in law and order, discrediting national heroes, exploding patriotic legends. Signed by A. V. Kuznetsov, it recalls that a permanent state of conflict exists between the Communist and non-Communist world. The only way to distinguish between true and false is to decide where each individual stands in that conflict. Thus he neatly "resolves" ethical problems of deceit.

VICTIMS OF
DECEPTIVE OPERATIONS

At the time of Gouzenko's death, a copy of the London *Daily Mail* with the headline SPY BOSS INTREPID HITS BACK arrived in the quiet Bermuda retreat where Stephenson sat, just as General Gubbins of SOE had described long ago: "Waiting for everybody . . . drawn by an unseen thread."

The *Mail* had published "a reply to the charges against Ellis which, says Sir William, *'are pure disinformation by the KGB.'* "

The newspaper commented: "It is a pleasure to watch this argumentative figure living up to his nickname of Machinegun Willy [sic] and lamming into his foes."

General Gubbins had written of people "coming like ancient Greeks to their oracle at Delphi to pose their multitudinous questions. . . . We always seemed to get from Bill a definitive answer."

There were no definitive answers this time, though. The oracle on an island six hundred miles off the North Carolina coast still pulled in his unseen threads. He saw the history of this century from the unique perspective of a man who had dealt with human aggression at every level, from close combat in the first Great War to the secret enemies in a conflict that seemed likely to be with us when the century ended. He knew the temptations of secret power. Secret warfare seemed to be overshadowed by the awful possibilities in atomic warfare. Gouzenko had exposed spies dealing with the Hiroshima bomb. Today, the equivalent of 525,000 Hiroshima bombs could be delivered within moments by a Soviet attack on the United States, killing 86 million Americans in that first strike.*

"The Corby Case might seem trivial, measured against such doomsday possibilities," said Stephenson. "Yet Gouzenko was a key to the secret warfare about which the public was allowed to know little: a form of warfare expanding as rapidly as the technology of nuclear weaponry. By re-examining the case today, the public can glimpse what's been happening inside that kingdom of spies, where a major weapon is deceit."

---

*Figures quoted by Stephenson from a 1982 study by *The New England Journal of Medicine*.

Gouzenko had been a victim of deceptive operations. The aim was to diminish his stature and limit discussion to the issue of atomic espionage in a period when the Soviet Union and the West were compelled to be partners. A secondary objective of the RIS was to give currency to the notion that secrets should be shared—but with the unspoken Russian proviso that "what's yours is mine but what's mine is my own."

The motivations of traitors were made to seem reasonable. One of the RIS informants who had been exposed through Gouzenko was Dr. Raymond Boyer, described in RIS traffic as "the best specialist on explosives on the American continent." Asked why he gave the Russians information that he was forbidden by his oath of secrecy to disclose, he replied: "I felt it was unfortunate that there was not clear scientific liaison in connection with such information between the Russian war effort and ours. . . . I was very anxious to see ABC, American-British-Canadian, technical missions in Russia and similar Russian missions here. I felt it was of great importance that the scientific war effort on two fronts should be coordinated." This disarming explanation echoed the views of the International Association of Scientific Workers, of whom Boyer was Canadian president. He testified that Professor Alan Nunn May was one of many Communists active in that organization pressing to give Russia the secrets of the bomb.*

Stephenson believed it was irrelevant whether or not Russia would eventually have built the bomb without help from its spies in the West. Gouzenko's actions should have raised the more vital issue of how to coexist with a world power that treated *all* its own affairs as state secrets, while using democratic arguments to convince its intended victims that secrecy played no part in democracy. Through Gouzenko, it had been possible to demonstrate that RIS operations in North America dated back to the 1920s; and his sensitive selection of documents covered every sphere of RIS activity, from military and atomic to political and diplomatic. Canadian government correspondence with its ambassadors, for instance, illustrated the invaluable guidance Moscow derived when it was leaked to the RIS. One example:

---

*From transcripts of the Royal Commission to Investigate the Facts Relating to and the Circumstances Surrounding the Communication by Public Officials and Other Persons in Positions of Trust of Secret and Confidential Information to Agents of a Foreign Power, published July 15, 1946. Dr. Boyer was sentenced to the penitentiary in 1946, was released after two years, became a millionaire, and now lives in Montreal.

From the Secretary of State for Dominion Affairs, London, to the Secretary of State for External Affairs, Ottawa, August 24, 1945: The problem of Bulgaria, Yugoslavia, Hungary and Rumania . . . Russia has never agreed to discuss it. All these countries are under the influence and supervision of Russia. . . . We have to gain the confidence and attention of these countries.

Such an exchange was obviously important for Soviet policymakers at that time, estimating the degree of Western opposition to their takeover of these Eastern European countries.

Gouzenko demonstrated that even if they seemed routine, confidential documents were important to an enemy determined to outwit and ultimately dominate the democracies. "Agents of influence," who were depicted by Soviet apologists as harmlessly passing "guidelines" over to Moscow, were in truth assisting an enemy to anticipate the West and to dispose diplomatic and military forces accordingly. In his first novel, Gouzenko sadly concluded that Moscow's best allies were men and women of innocent goodwill and considerable vanity, with access to policymaking papers. The rest could be left to the professional agents. As to resisting the powers of the secret police within the Soviet Union, Gouzenko showed how impossible it had become. He had beaten the KGB himself only by the enormous obstinacy and courage of himself and his wife, and by starting a new life that took a leaf from the KGB book. To be successful, a resister needed a new country and a new identity. Only then would he be relatively secure.

"COMPLETE SECURITY AND TOTAL DEMOCRACY ARE INCOMPATIBLE"

THIRTY-SEVEN

THE SEARCH FOR
THE SUPER-MOLE

When Gouzenko regained the world's attention in the year preceding his untimely death in 1982, he publicly condemned the misrepresentation of his responses to that SIS interrogation of 1946. Conducted in absolute secrecy, the questioning had concentrated on his conviction that Soviet moles had burrowed to the top of Western intelligence. His anonymous interrogator cloaked himself in such secret authority that nobody questioned his integrity nor his subsequent actions. Then, at long last, there came more visitors from London to meet Gouzenko's increasingly vigorous demands to hear just exactly what it was he had been reported as telling the first "gentleman from England." The second set of emissaries arrived in 1973, twenty-seven years late. Gouzenko was going blind, and it could be claimed that his memory was faulty. He listened to the official report on his 1946 interrogation with mounting anger.

"It was a fabrication," he confided. "Pages of rubbish designed to discredit me by pretending I said obviously ludicrous things, and by presenting me as claiming to have knowledge that was clearly beyond my powers." But it was only on the eve of his death, nearly a decade later, that he made these charges in the most public way he knew how. In the interval, he had tried to straighten out the record by less vociferous means. Why did he wait eight years to air his frustrations fully?

The bizarre position of a Russian defector should be kept in mind. The editor-in-chief of the Toronto *Sun*, Peter Worthington, described Gouzenko's mental state in 1973:

He came to my office and asked if I'd accompany him to the Royal York Hotel, where he said a couple of representatives of British intelligence wanted to question him about an earlier statement regarding high-level moles entrenched in MI5. . . . Gouzenko was uneasy that maybe the British intelligence types wanted to bump him off. . . . He was afraid, too, the Soviets would be impelled to send an assassin, afraid that *unwittingly* Gouzenko held the key to more Soviet spies.

Gouzenko asked Worthington to wait until he returned to the hotel lobby. "You can see I'm not suicidal," he said. "If I'm found dead, I didn't jump. I was pushed."

He was right to be worried. A Russian "sleeper" had been activated by Oleg Khomenko, a Soviet embassy counselor in Ottawa, to kill Gouzenko at the time of the Royal York meeting. But the "sleeper" had enjoyed the good life too long, and surrendered instead to the RCMP. He was known as "Anton Sabotki." In exchange for asylum, he gave a full account of the modern KGB successor to the SMERSH death squads.

The reasons for activating the sleeper were clear. Gouzenko had to be stopped from talking with the new "gentlemen from England." They were bonafide SIS investigators into KGB penetrations, reporting back to a secret SIS section known as K–7, set up to backtrack all the sixty or so intelligence officers then under suspicion, of whom a dozen had emerged with question marks after their names. What Gouzenko could reveal, once confronted with the KGB-doctored account of his original confidential statement, must set off a fresh spate of inquiries. *But how did the KGB know?*

The K–7 inquiries of the 1970s had been set in train by the hunt for a so-called super-mole. Sir Roger Hollis, onetime chief of MI5, was still alive but in retirement. He had been questioned harshly about the suspicion that he had used his power to halt inquiries that might expose Soviet activities. He had been described as interrogating Gouzenko, and as being the author of the distorted report. We are left, to this day, with the two contradictory statements: that Hollis did in fact question Gouzenko and was the original "gentleman from England," and the equally confident assertion from Sir William Stephenson that "I sent Hollis back to England before he got to Gouzenko, and had my own experts conduct the interrogation."*

All records had been destroyed. The London files on Gouzenko were gone. If Hollis returned to Canada by some other route, in the period when Stephenson and BSC were being pushed into dissolution, there was nothing to show for it. The old royal-court rule prevailed, that "Secret

---

*The summary of the Gouzenko transcripts, published in Ottawa in 1982, claimed that Roger Hollis interrogated Gouzenko in 1945–46, but offered no evidence of this.

services are secret and discussion of their work is inadmissible." Any discussion of Hollis's coming and going, in a Canada that still in 1945–46 acknowledged British security rules, would have been "inadmissible."

But by the 1970s, Gouzenko had learned Stephenson's lesson of "the deterrent of publicity." His trusted friend, Peter Worthington, also felt that the final meeting between Gouzenko and SIS was confidential. But when the first accusations were published in 1981 that both Hollis and Dick Ellis had been spies, nobody any longer felt obliged to keep silent. The report shown to Gouzenko in 1973, said Worthington, had clearly been written by a Soviet agent.

But who was he? The second ELLI? Or another member of an ELLI network?

The super-mole allegations in Britain were leveled in 1981 by the defense correspondent of two popular newspapers, Chapman Pincher, and appeared in his book, *Their Trade Is Treachery.* * Pincher offered to prove Dick Ellis was among those who betrayed the West.

But many readers were distressed. If the book reflected the way secret-intelligence offices built up a case against a suspect, there was cause for concern. The evidence seemed to be hearsay and circumstantial.

Stephenson was reminded of the refutation of FBI counterintelligence by Franklin D. Roosevelt, Jr., writing a foreword to the book about his mother, *Love, Eleanor,* by Joseph P. Lash. ** A rumor that she and Joe Lash were lovers supposedly caused a vengeful FDR to banish Private Lash in 1943 to a combat zone. Author Lash tracked the persistent lie through the Freedom of Information Act and found the entire canard had originated with an aggrieved counterintelligence officer who prompted the FBI to investigate. He found that White House counsel John Dean, trying to display precedents for President Richard Nixon's misuse of counterintelligence in Watergate, swallowed the Mrs. Roosevelt yarn and (with

---

*The title is taken from a British Security Service publication warning civil servants of Russian methods of entrapment. Pincher's book was published in the U.S. by Bantam, New York, 1982. At the same time, secret documents regarding Soviet procedures, slated for declassification in 1982, were placed under a further, indefinite ban. This applied to Burgess and Maclean, whose Soviet service, it might have been thought, would serve as a more cautionary tale than the government publication.

**New York: Doubleday, 1982.

the deep concern for accuracy that characterizes so many authors of unchallengeable secret reports) mislabeled it "The Case of Don Lash." The story was a salutory reminder, warned Stephenson, of the way untruths entered security files, producing monstrous offspring if the public never got the chance to refute them.

By the 1980s, the individual American's right to privacy was again under attack, according to those who found it difficult to challenge the contents of secret files.

But the professionals of security said the CIA had become virtually disarmed, and KGB defectors voiced alarm. Vladimir Sahkarov, a product of Moscow Center's elite (whose KGB posts, he said, "are handed down from father to son and whose cousins and uncles share the special privileges"), became a CIA agent. He subsequently made strong appeals in the United States for a more realistic appraisal of the new KGB.* It had grown into the Soviets' powerful Fourth Arm whose officers were sophisticated, highly trained, efficiently organized, and arrogant.

Counterintelligence, other professionals agreed, had been emasculated in 1973–74 when the proposed National Intelligence Act provided that all CIA work should be scrutinized through political committees on the public's behalf. The FBI's powers of surveillance, it was said, had been severely curtailed: no screening or investigation was possible without clear evidence of spying—which, as we have seen, is the most difficult evidence to obtain.

It was hard to balance individual liberty against security concerns. The difficulty was aired by Dr. Wilfred Basil Mann, a British-born nuclear scientist, now an American citizen who worked for the U.S. National Bureau of Standards. He wrote in 1982 about "attempts to identify me with the 'Basil' in a recently published book" about moles.

Dr. Mann will be recalled as the man who reported having discovered Philby and Burgess together in bed. He denied, though, that he was "the fifth man" in the Soviet spy rings of Philby, Burgess, Maclean, and

---

*Vladimir Sakharov with Umberto Rosi, *High Treason* (New York: Ballantine Books, 1981).

Blunt.* A new book, Andrew Boyle's *The Climate of Treason,* indicated
he was a Soviet spy. Dr. Mann wrote: "It is but the latest of several
attempts to mould such a character in the likeness of my own—that
of . . . an American citizen with special and esoteric ties with the CIA."
If Philby wished to sow more discord, suggested Dr. Mann, he had only
to play on these paranoid fears and unsubstantiated charges.

As an example of how KGB disinformation exploited the "touchy
subject of nuclear espionage," he quoted two reports on the front page
of the London *Times* of August 21, 1975. At the top of the page was the
allegation that "the CIA had given technological support to Israel to make
atomic bombs." Below was an account of Secretary of State Henry Kis-
singer's negotiations between Egypt and Israel.

"Was this a deliberate plant from a Soviet expert in the Middle East
in KGB propaganda, perhaps my old colleague Philby?" asked Dr. Mann.
"Did MI5 ever notice this strange juxtaposition?" The first report had
blamed James Angleton of CIA counterintelligence for supplying Israel
with a nuclear-bomb capability. Before long, Dr. Mann found himself
questioned by newsmen about allegations that he had helped Israel evade
the U.S.-sponsored Nonproliferation Treaty, "marking my entrance on
stage as suspect."

Dr. Mann concluded with a weighing of the balance to be struck
between freedom of speech and security in a liberal democracy. "It is a
problem which does not and could not arise in the Soviet Union," he
concluded. "But we in the Western world have to accept that complete
security and total democracy are incompatible. Insofar as a degree of
democratic freedom exists in our countries, Soviet intelligence services
have scope to operate. If the pack is not to be stacked too heavily in their
favor, they must be countered by some surveillance of our own people,
and this in itself is an encroachment on freedom. . . . In the process of
safeguarding national security *and* our freedom, the innocent cannot
always be protected from harassment."

*Professor W. B. Mann, *Was There a Fifth Man?* (New York: Pergamon Press, 1982).

THE GENTLEMAN FROM ENGLAND

Gouzenko's death, I thought, must mark an end to Intrepid's continuing investigation into his "last case."

I should have known better.

I flew from Washington to Bermuda in the spring of 1983 with reports that seemed to tie everything up except the mystery of the second ELLI. Many things now seemed clear:

> —Dick Ellis was vindicated. A former colleague, to clear Ellis's reputation, had shown a London newspaper the letter written by Britain's Prime Minister Margaret Thatcher to one of Ellis's children.
> —Three published obituaries dramatized a curious fact: spies in Soviet service, if they had the right and stylish background, had plenty of apologists; in contrast, the humble Gouzenko was damned with faint praise. The two most recent obits were those about Anthony Blunt and Donald Maclean.
> —And Soviet disinformation was openly acknowledged. A Communist party theoretician had written of the deliberate effort to discredit Western security by the publication of allegations against security chiefs.

These oddities from the tidying-up process in Intrepid's last case confirmed, in a way, Stephenson's faith in open information. An average citizen could discern, when the dust of argument died away, where the truth lay. But there was still the danger that the citizen could be misled by the luster of intellectual and social prominence.

Take the matter of the obituaries, for example.

Gouzenko may, as Peter Worthington had said, have won a final victory by dying in peace, but his departure from this earth was nonetheless shabbily covered. He was buried in the august columns of the *Times* of London with a brisk, brief tribute.

Anthony Blunt, on the other hand, was memorialized by the same newspaper with what a former MI5 chieftain described as "an obituary on a scale normally deployed for only the greatest and best." Blunt was stuck, for all time now, with posthumous whitewash and extravagant Marxist quotes. "A new art is beginning to arise," this world-renowned art expert was now officially chronicled as having said, "the product of the proletariat, again performing its true functions of propaganda. . . . Artists are gripped by the central realities of corn, copulation, revolution, water and space."

And Donald Maclean, the British diplomat who spied for the Soviets and conveyed behind-the-scenes intelligence on the progress of the Gouzenko inquiries, was eulogized by the *Morning Star* of London as "a man of high moral qualities." Admittedly, the *Star* was a Communist mouthpiece and went on to praise Maclean as a "dedicated party man." However, it was not the only newspaper to reprint *Izvestia's* official Soviet obituary, stating that Maclean "devoted all his conscious life to the high ideals of social progress and humanism, peace and international cooperation." (The implication was that Maclean had been less than conscious when he finally voiced doubts. I thought of Gouzenko's fictional hero, the writer Gorin, whose final revulsion for the party was quickly concealed with a sharp and fatal crack across his skull by an assassin. With Gorin safely dead, Stalin could proclaim him "the great patriot devoted to party ideals.")

As a relief from Newspeak, Ellis's attackers had been answered in a gracious statement by his old friend and SIS colleague, H. Montgomery Hyde. The London barrister, a distinguished historian and successful writer, had read renewed allegations in April 1983, and wrote in the *Daily Telegraph* of London under the headline ELLIS'S SERVICE TO THE CROWN: "I knew him intimately for 35 years. . . . Never did he give me the slightest indication that he was other than completely loyal to the Crown and the service."

Mrs. Thatcher had written to Ellis's daughter: "I am very sorry for the distress that you are suffering on account of the reference to your father in Chapman Pincher's book, and I deplore as strongly as you do his attacks on the memories of those who are no longer living and who cannot defend themselves." The prime minister explained that it was difficult to comment specifically on insinuations and allegations against ex-SIS officers in general without implicitly indicating (by omission) where suspicion might be better directed. She had commented on the allegations against Sir Roger Hollis only because he had been director-general of the Security Service.

Allegations against Sir Roger Hollis had been aired again on March 31, 1983, in the *Morning Star*, together with wild accusations that another director-general, Sir Michael Manley, and a deputy director-general, Graham Mitchell, had also helped the Soviets. A *Star* writer, the British Communist party ideologue George Matthews, gazed at the rubbishy work of the accuser and suggested that if he "were a left-winger, he would be accused of deliberately trying to discredit Britain's Security Services."

The lingering stench from these catfights called for the antidote of Stephenson's good cheer and forbearance. I was glad to see Bermuda's serene waters again slide under the wingtips. Here was a multiracial community whose struggle to prosper made each islander tolerant of his neighbor. The result was a sense of calm.

The routine seldom varied. Stephenson rose at the crack of dawn, checked the telex machines for messages, monitored foreign broadcasts, fed the shrill kiskadees in the lush garden, and by degrees worked his way to the study, to his books and correspondence. His firm progress through the day was like his life itself. As he advanced across the 1980s, himself older than the century, he seemed to grow sprightlier.

He was rehearsing the speech he planned to make on board the USS *Intrepid*, now permanently berthed at Pier 86, not far from his old New York headquarters at Rockefeller Center. In these illustrious surroundings, he was to receive the General William J. Donovan Award from veterans of the OSS.

How was he going to get to the aircraft carrier?

"Navy plane, and then helicopter," said the octogenarian without batting an eyelid.

As men grow older, their speeches often become more backward-looking. Not so with Stephenson. He planned to attack Yuri Andropov, the former KGB chief who now ruled all the Russias. Andropov dominated an empire built upon treachery, held together by informers and spies. The world had fallen under the shadow of this monstrosity since the days of Gouzenko.

I realized Stephenson was not yet ready to close his last case. "Gouzenko was the first to tell us about modern traitors," said Stephenson. "He tried to help us understand what makes them tick."

Gouzenko had stumbled across a real, live example of the success of such a traitor, the second ELLI, whose story might someday provide a complete blueprint of how such men and women were protected, as well as how they were recruited and inserted into the most sensitive branches of Western defense. But the second ELLI had been used as a red herring, so safe did the real traitor and his comrades feel from being detected. The evidence of their activities was everywhere to be seen, making it no longer possible to dismiss them as phantoms. "The gentleman from England" had been real enough. This part of the case, which once seemed a footnote, had become an abiding mystery. And Stephenson still loved a good mystery.

THIRTY-NINE

ARE THERE NO SECRETS?

Stephenson liked to tell a story about a mystery—a book, this time—fictional traitors and real suspicions. Agatha Christie seemed to know too much when she wrote the following dialogue:

"But there are those for whom we have neither respect nor liking—the traitors within our own ranks."

"My God, I'm with you, sir. That's a skunk's trick."

"And deserves a skunk's end."

"There really are these swine?"

"Everywhere. . . . In our Secret Service. In the fighting forces. . . . It's the big bugs we want, the people who can do untold damage . . . throwing us into just the state of confusion necessary."

This dialogue from Agatha Christie's N or M? was written during the wartime development of ULTRA cryptops at Bletchley Park and published in 1941. One of her characters was named Bletchley, which threw a scare into allied counterintelligence. Was Agatha Christie signaling knowledge of Bletchley as the most highly secret heart of that vital ULTRA secret, the biggest single weapon in modern secret warfare? The distinguished author had to be approached with infinite subtlety. A famous don, banging out his brains on ULTRA, was a personal friend and engineered an afternoon with the lady. He stalked the subject through crumpets and marble-cake and endless cups of tea. Finally he let drop the sacred name in hushed tones. Agatha Christie burst out laughing.

"Bletchley? My dear, I was stuck there on my way by train from Oxford to London, and took revenge by giving the name to one of my least lovable characters."

"Too much suspicion destroys those things worth preserving in our society." That was the lesson Stephenson drew from the anecdote. He remembered it as a cautionary tale from wartime BSC days. But after reviewing the subsequent years of betrayal, the lesson he drew was that "too little suspicion is equally dangerous."

Not even Gouzenko's wildest nightmares in 1945 could match the reality today. He had come over with news of treachery on a comparatively small scale. Today, there is an escalation of Soviet operations in the very region where Gouzenko's disclosures had caused such shock. "In the United States, the number of official representatives of governments undertaking hostile intelligence activities has increased by four hundred percent in the last dozen years," insisted U.S. Attorney General William French Smith. "At one time the FBI could match hostile agents on a one-to-one basis. Now the number of hostile agents has grown so much that our FBI counterintelligence are outnumbered."

Smith was talking about more than Communist diplomatic posts eavesdropping on public telephones, stealing U.S. industrial secrets, and buying commercial information from Manhattan to the "silicon valley" in California. That sort of thing also happened in London, Paris, and other Western capitals, and became evident in the publicized expulsion of Soviet agents masquerading as diplomats. Many more were squeezed out by what the FBI director in 1983, William Webster, called "neutralizing techniques." More than a hundred Communist agents had been quietly neutralized, he disclosed, in the previous three years. One in three Soviet-bloc diplomats had been identified as having intelligence responsibilities. Once they were known, the FBI could select from a wide range of techniques for making their lives uncomfortable, or rendering their presence in the United States so unproductive that they were withdrawn.

Had Gouzenko's actions led essentially nowhere? Soviet-run operations were now on the grandest scale. But Gouzenko had been saved by publicity; and it was the free circulation of information that finally put the West on guard. Gouzenko himself believed it was only the proximity of the United States and its free press that forced Canada to tighten security procedures. His story had begun while he was still working inside the Soviet embassy, when alert radio monitors, still concerned with enemy secret-intelligence transmissions of World War II, caught the first whispers of a new era of treachery. BRIDE and other cryptops were now put in the shade, but their coordination forged the links that held during Soviet onslaughts against the Atlantic alliance. The U.S. National Security Agency now worked closely with British Communications headquarters to scan Soviet telecoms, despite spy scandals exploited for the harm they might do to the partnership. The U.S. National Reconnaissance Office digested for its allies the intelligence gathered by satellites using heat, radiation, light, and sound to detect Soviet activities. The U.S. Defense Intelligence Agency coordinated the work of friendly governments and shared with them its assessments of what an enemy might plan to do.

That is basically the purpose today of Western secret intelligence: to see beyond the totalitarian barricades. It gives free societies a fighting chance, when confronted by the secret power of a closed society whose vast empire was, by 1983, governed by Yuri Andropov, the veteran of fifteen years at the head of the world's most pervasive and powerful intelligence Fourth Arm, the KGB.

Andropov had used history's largest political power base to claim the Soviet Party's top job. His enormous bureaucracy was calculated by foreign experts to number 40,000 clerks to service 90,000 supervisory and administrative staff behind 1,500,000 KGB informers, officials and agents executing the KGB's primary task—*internal control*. For external operations, there were known to be 250,000 KGB operatives in embassy, legation, consular, trade, and airline functions, or in foreign employ. These were minimum CIA and SIS estimates. They conveyed a sense of Andropov's awesome powers, but also a measure of his anxieties about internal unity. The emphasis was on the KGB's role of killing dissent within Soviet borders, a reaffirmation of Stalin's old obsessive fears of a revolt that, once it began, would look for Fourth Arm help from abroad.

To see into the heart of the KGB required more than inadvertent leaks or new advances in technology. Gouzenko had called for a program to win over defectors. When he himself crossed the line, there were no guidelines for handling such "storm petrels." By the 1980s, defectors were recognized as a single rewarding source of ground-level intelligence from inside the Soviet empire. Cameras in space could do no more than confirm material coming directly from the Kremlin. And of course Moscow Center knew this too, and now had an elaborate program for training bogus defectors who would, to paraphrase Lenin, "tell the West what the West wants to hear."

If Gouzenko's proposals for encouraging and handling defectors had been adopted, the battle of wits might have moved more certainly in our favor. The Soviets made empty promises of dignified retirement and pensions to those the KGB recruited abroad. The wife of a CIA man caught selling secrets said later, "My husband and the KGB recruiter shared the same professional problems. . . . But of course the KGB man was cultivating my husband. . . . Still, they had more in common with each other than with the outside world."

Her statement came thirty years after Gouzenko had formulated a plan that would guarantee, for defectors from the Soviet bloc, decent living conditions, a chance to work, new citizenship, and tangible recognition. Instead, Gouzenko himself had been neglected, a victim of KGB smears: a fate unlikely to popularize his mode of defection.

"There are no secrets!" the KGB repeated over and over again, while

destroying lives and reputations of any who gave away whatever the Soviets designated as secrets, which was almost everything that wasn't official propaganda.

In democratic societies, it was true that *there ought not to be secrets.* But when half the world sealed itself off, and waged secret wars against the rest, secrecy became universal. What the "father of the atom bomb," J. Robert Oppenheimer, had said about atomic scientists might be said about secret-intelligence experts: "In some sort of crude sense which no vulgarity, no humor, no overstatement can quite extinguish, they have known sin. And this is a knowledge they cannot lose."

Stephenson now concluded that, with all the secrets seemingly violated by the KGB, the West must rely on its exclusive weapon, one he had always advocated, one the Soviets could not match: freedom of the press. "Newspaper files don't vanish," he said. "The clippings are filed on the day of publication. They can't be doctored."

In time of war, disclosures might have to be delayed. In those instances, the sanctity of the secret files had to be guaranteed. But at other times, the best defense against KGB misrepresentation was public disclosure. Editors had a consuming respect for the truth. Stephenson quoted C. P. Scott of the Manchester *Guardian*: "Facts are sacred, opinion is free." History was written in the raw by reporters. A newsman's reports were hung up for all to read and, if necessary, to challenge. In contrast, secret informers left their little lies to pollute the opinions of those in power. The rewriters tailored history for their own ends.

To counter the danger of a supreme alliance of intelligence bureaucrats, to counter real threats to democracy, to maintain moral rectitude and keep our secret agencies "straight," the public had *the need to know.* The phrase had become intelligence jargon, meaning a secret project, restricted to those with a demonstrable need to know.

But wasn't Stephenson advocating a contradiction? How could anything be kept secret if the need to know was a public one?

"That, of course, is the heart of the matter," said Stephenson. "Since Gouzenko's defection, an international elite has controlled the destructive power of the atom and of secret intelligence. The ordinary citizen clings to the ball of Earth against a flood of information, suspecting that not all the truth seeps through the fences of security. The Hiroshima bomb devastated lives in ways officially concealed until 1955, when the elitists decided the public could handle the truth about radiation.* Now, that same public handles the far more disturbing truth that a one-megaton bomb (equal to a million tons of TNT) can scatter radioactive fallout over populations living within one hundred miles of ground zero.

"The secret-warfare techniques born out of the same secrecy, however, came to light only through democracy's need for truth. The security investigations of the past two decades disclosed disasters and humiliations bred of misguided 'covert action.'

"The public now knows that the same Germany occupied by the West when Hiroshima was atomized has become an arsenal of six thousand nuclear warheads crammed into a region no larger than Oregon. But what does the public know about the buying and selling of secrets in West Germany by professional intelligence prostitutes? Of the buying and selling of Nazis? Of secret spy swaps? Of marketing 'patriotism'?"

The Corby Case could not be closed. Concealment continued. I sat with Stephenson in his Bermuda library. He recalled Herbert Lyons, "who made the Nieman Foundation at Harvard a force for objectivity in Amer-American journalism." Lyons, in the early days of television, had been commenting on the day's news when time ran out. A director tried to stop him. "Don't wave your arms at me, young man," said Lyons. "I'll tell you when I'm finished."

Stephenson would tell us when he was finished.

---

*Except in China. Official propaganda films still showed how Chinese Red Army troops emerge unscathed from radiation fallout after a test explosion. The author, challenging the mythology that radiation sickness was an American propaganda lie, was told by Peking that the judgment was based on U.S. studies playing down radiation aftereffects. The studies came out of the 1945–55 coverup. Another case of biter bitten.

WITH BOTH EYES OPEN

He represented another period, when intelligence assessments were made by individuals, not by committees or computers. It now appeared that the postwar intelligence agencies had not always known how to make use of the information flooding out of the technology Stephenson had helped to develop. Satellites and spy-planes could photograph anything on earth. Down there, among tall buildings, laser beams invisibly conveyed conversations by picking up window vibrations. Most o the world's communications were vulnerable to eavesdroppers. Yet what was done with the masses of intelligence that high technology produced? Analysts were often recruited straight from college campuses. They joined because the pay was good and family security guaranteed. Dick Ellis had never been paid more than a bus-driver's salary. His meager pension had been cut arbitrarily because he had taken risks—such risks that now his reputation was smeared, and future secret-intelligence analysts would think twice about making a controversial, individual decision. If the KGB had planned to destroy the creative eccentrics and the individuals who sensed where the truth lay, they had succeeded.

A former CIA man, Ray Cline of the Georgetown Center for Strategic Studies, had proposed that the CIA drop covert action and devote itself to producing true intelligence, largely in the open.

Well, said Stephenson, that was pretty much what the good newsman did now. "Our natural world is an open one," said the old spymaster, and again he quoted M. Dolivet, the French spy-who-never-was: "In the great battle for the maintenance of freedom and true peace, where the aggressor will be opposed by free men and women, the free press must be bound by the noble rules of democratic ethics."

An old Russian proverb came to mind. Stephenson sighed. "Old men forget. . . ." His voice trailed away. He shaded his eyes against the Bermuda sun. "Alexander Solzhenitsyn?" he said questioningly. Yes, it was Solzhenitsyn who had quoted the proverb. Poor man! They said the Russian writer feared he might die before his time, with so much important work still to do. "Life's unfair," said Stephenson. "Here I am, eighty-seven, and it'll take a bullet to kill me."

Why not enjoy what life remained, as he insisted Solzhenitsyn should?

"But I *am* taking it easy," protested Stephenson. "I'm cemented to this chair."

His secretary appeared in the doorway. "Now then, Sir William, shall we go out today?" She glanced at me for help. "He hasn't been out for lunch in nearly a week."

I knew those lunches. He'd attend to his guests and eat nothing himself.

He levered himself up, and punched his stomach. "Look! I can still take it, thanks to those Canadian air-force exercises." He glanced up, eyes bright, a rebellious elf. "An old crock who won't crack—"

"Lunch?" prompted the secretary. Then the phone rang.

"That Russian proverb," said Stephenson to me. "It goes—"

But the secretary was back. "Someone to talk with you about that case, Sir William."

Stephenson's chin came up. He filled visibly with some fresh spirit of resistance, leaned his weight forward on his cane, and began toward the door. Then, hearing the clatter of the distant teleprinter, he paused to change direction.

"That Russian proverb!" he called back to me.

I was standing too, trying not to betray anxiety about his precarious balance.

"I remember it now," said Sir William, twinkling.

That, I had never doubted.

"It goes—'Dwell on the past and you'll lose an eye! Forget the past and you'll lose both eyes!' "

And brandishing his cane, Intrepid was off to see what new snippet might be hanging from his unseen threads. This time, perhaps, he would find the final clue to the true identity of Gouzenko's "gentleman from England."